Promoting Mental Health Through Imagery and Imagined Interactions

Health Communication

Gary L. Kreps, Series Editor

Vol. 14

The Health Communication series is part of
the Peter Lang Media and Communication list.
Every volume is peer reviewed and meets
the highest quality standards for content and production.

PETER LANG
New York • Bern • Berlin
Brussels • Vienna • Oxford • Warsaw

Promoting Mental Health Through Imagery and Imagined Interactions

James M. Honeycutt
EDITOR

PETER LANG
New York • Bern • Berlin
Brussels • Vienna • Oxford • Warsaw

Library of Congress Cataloging-in-Publication Data

Names: Honeycutt, James M., editor.
Title: Promoting mental health through imagery and imagined interactions / edited by James M. Honeycutt.
Description: 1 Edition. | New York: Peter Lang, [2019]
Series: Health communication: volume 14 | ISSN 2153-1277
Includes bibliographical references and index.
Identifiers: LCCN 2018042885 | ISBN 978-1-4331-5363-1 (hbk: alk. paper)
ISBN 978-1-4331-5409-6 (pbk: alk. paper) | ISBN 978-1-4331-5410-2 (epdf)
ISBN 978-1-4331-5411-9 (epub) | ISBN 978-1-4331-5412-6 (mobi)
Subjects: LCSH: Mental health promotion. | Imagination.
Classification: LCC RA790 .P785 2019 | DDC 616.89—dc23
LC record available at https://lccn.loc.gov/2018042885
DOI 10.3726/b14785

Bibliographic information published by **Die Deutsche Nationalbibliothek**. **Die Deutsche Nationalbibliothek** lists this publication in the "Deutsche Nationalbibliografie"; detailed bibliographic data are available on the Internet at http://dnb.d-nb.de/.

29 Broadway, 18th floor, New York, NY 10006
www.peterlang.com

This book is dedicated my family including Frank, Susan, and Judy. I thank Elizabeth and Abby as well as those who use the power of imagination to create new solutions to everyday problems through the power of human resilience, motivation, and creativity. I also dedicate it to loyal doctoral, MA, and undergraduate students over the years. You know who you are.

JMH

CONTENTS

TABLES

ACKNOWLEDGEMENTS

We wish to acknowledge students in our imagined interaction classes including those who have interviewed others about their mental imagery and discussed the power of imagined interactions in providing solace and optimism. We thank Ryan Rasner along with our research teams in the Matchbox Interaction Lab who is pursuing quantum relational observation theory in which people use mental imagery to observe themselves with their relational partners. We acknowledge all of our research participants in the Matchbox Interaction Lab including the participants from the various universities represented in this exciting volume. We thank all of the contributors to this volume for their enticing topics in dealing with trauma through imagined interaction.

I would like to thank Gary Kreps, whose inspiration has created the exciting, health communication series for Peter Lang Publishing, Inc. I am also indebted to Kathryn Harris of Peter Lang Publishing for her encouragement in the books that I have written for Peter Lang.

SERIES EDITOR'S PREFACE

Communication and the Neurobiology of Health

I am very pleased to include this important new book about *Promoting Mental Health Through Imagery and Imagined Interactions* as an important part of the Health Communication book series that I edit for Peter Lang Publishers. This exciting book breaks important new ground in health communication research and applications, examining the ways that individuals can use intrapersonal communication processes to address personal trauma through mental imagery. My friend and forward-thinking communication scholar Jim Honeycutt has worked closely with the chapter authors of this book to report an impressive array of studies examining the influential applications of imagery and imagined interactions in promoting recovery from personal trauma to promote mental and physical health. The implications of the chapters in this book suggest that there is much we each can do ourselves to promote health and wellness, even when addressing deep-seated mental health problems.

Typically, when we address health issues, we only think about physiological health issues and not about the broader emotional and cognitive psychological bases of health. Health care must be addressed holistically, clearly recognizing and responding to the interplay between individual physiology and psychology. Every physical ailment has significant psychological implications. For example, personal responses to serious health issues (such as heart disease, cancers, and paralysis) often influence psychological as well as physiological functioning, including the personal experiences of trauma, depression, and stress. To treat physiological health issues effectively, we must also treat the psychological dimensions of health and illness. Similarly, the ways we think and feel have powerful influences over our physiology. Serious mental health problems (such as stress disorder, psychosis, and bi-polar disease) invariably influence our physiology, including individual immune responses, sleep cycles, digestive processes, and pain responses. Directed intrapersonal and interpersonal communication practices can help address both mental health and related physiological health issues!

Too often, the modern health care system tends to focus primarily on the use of (often invasive) external biomedical therapeutic processes for addressing health problems, such as surgical and pharmacological interventions. This book takes a unique self-directed approach to therapy, focusing on how intrapersonal and interpersonal communication can be harnessed to help address mental health issues, especially to reduce the debilitating influences of trauma on wellbeing. The book vividly illustrates that we each have tremendous opportunities to influence our own health through directed application of intrapersonal communication processes such as the use of imagery and imagined interactions. This communication process illustrates the powerful neurobiological mechanisms of meditation, mindfulness, and imagery (see: Tang, Holzel, & Posner, 2015; Vago, 2013). The interesting chapters of this book address a broad range of relevant traumatic mental health threats experienced by many people, including teasing and bullying, victimization and abuse, jealousy, bereavement and loss, stress, body image and eating disorders, environmental degradation and hazards, violence and difficult interactions with police, as well as personal disappointments from losing political elections and other losses. There are clearly many opportunities to use the communication strategies described in this book to improve mental health and enhance quality of life.

Overall, this book helps to expand our understanding of the psychological dimensions of health and illness, indelibly connecting communication practices and mental health. It encourages a holistic approach to examining and addressing neurobiological aspects of health and illness. It promotes personal consumer responsibility and self-directed communication action to address individual health threats. It helps increase personal control and advocacy in delivering non-invasive health care. The book also increases access to care for those who are suffering. In addition, I hope this book also encourages careful empirical investigations of future applications of mental imagery and imagined interactions for addressing serious health concerns.

Gary L. Kreps
Gaithersburg, Maryland

References

Tang, Y. Y., Hölzel, B. K., & Posner, M. I. (2015). The neuroscience of mindfulness meditation. *Nature Reviews Neuroscience, 16*(4), 213–225.

Vago, D. R. (2013). Clarifying Habits of Mind: Mapping the Neurobiological Substrates of Mindfulness through Modalities of Self Awareness. Annals of the New York Academy of Sciences, 1–15. doi: 10.1111/nyas.12270

INTRODUCTION

Types of Trauma and Overview of Imagined Interaction Theory

James M. Honeycutt

Every day we live with stress and trauma in varying degrees ranging from the most minute of stressors (e.g., getting up when still tired as the alarm sounds, standstill traffic) to more serious injuries (e.g., concussions, breaking a leg) including mental effects of trauma such as depression, helplessness, anger, and resiliency. Common types of trauma are sexual abuse/assault, physical abuse, bullying, emotional or psychological abuse, neglect, accident, chronic illness, and domestic violence, Interestingly, historical trauma occurs when groups or communities are subjected to traumatic events such as terror (911 terror incident) including adverse environmental or weather events such as tornadoes, hurricanes, tsunamis, wildfires, or earthquakes. Furthermore, trauma is subjective events that are perceived as traumatic for someone may not be traumatic for others (SAMHSA, 2014).

Definitions of Trauma

There are different definitions of trauma depending on the context in which the term is used. For example, trauma refers to any event and the consequences that occur afterward, which result physical and mental emergency problems (Honarpisheh, 2012). Psychological trauma occurs "from an event, series of events, or set of circumstances that is experienced by an individual as physically or emotionally harmful or life threatening and that has lasting adverse effects on the individual's functioning and mental, physical, social, emotional, or spiritual well-being" (Substance Abuse and Mental Health Services Administration [SAMHSA], 2014, p. 7). Additionally, the Diagnostic and Statistical Manual of Mental Disorders (5th ed.; DSM–5; American Psychiatric Association, 2013) uses the following clinical definition:

> Exposure to actual or threatened death, serious injury, or sexual violence in one (or more) of the following ways: directly experiencing the traumatic event(s); witnessing, in person, the traumatic event(s) as it occurred to others; learning that the traumatic event(s) occurred to a close family member or close friend (in case of actual or threatened death of a family member or friend, the event(s) must have been violent or accidental); or experiencing repeated or extreme exposure to aversive details of the traumatic event(s). (p. 271)

Traditional ways of dealing with trauma are cognitive behavioral therapy (CBT) or what is commonly known as talk therapy (Brink, 2019). Additional methods are relaxation, exercise, lifestyle changes (e.g., diet), meditation, and medication. Table 0.1 presents a sample list of these techniques relative to each chapter in this volume. Related to CBT, is biofeedback which is used to treat PTSD through cardiac coherence in the form of regulating heart-rate variability.

Indeed, heart-rate variability is associated with better health, security, and stable relationships according to the poly-vagal theory of Porges (2001). The Institute of HeartMath (www.heartmath.org) has conducted decades of research on how positive emotions improve health. They advocate the use of what is known as the "quick-coherence" technique where you focus on your heart and breathing while dealing with stress (Honeycutt & Sheldon, 2018).

Stress versus Trauma: Similarities and Differences

The terms are often interchanged. However, trauma can be viewed as a sudden event that enters our lives and changes the way we perceive the world. Conversely, stress, is a reaction to less dramatic and often daily events that are perceived as threatening such as a job interviews, deadlines, finances, or worries related to an ongoing security situation. On a scale of intensity, trauma is more intense while stress is less intense. Indeed, so-called positive stress is referred to as "eustress" while distress reflects bad stress.

Depending on the severity of traumatic events, some people have a sense of learned helplessness and experience intrusive memories of the event and often feel that they cannot control their thoughts. People experiencing post-traumatic symptoms relive the event again and again in their imagination and dreams, and can impede in their ability to live their lives. Hence, this reasoning leads into the idea that people can use a self-type of therapy in the form of imagined interactions to deal with trauma.

Imagined Interactions (IIs)

Honeycutt (2003) defines imagined interactions as type of social cognition and mental imagery that are theoretically grounded in symbolic interactionism and cognitive script theory in which people think about encounters with significant others. Honeycutt and Sheldon (2018) discuss how scripts are a type of automatic pilot providing guidelines on how to act when one encounters new situations. Scripts are activated mindlessly and created through IIs as people envision contingency plans for actions.

They have many of the same characteristics as real conversations to the extent that they can be fragmentary, extended, rambling, repetitive, or coherent. There are fourteen features of IIs which include eight attributes and six functions. The attributes of IIs include the following:

1. frequency (how often persons experience IIs)
2. emotional valence (how enjoyable or uncomfortable they are)
3. discrepancy (the degree to which IIs are different from actual communication)
4. dominance (the amount that the self or other dominates the talk)
5. proactivity (whether IIs precede anticipated encounters)
6. retroactivity (whether IIs follow encounters)
7. specificity (the amount of detail in IIs)
8. variety (the number of different topics and partners experienced). (Honeycutt, 2015; pp. 75–76).

The functions include:

1. Rehearsal (message planning)
2. Catharsis (Release of emotions for venting and dealing with anxiety and uncertainty)
3. Compensation (They substitute for actual encounters)

4. Self-understanding (Helps us understand the etiology and motivation of our attitudes, values, and beliefs)
5. Relational maintenance (They psychologically helps us maintain relationships with others within the human mind)
6. Conflict-linkage (People ruminate about disagreements, arguments, grievances in functional and dysfunctional ways (I cannot forgive or forget).

Furthermore, Honeycutt (2015) discusses how the term "imagined interaction" is strategically used instead of "imaginary conversation" or "internal dialogue"; because imagined interactions is a broader concept that takes into account nonverbal and verbal imagery. Visual imagery reflects the scene of the interaction (e.g., office, den, and car). Verbal imagery reflects lines of dialogues imagined by the self and by others (e.g., I recall speaking to my boyfriend on my cell phone when he told me that he had just gotten tickets to a concert that we wanted to attend. I was happy at the news since the performance was in demand.

General Benefits of IIs

IIs can be measured as a personality traits using the Survey of Imagined Interactions as well as state in which a particular situation prompts their use. For example, as you go to pick someone up at the airport in which you haven't seen them in a while, you could envision the greeting (proactivity). They may also occur in short, quick intense bouts. A bouting behavior is defined as an activity that may occur over a time period that is relatively infrequent. For example, eating is a classic bouting behavior that occurs infrequently over a day. Yet, for many people, it occurs regularly at three time periods, morning (breakfast), noon (lunch) and evening (dinner). Similarly, IIs may occur infrequently, but then after an intense argument, the person is caught in an absorbing state where they ruminate about the conflict. Future research should examine if IIs examined as a bouting behavior occur in relation to certain days, topics, and interaction partners. Which functions are associated with these bouts? Are people more cognitively complex or less differentiated during these bouts? We need to know if IIs dealing with trauma occurs in a trait or state function.

Individuals who imagine conversations increase competence in a variety of communicative encounters. For example, reading between the lines of what others are saying is one indicator of communication competence. Sensitive people listen for feelings besides the literal content of what is said. This may be why women, who tend to spend more time imagining conversations, are better able to keep real conversations going. (Honeycutt, 2000).

Individuals gain more self-understanding by thinking about interactions. It is a process Daryl Bem (1972) calls self-perception. It helps clarify feelings about people and topics. For example, as George keeps imagining an upcoming conversation with Mary, he realizes devoting attention to it must mean he likes her.

As indicated above, IIs help keep relationships alive despite physical separations. "Out of sight, but in mind" reminds lovers of others' delightful qualities. For example, one of my students wrote "Because my present girlfriend is living in New Orleans this semester, I often have imagined interactions about the two of us. For instance, I often imagine us embracing and kissing when we see each other on Fridays. These imagined interactions are often fulfilled and then some."

IIs can improve mood by reducing tensions through the catharsis function. For example, another student fantasized an II with a man who had terminated their relationship. He apologized for the hurt he caused and admitted he was wrong to let her go. She responded that she hated him and was better off with her present boyfriend. This II, which occurred in the post-termination.

Sections of the Book

The book is divided into three sections. Table 0.1 previews the chapters with examples of types of trauma and common coping strategies. Section 1 discusses how IIs can deal with teasing, bullying, abuse and conflict. Chapter one and two by the editor of this volume precisely discuss how selected functions of IIs function in everyday life to help people cope with trauma. The third chapter by Ryan Rasner discusses jealousy from an evolutionary view and how people use IIs to replay jealousy episodes while preparing them to deal with the cognitive ramifications of jealousy.

Section two deals with physical, emotional and material loss. The fourth chapter by Jonathon Frost reviews studies on using IIs to deal with bereavement in terms of sudden loss and expected death. Chapter five, by the editor and Jake Harwood, discusses how IIs and music therapy are used to deal with stress. Music invokes visual, verbal, and auditory imaging. People listen to music and often have IIs to reinforce existing moods or use the ISO principle

Table 0.1. Common Types of Trauma and Treatment.

Chapter/Topic	*Type of Trauma*	*Common Coping Strategies* Treatment*
Abuse and Conflict		
1. Teasing/Bullying	Physical/Emotional	Cognitive behavioral therapy (CBT) (Cry, exercise, martial arts), biofeedback
2. Physical Abuse	Physical/Emotional	Antidepressants, CBT (Talk with empathic listeners)
3. Jealousy	Emotional	Control; (Mobilize support system)
Physical & Emotional Loss		
4. Bereavement	Traumatic loss	Social support networking (Talk with empathic listeners)
5. Stress & music therapy	Emotional	Performance & listening (Engage in arts)
6. Eating Disorders	Disease/Emotional	CBT, Social networking, (Balanced diet)
Policy Concerns		
7. Environmental activism	Disease/Emotional	Community protests (Cry, Talk with empathic friends, Social posting)
8. Hurricane Evacuations	Emotional	FEMA, Repression, Fortification (Talk with empathic listeners)
9. Police Encounters	Physical/Emotional	Politeness, Conformity, IPhone videoing, Media exposure
10. Political losses	Emotional/ Financial	Exposure to media reinforcement, Media avoidance, (cry, protest, castigate opposition)

*Parentheses represent more informal strategies used by individuals as opposed to more structured or clinical therapies.

of music to alleviate emotional change. Chapter six by Pavica Sheldon concerns the eating disorders that are so prevalent in societies where body image is valued. People use IIs to deal with their eating dilemmas.

The third section is concerned with policy concerns. The seventh chapter; coauthored by Andrea Vickery, Michael Rold, Kayla Hastrup, and Stephanie Houston Grey discusses fracking and the fear of environmental degradation. Hence, some individuals rehearse their concerns with oil company officials and politicians as they actively engage in environmental activism; hoping to change resistance to understanding of community needs. Chapter 8 deals with hurricane evacuation notices in the classic, fight, flight, or freeze reaction to impending storms. People who are prompted to use IIs upon receiving an evacuation warning were more likely to comply.

Chapter 9 by Laura Carper deals with police encounters in which a series of hypotheses are tested. It is common to view videos of police encounters where the officers and the people who are dealing with the police are in verbal or life-threatening conflict. The final chapter co-authored by Phil Madison, the editor, Emily Covington, and Philip Auter concerns how have depression after their favored candidate in a political election is defeated. This study explores the role of parasocial relationships (PSRs) in the form of imagined interactions (IIs) among those experiencing depression and learned helplessness as results of electoral defeat. We identify the functions and attributes of IIs that predict affective discomfort and offer suggestions for how people may use visualization and imagination to overcome the despair of unprecedented election results. Although the times may be terrifying for some, human imagination remains a powerful tool for coping with the past, the present, and the future.

It is hoped that this volume will inspire some people to use IIs as a type of self-therapy and to realize that having IIs in everyday life is a normal part of daydreaming and mental imagery. IIs can be used productively as well as dysfunctionally. Hence, it is up to the individual to decide how they use IIs to deal with stress and trauma. "Logic will get you from A to B. Imagination will take you everywhere." —Albert Einstein (www.brainyquote.com/topics/imagination)

References

Bem, D. J. (1972). Self-Perception theory. In L. Berkowitz (Ed.), *Advances in experimental social psychology* (Vol. 6, pp. 1–62). New York, NY: Academic Press.

Brink, N. E. (2019). *The constructivist approach to cognitive therapy: Resolving the unconscious past.* New York, NY: Routledge.

Honarpisheh, H. (2012). A comprehensive model for trauma research design. *Archives of trauma research, 1*(1), 3–13. doi: 10.5812/atr.5288

Honeycutt, J. M. (2000). It's the thought that counts. In C. G. Waugh (Ed.). *Let's talk: A cognitive-skills approach to interpersonal communication* (pp. 18–20). Newark, Del.: Kendall-Hunt.

Honeycutt, J. M. (2003). *Imagined interactions: Daydreaming about communication.* Cresskill, NJ: Hampton.

Honeycutt, J. M. (2015). Imagined interaction theory: Mental representations of interpersonal communication. In D. O. Braithwaite, & P. Schrodt (Eds.). *Engaging Theories in Interpersonal Communication (2nd ed.) (pps. 75–87)*. Thousand Oaks, CA: Sage.

Honeycutt, J. M., & Sheldon, P. A. (2018). *Scripts and communication for relationships* (2nd ed.). New York, NY: Peter Lang.

Substance Abuse and Mental Health Services Administration (2014). SAMHSA's concept of trauma and guidance for a trauma-informed approach. Rockville, MD: SAMHSA's Trauma and Justice Strategic Initiative. Retrieved from https://nrepp.samhsa.gov/Docs/Literatures/Behind_the_Term_Trauma.pdf

SECTION 1

USING IIs TO DEAL WITH ABUSE AND CONFLICT

· 1 ·

USING IMAGINED INTERACTIONS TO DEAL WITH TEASING AND BULLYING

James M. Honeycutt

Teasing and bullying can be very traumatic for children and adults. One of the rubbish nursery rhymes that should be banned for its utter naiveté and deception is "Sticks and stones may break my bones, but names will never harm me." A meta-analysis of over 315 studies reveal that there is strong evidence for victimization from bullying resulting in mental health afflictions, and chemical dependency (Moore et al., 2017). Specifically, these studies demonstrate that bullying victimization in children and adolescents has health outcomes including anxiety, depression, poor general health, non-suicidal self-injury, suicidal ideation and suicide attempts. Research suggests that being bullied can have worse longitudinal effects on young adults' mental health than being maltreated (Lereya, Copeland, Costello, & Wolke, 2015).

Evolutionary View

The origin of the word, "bully" can be traced back to the 14th century. Bullying may be done through physical assault (e.g., hitting, throwing, pushing, slapping, kicking), verbal (e.g., ridicule, taunts, mockery, threats) and indirect communication through rumors and gossip. The desire to survive is instinctual and common among all living things. Teasing and bullying can be used as a tool for competitive advancement due to limited and diminishing resources on the planet (see Chapter 9). From the time, a child enters school, he or she is taught to be the best he or she can. Conventional views of bullying have proposed that it is the result of underprivileged individual or environmental factors resulting in maladaptive development. However, an evolutionary adaptive view complements this view by arguing that some people engage in bullying for somatic resources, mates, and/or dominance and status (Volk, Camilleri, Dane, & Marini, 2012). Indeed, bullying occurs in all cultures, throughout history, and across species. Volk and his associates (2012) discuss the genetic heritability of bullying and how bullying provides some rewards despite potential costs to the behavior. In terms of early socialization, children often learn corrupt ways to get ahead in the highly competitive educational and social environments presented in grade school. Cyberbullying has increased with the popularity of social media and has resulted in some suicides (Sheldon, Rauschnabel, & Honeycutt, 2019).

This chapter will distinguish between teasing and bullying, as well as overviewing cyber mechanisms for these behaviors. Imagined interactions (IIs) studies are reviewed including brief overview of the use of visual imagery to deal with trauma. Bullying through road rage is discussed as well as the use of the catharsis function to deal with teasing. Therapeutic intervention is mentioned. The chapter concludes with applied interventions for using IIs to cope with teasing and bullying.

IIs, Teasing, and Bullying

Teasing is related to bullying. Bullying is a blatant act of aggression in which the goal is to harm the victim (Juvonen & Graham, 2014). The Center for Disease Control (CDC) and Department of Education defined bullying in 2014 in terms of the following: unwanted aggressive behavior; observed or perceived power imbalance; and repetition of behaviors or high likelihood of repetition (Gladden, Vivolo-Kantor, Hamburger, & Lumpkin, 2014). The CDC definition acknowledges two modes and four types by which youth can be bullied or can bully others. The two modes of bullying include direct (e.g., bullying that occurs in the presence of a targeted youth) and indirect (e.g., bullying not directly communicated to a targeted youth such as spreading rumors). Indirect bullying can reflect cyberbullying that is discussed below. In addition to these two modes, the four types of bullying include broad categories of physical, verbal, relational (e.g., efforts to harm the reputation or relationships of the targeted youth), and damage to property.

Conversely, teasing involves more ambiguity because it can be friendly or negative (Kowalski, 2007). Although the terms teasing and bullying are frequently used interchangeably, they are actually distinct (Bishop & Carwile, 2009). Bullying is a definitively negative pattern of behavior that involves repeated hostile or aggressive acts in an attempt to ridicule, embarrass, or exclude others (Hanish & Guerra, 2004). Although teasing can be used for similar purposes, characterized by Honeycutt and Wright (2017) as aggressive teasing, bullying is indicative of a larger imbalance of power evidenced through frequent and targeted aggressive behaviors. Teasing, on the other hand, typically refers to isolated events, and can be used both positively and negatively.

Teasing can turn into bullying when an individual's goal of teasing is to intentionally hurt the other (Honeycutt & Wright, 2017). Further, Kowalski (2007) reported that individuals who are negatively teased tend to have increased stress along with a lower self-esteem. The epidemic of teasing and bullying have been documented in both adolescents and adult relationships. For example, Creedon, Ray, and Harkins (2009) found that adult women who tease others about their physical appearance are more likely to suffer from low self-esteem. Adolescents in high school have discussed grades, study habits, physical appearance, and friends as common topics for teasing other individuals (Mottet & Thweatt, 1997). These two examples illustrate that bullying and teasing are not something an individual does only as a child, but something that can be experienced in adulthood. But, it is important to note that while teasing and bullying are related, they are not the same thing. For instance, teasing can serve to enhance a relationship, while it can also serve to humiliate another individual (Bishop & Carwile, 2009). Bullying in contrast, is not used to enhance a relationship.

Affectional Teasing

Honeycutt and Wright (2017) examined the motivation behind teasing episodes among college students. Participants were instructed that part of human existence is to kid others as well as be the object of teasing. They were told that there a few questions about esteem since some people like teasing while others do not like it as much. Indeed, teasing can be playful and enjoyable as well as hurtful. Affectionate and hurtful teasing were predicted in two regression analyses. The results revealed that self-esteem, retroactivity, and rehearsal were positively associated with affectionate teasing. Hence, people go back and replay the positive episode. In a sense, the retroactivity here is associated with relational maintenance in which the relationship is psychologically maintained within the mind (Honeycutt, 2003).

Aggressive Teasing

Aggressive teasing was predicted by low self-esteem in which individuals have a variety of IIs concerning the hurtful episode in which they strategize and plan out the aggression (rehearsal function). Additionally, aggressive teasing is associated with catharsis in which the teaser feels that he or she is able to release their tension and feel better about him or herself. Hence, the aggressive teaser is releasing pent-up, frustrations throughout the teasing episode.

Research findings pertaining to narcissism, personality, and IIs are helpful here. Narcissism defined in terms of hypersensitivity to criticism and overcompensating with inflated self-exaggeration has not been examined in terms of personality and communication (Sheldon et al., 2019). Results revealed that anxiety and anger are associated with narcissism as well as indulging in fantasies, lack of perspective taking, being disagreeable and ruminating about conflict (Honeycutt, Pence, & Gearhart, 2014). Narcissists may desire entitlement in the form of recognition which would be evident in aggressive teasing. Honeycutt and his colleagues (2014) note that narcissists feel enhanced feelings of superiority by feeding off of others and seeking constant affirmation. Aggressive teasing could be a manifestation of this need. Continuing research is warranted on the traumatic effects of teasing.

Bullying Trauma and IIs

The longitudinal effects of bullying are robust. People who lack empathy are more likely than to engage in bullying and less likely to volunteer to help people in need compared to those with higher levels of empathy (Konrath, O'Brien, & Hsing, 2011). Many children fail to mature and outgrow the pain of bullying because the bullying is severe. Hence, as adults, they are less mentally healthy (Wolke, Copeland, Angold, & Costello, 2013). Involvement in any role in bullying was associated with compromised adult health, less socioeconomic status, risky/illegal behavior, impairment in social relationship, less empathy and less likely to help people in need (Konrath et al., 2011). Even controlling for family hardship and childhood psychiatric disorders; bully-victims (e.g., those who are bullied and have been targets) continued to be impaired in health, wealth and social relationships in adulthood. Conversely, pure bullies (e.g., those who are not victims) were not at an increased risk of poor adult outcome once, other family and childhood risk factors were controlled for.

Those who were not involved in bullying, were more likely to experience depression, anxiety, panic attacks and agoraphobia than those were involved in bullying (Wolke et al., 2013). Additionally, pure victims were four times as likely to develop an anxiety disorder in adulthood compared with kids who were uninvolved in bullying. Bully/victims had a five-times greater risk of depression than uninvolved kids, as well as 10 times the likelihood of suicidal thoughts or actions as well as 15 times the likelihood of developing a panic disorder.

While the numbers vary as a function of the sample and location, at least 25% of students are involved in some form of bullying. When bullying is thought of or portrayed in pop culture, the victimization is typically a verbal action (e.g. teasing) or a physical action (e.g. shoving or hitting). Past literature has investigated the characteristics and effects of bullying victimization. For example, Radliff, Wang, and Swearer (2016) found that bully victims have a significantly higher external-locus of control than individuals who were not involved in bullying. This means that victims of bullying believe that they have little control over the situations that they are involved in or what happens to them. Radliff and associates (2016) also found that that victims of bullying report high levels of hopelessness. The hopelessness could be driven by the individual's external locus of control because they feel they have no ability to better their situation.

Bullying and IIs have been examined in a sample of over 300 participants in which the goal was to predict bullying based on the use of II attributes (Krawietz & Honeycutt, 2018). A stepwise regression analysis revealed that bullying was predicted by the II attributes of retroactivity and positive valence. Hence, bullies are reliving the bullying episode in their mind and they are enjoying the memory recall. This interpretation reflects theorem 1 and 2 of imagined interaction conflict theory which state:

1. Recurring conflict is maintained through retroactive and proactive IIs.
2. The current mood of the individual is associated with whether or not his or her IIs are positive and negative. The better a person's mood, the more positive his or her IIs will be as well as the inverse (Honeycutt, 2010, p. 19).

Conflict-linkage theory has received support in various studies (review Honeycutt, 2004; Hample, Richards, & Na, 2012). It is also discussed in the ensuing chapter. Conversely, the rumination by victims could possibly be caused by their feelings of helplessness and external locus of control (Radliff et al., 2016). Moreover, Sutton, Smith, and Swettenham (1999) discovered that bullies know when is the best time to strike and what exactly to use when striking. The bully could be using a form of bullying that hurts the victim more psychologically, which in turn could make it hard for these past transgressions to exit their minds. Since these victims are ruminating about the conflict, this could result in a lack of forgiveness, which in turn could continue the negative loop of bullying. By not forgiving their bully for past transgressions; these individuals are attributing past conflicts with the other to present conflicts. Gunny sacking happens when people in an argument do not focus on the initial complaint and start to criticize as other issues are brought up out of frustration that are unrelated to the initial complaint. As Gottman, Gottman, and DeClaire (2006) argue (pun intended), complaints are good in arguing because they are focused on the issue. Conversely, criticisms are destructive because they reflect personal attacks on another person's personality. Criticisms are also easily viewed as verbal bullying.

In terms of retroactivity and, bullies could possibly be thought of as basking in their glory in accordance with game theory. Game theory investigates interactions between individuals in which they make decisions that can each other based on prior moves (Rasmusen, 2007). Hence, a bullying encounter could be thought of as a game in which the bullies are making decisions that affect victims. The qui-pro-quo line of reciprocity would argue that if a person was bullied, he/she may use retaliatory bullying. Furthermore, the psychological notion of transference and social-learning theory would posit that if a person has been bullied by someone that they are unable to retaliate against; they could transfer the motive to someone whom they see as weaker.

Another reason for the positively affected retroactive IIs for bullies may be because they have reached an outcome or payoff that benefits them the best. One speculation for satisfaction comes from research conducted by Berger and Caravita (2015) in which they discovered that Machiavellianism and perceived popularity are associated with bully. So, based off their findings, individuals who bully could replay these encounters in their mind and determine how successful their manipulative tactics were. If these tactics were in fact successful, a result could be positive IIs. Another possible explanation for their positive IIs could be in their thought of gaining status. If the bullies following the encounter believe their peers now view them more favorably, it could be speculated that they would be more likely to review this interaction as going well.

The regression analysis revealed that involvement in fighting was predicted by valence, conflict-linkage, bullying, and it was negatively predicted by rehearsal. This research found that fighting was associated with a lack of rehearsal, while it was positively predicted by conflict-linkage and positive valence. When faced with a conflict they make a snap decision to fight rather than to flee the scene. We believe that these individuals are likely to flee the scene when fighting is about to occur. This could lead to adverse effects in these individuals, but additional research is needed to determine the fight, flight, or freeze response that goes on between bullies and victims in the context of fighting. Yet, for there to be a fight, more than one individual is needed in the interaction, which makes the lack of association between fighting and victimization interesting. The high correlation between bullying and victimization could suggest that individuals who are bullies and victims of bullying are likely to be involved in fighting situations rather than individuals who are just victims. But, this assertion holds no empirical evidence based on the present study, and future research is needed to address this situation.

Cyberbullying

Cyberbullying is also traumatic and has resulted in suicides. This type of bullying involves primarily verbal aggression through threats and spreading rumors electronically (Sheldon et al., 2019). Entire foundations have been created due to cyberbullying suicide. The Megan Meier Foundation was created in memory of a fourteen-year old girl who hung herself after being misled and tormented in a series of messages (https://www.meganmeierfoundation.org/megans-story.html). This young girl dealt with depression and used the old social media platform, Myspace. According to the website, a neighbor down the street created an imaginary, 16 year old boy by the name of Josh Evans. Unfortunately, on that fateful day of her suicide, the created character of Josh Evans and Megan began to have an argument over MySpace. A few others joined in and horrible and hurtful messages and bulletins went out publicly to hundreds of kids. The last words that were said to Megan from fictional Josh were, "The world would be a better place without you" and "Have a shi**y rest of your life." (Retrieved from https://www.meganmeierfoundation.org/about-tina-meier.html)

When reading the case history of this girl, it is clear that Megan had imagined interactions dealing with the numerous functions of IIs including catharsis, conflict linkage, self-understanding and relational maintenance. She constantly thought about the fictional boy. In a recent study, approximately 34% of students reported experiencing cyberbullying during their lifetime and 15% of students admitted to cyberbullying others during their lifetime (Patchin & Hinduja, 2016).

Social media is associated with mental health problems, which includes depression, sleep disturbances, and eating disorders, among young adults (Sheldon et al., 2019). Additionally, cyberbullying has negative effects on victims, such as lowering self-esteem, increasing depression and producing feelings of powerlessness (Anderson, Bresnahan, & Musatics, 2014). Social media allows for bouts of imagined interactions to occur while individuals are posting, texting, and reading others' blogs. While typing a message, you are literally having an imagined interaction with the recipients in the seconds and milliseconds before your press the send button. Hence, you can live in a virtual world of bullying rather than orally taunting another. Interestingly, oral communication is revealed through videos and platforms such as YouTube in which we can google clips of teasing and bullying (see https://www.youtube.com/watch?v=jKA1KzwyhtU).

Visual Imagery and Trauma

Imagined interactions typically occur in three imagery modes; verbal, visual, and mixed imagery (Honeycutt, 2003). Verbal imagery occurs when an individual imagines the alternating lines of dialogue uttered by self and other in terms of the classic Lasswell (1948) model of communication (e.g., Who said what in which channel to whom with what effect). Indeed, this phrase has been described as "perhaps the most famous single phrase in communication research (McQuail & Windahl, 1993, pp. 13–15).

Most imagined interactions begin with the self-uttering the first statement, which is known as agenda initiation (Honeycutt & Sheldon, 2018). The topic of the imagined interaction and the content of the II reflect "said what" in the Lasswell model. The channel is internal introspection because the self is communicating with oneself. Interestingly, IIs can be observed when others watch a person who speaks out loud to oneself (Honeycutt, 2010). Identifying the other party in the II reflects the "whom" in the Lasswell model while "the effect" is the outcome of the II. Honeycutt (2003) reviews myriads of studies indicating how some of the attributes such as discrepancy and valence can be viewed as outcome. For example, discrepancy is an outcome when what is imagined is different from what occurred. Relatedly, after an II, the outcome can be positive or negative.

Early research revealed that conflict verbal imagery is associated with ruminating about conflict (Zagacki, Edwards, & Honeycutt 1992) while visual imagery is associated with more positive topics. Visual imagery reflects nonverbal elements of the scene in which the II occurs. For example, a person coping with PTSD may recall specific scenes of the traumatic incident. This is quite common among police officers and those serving in the armed forces (Colwell, Lyons, Bruce, Garner, & Miller, 2011). For example, Colwell and her colleagues analyzed the underlying dimensions of coping using a survey and a technique called factor analysis. One of the underlying factors, which they called "Personal and Familial Impact" essentially, consisted of items reflecting II functions of relational maintenance (e.g., I could not stop thinking about my family during or immediately following the event. I kept thinking about how my family would be affected by what happened.) and catharsis (e.g., I suffered some harm—either physically or mentally—as a result; It was difficult to control my emotions during or immediately following the incident because the people involved reminded me of people I love.) Additionally, the II retroactivity attribute was invoked. This event brought back memories of similar people or events from my personal life.

There are approximately 900,000 sworn officers in the United States. Depending on the study, the range of PTSD occurrence is 19% to 34%, which includes officers that do not meet the standards for the full diagnosis (Kirschman, 2017). Most of the visual imagery involves reliving death to children, serious line-of-duty injury, and shootings. The culture is replete with media portrayals of cops bullying citizens.

Most IIs contain a combination of visual and verbal imagery, which reflects mixed imagery (Honeycutt, 2003). However, the argument can be made that the severity and type of trauma can influence the mode of imagery. For example, imagine a situation where you were involved in a car accident in which you were arguing with someone (e.g., another passenger, road rage at a so-called offending driver). Road rage as a type of teasing and bullying is discussed next.

Bullying Through Road Rage

Using the car as a weapon is one of the ultimate types of bullying; commonly referred to as road rage. Road rage reflects the catharsis function of IIs since drivers release emotional anxiety and tension. Typical signs are gestures, verbal aggression, threats or dangerous driving targeted toward another driver. The outcome can be severe including altercations, assaults and collisions that result in physical injuries, death and incarceration. Anyone who has had road rage or been a passenger of a road-rage driver, may recall instances in which the driver was yelling at the offending driver and speaking to the person as if they were communicating face-to-face. Obviously, road rage reflects an intense form of stress in which the reaction is chaotic, disturbing, and potentially hostile. In fact, anyone can have incidents of situation road rage as well as habitual rage (give source). There is even the case of an Episcopalian priest driving a red corvette in Florida who pointed a pistol at a driver who had passed him on a highway. The priest "brake checked" another driver when the other driver attempted to pass him which resulted in the priest pulling out his weapon (DeGrave, 2017). After initially pleading not guilty to more serious charges of aggravated assault with a deadly weapon and facing 10 years in prison; the priest accepted a plea deal by pleading no contest to charges of improper exhibition of a firearm, a first-degree misdemeanor. The plea agreement resulted in one year of probation and adjudication was withheld.

We have assessed the relationship between road rage bullying, emotional intelligence, and IIs in conjunction with the Louisiana State Police using driver simulators (Honeycutt, 2010). In the scenario, automobile drivers are "venting" at so-called offending drivers in heavy traffic conditions when they are late for an important meeting with business clients. This research reveals that there are individual differences in having imagined interactions while driving. Some of these differences are personality differences in driving profiles such as being an angry driver, impatient, competing, or punishing driver. IIs were used for venting at offending drivers including the use of the catharsis function as tension is relieved. The presence of passengers, music, weather conditions, and drinking patterns, and personality profiles in terms of driving behaviors are correlated with aggressive driving tendencies including acceleration, braking, swerving, and tailgating. Using IIs to vent at other drivers is associated with being a punishing driver such that the car is used as a weapon, being an impatient driver, and being a competitive driver. In fact, during an interview after participating in the driving scenario, one of the participants reported the following in terms of bullying:

> When other cars cut me off in traffic, I see this as asinine bullying. I feel stress because my daughter was killed in an auto accident when a person who was speeding, lost control of the car and struck her car. Many of these drivers couldn't pass a new driving test with knowledge of how to properly change lanes, how to pass, the meaning of road markings and using Wi-Fi instead of holding their phones. The double-yellow line on the road, which means do not pass, and other basic rules are oblivious to many drivers. May they reap what they sow as the Good book says.

In terms of using IIs to cope with trauma, rather than ruminating about negative outcomes with other drivers, we gave her counseling in the attempt to empower herself through emotional self-control and discussed how catastrophizing about worst-case scenarios often are futile (Honeycutt, 2000). She is taught the power of positive thinking through imagining productive outcomes. Furthermore, she is presented with research studies revealing how pessimism is associated with depression and negative health indicators such as earlier morbidity while optimism is associated with overall life happiness and specific outcomes including faster recovery after coronary surgery. Additonally, in Chapter 7, we will discuss how music therapy in alignment with IIs can be used to mollify stress and trauma.

Catharsis and Dealing with Bullying Trauma

IIs can be used in functional and dysfunctional ways. As noted above, ruminating about conflict may result in depression. Various longitudinal studies reveal the negative aspects of rumination (Hamilton, Farmer, Fogelman, & Gotlib, 2015). For example, classical research by Nolen-Hoeksema, Parker, and Larson (1994) revealed that rumination predicted major depression among 455, 18 to 84-year-olds who had lost family members to terminal illnesses. Those who ruminated more often became depressed and were still depressed as long as 18 months later. They would constantly stew due to the loss and lack of comparison alternatives in terms of social exchange theory. Other research has revealed how rumination predicts new onsets of depressive episodes (Nolen-Hoeksema, 2000).

Recall that catharsis is concerned with the alleviation of tension and anxiety while using mental imagery. Journal accounts over a month-long period, reveal that catharsis is the most reported function in a sample of over 562 analyzed entries, as it was present in 20 of the 37 diaries of those who were studied and represented by 296 individual instances across all entries (Honeycutt, Vickery, & Hatcher, 2014). Moreover, cognitive complexity is associated with the use of the catharsis function. Cognitive complexity reflects individuals' ability to categorize and process social information (Burleson & Caplan, 1998). These differentiations occur cognitively, similar to IIs. Thus, variations in how individuals report using multiple functions over time are associated with differences in cognitive complexity (Honeycuttet al., 2014). Research reveals that conflict linkage and cathartic IIs are more negatively valenced than those used for compensation and relational maintenance (Bodie, Honeycutt, & Vickery, 2013). Hence, while ruminating about teasing and bullying, negative valence is represented. Using IIs to provide emotional catharsis, although often resulting in positive emotional improvement, is marked primarily by negative emotions surrounding past traumatic events (e.g., Honeycutt, Nasser, Banner, Mapp, and DuPont, 2009). Thus, IIs that are used to cope with trauma may be relatively unpleasant. Similarly, imagined interaction conflict linkage theory posits that imagining conflict or recalling a past conflict often results in negative feelings and emotions, a prediction that has been supported with empirical data (Hample et al., 2012; Honeycutt, 2010).

Imagery and Trauma: Imagined Interaction Interventions

Intrusive mental imagery is a trans- diagnostic process present in various psychological disorders including trauma-related disorders involving anxiety, mood, and eating disorder (see Sheldon, Chapter 10) as well as severe mental health problems, such as bipolar disorder and psychosis (Brewin, Gregory, Lipton, & Burgess, 2010). Intrusive images are based on memories of past adverse experiences. Hence, retroactive IIs are occurring along with the use of the catharsis and conflict-linkage functions. Çili and Stopa (2015) review studies in which post-traumatic stress disorder, agoraphobia, and health anxiety are often associated with traumatic experiences including physical and sexual abuse. Additionally, visually imagery is used with less intense experiences including arguing with significant others and being teased or bullied.

While IIs can be used to deal with aggressive teasing and bullying through the catharsis function as earlier noted, the self-understanding function can be used as well. This function reflects self-understanding, which helps people to understand themselves better as they help to uncover opposing or differing aspects of the self-concept (Honeycutt, 2015). People can explore the basis for their beliefs, attitudes, values, opinions, and ideology. For example, why is this person teasing or bullying me? This function may be used to understand the etiology of your own beliefs as well as exploring the motivation for other's aggressive behaviors.

Summary

Teasing and bullying are endemic in human existence. We see this in elementary schools. There can be affectionate and aggressive teasing. Affectionate teasing can enhance relational bonding while aggressive teasing signifies competition. Bullying is an intensification of aggressive teasing. The typology of bullying includes verbal taunting, physical force, and indirect means through spreading rumors. Road rage is bullying by using the car as a weapon. We can use IIs to deal with aggressive teasing and bullying. However, IIs can also be used destructively. A recurring theme in this book will be the use of the catharsis function of imagined interactions to deal with trauma. This next chapter will examine signal detection theory and abuse as people use IIs to reflect on coercion and for the survival purposes.

Discussion Questions

1. *Have you ever been teased or bullied? What was the nature of these incidents? Were the effects short or long-term?*
2. *Have you used the catharsis, understanding, or conflict-linkage functions of IIs to deal with aggressive teasing or bullying? Do you ever have recurrent IIs in the form of memory recall with the source of these episodes?*
3. *Have you been cyberbullied? Did you have imagined interactions to deal with the source of the bullying?*
4. *Compare the use of IIs as a type of therapeutic intervention for repeated instances of aggressive teasing or bullying compared to social media website forums, talking with friends, psychotherapy, or other modalities.*

References

Anderson, J., Bresnahan, M., & Musatics, C. (2014). Combating weight-based cyberbullying on Facebook with the dissenter effect. *Cyberpsychology, Behavior, and Social Networking, 17*(5), 281–286. doi: 10.1089/cyber.2013.0370

Berger, C., & Caravita, S. C. S. (2015). Why do early adolescents bully? Exploring the influence of prestige norms on social and psychological motives to bully. *Journal of Adolescence, 46*, 45–46. doi: 10.1016/j.adolescence.2015.10.020

Bishop, C. M., & Carwile, A. M. (2009). The good, the bad, and the borderline: Separating teasing from bullying. *Communication Education*, 58(2), 276–301. doi: 10.1080/03634520902783666

Bodie, G. D., Honeycutt, J. M., & Vickery, A. J. (2013). An analysis of the correspondence between imagined interaction attributes and functions. *Human Communication Research, 39*(2), 157–183. doi: 10.1111/hcre.12003

Brewin, C. R., Gregory, J. D., Lipton, M., & Burgess, N. (2010). Intrusive images in psychological disorders: Characteristics, neural mechanisms, and treatment implications. *Psychological Review, 117*, 210–232. doi: 10.1037/a0018113

Burleson, B. R., & Caplan, S. E. (1998). Cognitive complexity. In J. C. McCroskey, J. A. Daly, M. M. Martin, & M. J. Beatty (Eds.), *Communication and personality: Trait perspectives* (pp. 233–286). Cresskill, NJ: Hampton Press.

Çili, S., & Stopa, L. (2015). Intrusive mental imagery in psychological disorders: Is the self the key to understanding maintenance? *Frontiers in Psychiatry*, 6, 103. doi: https://doi.org/10.3389/fpsyt.2015.00103

Colwell, L. H., Lyons, P. M., Bruce, A. J., Garner, R. L., & Miller, R. S. (2011). Police officers' cognitive appraisals for traumatic events: Implications for treatment and training. *Applied Psychology in Criminal Justice*, 7(2), 106–132. doi:http://dev.cjcenter.org/_files/apcj/APCJ%207-2pdfcOLWELL.pdf_1324066232.pdf

Creedon, M. T., Ray, S., & Harkins, D. A. (2009). Peer teasing, body-image and eating problems among women. *American Journal of Psychological Research*, 5(1), 111–130.

DeGrave, S. (2017, December 12). Fletcher priest to enter plea deal for lesser sentence in Florida road-rage case. *Citizen Times*. Retrieved on December 20, 2017 from http://www.citizen-times.com/story/news/local/2017/12/12/road-rage-rector-fletcher-priest-change-not-guilty-plea-florida-assault-case/943560001/

Gladden, R. M., Vivolo-Kantor, A. M., Hamburger, M. E., & Lumpkin, C. D. (2014). *Bullying surveillance among youths: Uniform definitions for public health and recommended data elements, Version 1.0*. Atlanta, GA: National Center for Injury Prevention and Control, Centers for Disease Control and Prevention and US Department of Education.

Gottman, J. M., Gottman, J. S., &DeClaire, J. (2006). *Ten lessons to transform your marriage.* New York, NY: Crown.

Hamilton, J. P., Farmer, M., Fogelman, P., & Gotlib, I. H. (2015). Depressive rumination, the default-mode network, and the dark matter of clinical neuroscience. *Biological Psychiatry*, 78(4), 224–230. doi: 10.1016/j.biopsych.2015.02.020

Hample, D., Richards, A. S., & Na, L. (2012). A test of the conflict linkage model in the context of serial arguments. *Western Journal of Communication*, *76*, 459–479. doi: 10.1080/10570314.2012.703361

Hanish, L. D., & Guerra, N. (2004). Aggressive victims, passive victims, and bullies: Developmental continuity or developmental change? *Merrill-Palmer Quarterly*, *50*, 17–38. doi: 10.1353/mpq.2004.0003

Honeycutt, J. M. (2000). It' s the thought that counts. In C. G. Waugh (Ed.), *Let's talk: Acognitive-skills approach to interpersonal communication* (pp. 18–20). Newark, DE: Kendall-Hunt.

Honeycutt, J. M. (2003). *Imagined interactions: Daydreaming about communication*. Cresskill, NJ: Hampton Press.

Honeycutt, J. M. (2004). Imagined interaction conflict-linkage theory: Explaining the persistence and resolution of interpersonal conflict in everyday life. *Imagination, Cognition, and Personality*, *23*, 3–25. doi: 10.2190/240J-1VPK-K86D-1JL8

Honeycutt, J. M. (2006). Enhancing EI intervention through imagined interactions. *Issues and Recent Developments in Emotional Intelligence*, [Online serial], *1*(1), 1–4. Available at http://www.eiconsortium.org

Honeycutt, J. M. (2010). Forgive but don't forget: Correlates of rumination about conflict. In J. M. Honeycutt (Ed.), *Imagine that: Studies in imagined interaction* (pp. 17–29). Cresskill, NJ: Hampton.

Honeycutt, J. M. (2015). Imagined interaction theory: Mental representations of interpersonal communication. In D. O. Braithwaite & P. Schrodt (Eds.), *Engaging Theories in Interpersonal Communication* (2nd ed.) (pp. 75–87). Thousand Oaks, CA: Sage.

Honeycutt, J. M., & Sheldon, P. (2018). *Scripts and communication for relationships* (2nd ed.). New York, NY: Peter Lang.

Honeycutt, J. M., Vickery, A. J., & Hatcher, L. C. (2014). The daily use of imagined interaction features. *Communication Monographs*, *82*(2), 201–223. doi:10.1080/03637751.2014.953965

Honeycutt, J. M., & Wright, C. N. (2017). Predicting affectionate and aggressive teasing motivation on the basis of self-esteem and imagined interactions with the teasing victim. *Southern Communication Journal*, *82*, 15–26. doi: 10.1080/1041794X.2016.1265577

Honeycutt, J. M., Nasser, K. A., Banner, J. M., Mapp, C. M., & DuPont, B. W. (2008). Individual differences in catharsis, emotional valence, trauma anxiety, and social networks among hurricane Katrina and Rita victims. *Southern Communication Journal*, *73*, 229–242. doi: 10.1080/10417940802219728

Honeycutt, J. M., Pence, M. E., & Gearhart, C. G. (2014). Associations between narcissism, empathy, personality, and imagined interactions. In A. Besser (Ed.), *Handbook of the Psychology of Narcissism: Diverse Perspectives* (pp. 333–346). New York, NY: Nova Science.

Juvonen, J., & Graham, S. (2014). Bullying in schools: The power of bullies and the plight of victims. *Annual Review of Psychology*, *65*, 159–185. doi:10.1146/annurev-psych-010213-115030

Kirschman, E. (2017, June 26). Cops and PTSD. *Psychology Today*. Retrieved on March 28, 2018 from https://www.psychologytoday.com/blog/cop-doc/201706/cops-and-ptsd-0

Konrath, S. H., O'Brien, E. H., & Hsing, C. (2011). Changes in dispositional empathy in American college students over time: A meta-analysis. *Personality and Social Psychology Review, 15*(2), 180–198.

Kowalski, R. M. (2007). Teasing and bullying. In B. H. Spitzberg & W. R. Cupach (Eds.), *The dark side of interpersonal communication* (pp. 169–197). Mahwah, NJ: Lawrence Erlbaum.

Krawietz, C. E., & Honeycutt, J. M. (2018, online). An investigation of bullying and imagined interactions. *Imagination, Cognition, and Personality*. https://doi.org/10.1177/0276236618806663

Lasswell, H. D. (1948). The Structure and Function of Communication in Society. In L. Bryson (Ed.), *The Communication of Ideas: A Series of Addresses*. New York, NY: Institute for Religious and Social Studies.

Lereya, S. T., Copeland, W. E., Costello, E. J., & Wolke, D. (2015). Adult mental health consequences of peer bullying and maltreatment in childhood: Two cohorts in two countries. *The Lancet Psychiatry, 2*, 524–531. doi: http://dx.doi.org/10.1016

McQuail, D., & Windahl, S. (1993). *Communication models for the study of mass communications* (2nd ed.). New York, NY: Longman.

Moore, S. E., Norman, R. E., Suetani, S., Thomas, H. J., Sly, P. D., & Scott, J. G. (2017). Consequences of bullying victimization in childhood and adolescence: A systematic review and meta-analysis. *World Journal of Psychiatry, 7*(1), 60–76. doi: 10.5498/wjp.v7.i1.60

Mottet, T. P., & Thweatt, K. S. (1997). The relationships between peer teasing, self-esteem, and affect for school. *Communication Research Reports, 14*, 241–248. doi:10.1080/08824099709388666

Nolen-Hoeksema, S., Parker, L. E., and Larson, J. (1994). Ruminative coping with depressed mood following loss. *Journal of Personality and Social Psychology, 67*, 92–104. doi:10.1037/0022-3514.67.1.92

Nolen-Hoeksema, S. (2000). The role of rumination in depressive disorders and mixed anxiety/depressive symptoms. *Journal of Abnormal Psychology, 109*(3), 504–511. http://dx.doi.org/10.1037/0021-843X.109.3.504

Patchin, J. W., & Hinduja, S. (2016). *Bullying Today: Bullet Points and Best Practices*. Thousand Oaks, CA: Sage Publications.

Radliff, K. M., Wang, C., & Swearer, S. M. (2016). Bullying and peer victimization: An examination of cognitive and psychosocial constructs. *Journal of Interpersonal Violence, 31*(11), 1983–2005. doi: 10.1177/0886260515572476

Rasmusen, E. (2007). *Games and Information: An Introduction to Game Theory* (4th ed.). Malden, MA: Blackwell Publishing.

Sheldon, P. A., Rauschnabel, P., & Honeycutt, J. M. (2019). *The darkside of social media: Psychological, managerial, and societal perspectives*. Amsterdam, The Netherlands: Elsevier Academic Press.

Sutton, J., Smith, P. K., & Swettenham, J. (1999). Social cognition and bullying: Social inadequacy or skilled manipulation? *British Journal of Developmental Psychology, 17*(3), 435–450. doi: 10.1348/026151099165384

Volk, A. A., Camilleri, J. A., Dane, A. V., & Marini, Z. A. (2012). Is adolescent bullying an evolutionary adaptation? *Aggressive Behavior, 38*(3), 222–238.

Wolke, D., Copeland, W. E., Angold, A., & Costello, E. J. (2013). Impact of bullying in childhood on adult health, wealth, crime, and social outcomes. *Psychological Science, 24*, 1958–1970. doi: http://doi.org/10.1177/0956797613481608

Zagacki, K. S., Edwards, R., & Honeycutt, J. M. (1992). The role of mental imagery and emotion in imagined interaction. *Communication Quarterly, 40*, 56–68. doi:10.1080/01463379209369820

· 2 ·

RUMINATION, VICTIMIZATION, AND ABUSE DETECTION

James M. Honeycutt

Abuse is traumatic. People use Imagined Interactions (IIs) to cope with abuse due to being violated, alienated, and frustrated. The preceding chapter discussed one type of abuse, bullying. Abuse includes psychological (emotional degradation, attacking self-concept), verbal (taunting, ridicule, name-calling, yelling, cursing, insults), social (preventing contact with others), sexual (forced vaginal, oral, and anal sex), and physical coercion (shoving, slapping, scratching, biting, hitting, kicking). It permeates across the lifespan from child to elderly abuse (caregiver or self-neglect as well as sexual abuse in some cases). According to the World Health organization, 40 percent of all murders of women worldwide are carried out by an intimate partner (Alfred, 2014). The World Health Organization indicates that 33 percent of women across the globe have experienced physical or sexual violence at the hands of a partner. Additionally, the National Intimate Partner and Sexual Violence Survey of 2017 reports that approximately 25 percent and 1 in 7 men in the United States report some violence victimization from an intimate partner in their lifetimes. More than 2 million injuries related to intimate partner violence are reported annually in the United States (Retrieved from https://www.cdc.gov/violenceprevention/nisvs/summaryreports.html also see Breiding, Black, & Ryan, 2008). Here we examine how people can use IIs as conflict escalates to the point of physical coercion. We report on studies of physiological arousal while watching conflict escalation. We discuss how catharsis can be used to deal with escalating conflict.

When using IIs to deal with the trauma of verbal and emotional abuse, it is important to point out that many IIs deal with more pleasant experiences (e.g., Honeycutt, 2003; 2015). Additionally, we have made the arguments that IIs can occur in bouts. A bout behavior is an activity that may occur over a time period that is relatively infrequent. Hence, people may not ruminate on conflict and trauma a lot over a 24-hour period, but when they do, it occurs in quick, intense bouts (Honeycutt, Vickery, & Hatcher, 2015). Data that I am analyzing reveals that II conflict defined in terms of dealing with conflict in bouts (e.g., Imagined interactions in bouts help me deal with conflict). Past arguments are not completely resolved and that is why I have arguing bouts to constructively deal with it. It is negatively correlated with being in a quality relationship (r (158) = −.29, p = .006). What this means, is that you have a less quality relationship to the extent that you engage in ruminating about conflict. II conflict linkage is associated with verbal (r (158) = .32, p = .000) and emotional abuse (r (158) = .27, p = .000). It is also associated with systolic blood pressure after viewing a domestic argument that ends in physical coercion (r (158) = .17, p = .029) Therefore, you are using IIs to cope with these episodes.

Honeycutt, Sheldon, Pence, and Hatcher (2015) conducted research on game theory and conflict escalation. People are able to predict aggressive tendencies and conciliatory tactics as conflict escalates. For example, after a grievance is aired, how is the partner going to respond; with aggression or conciliation? The implications are that people with a history of victimization may be desensitized to cues of aggressive signaling as well as being early detectors of escalating conflict due to their experience in terms of social learning theory, or they can be more sensitized to aggressive signaling. The mediating variable in this is the role that imagined interactions play as people replay and forecast signals of conflict escalation (Honeycutt, Keaton, Hatcher, & Hample, 2014; Honeycutt & Eldredge, 2015).

Advising Conciliation and Aggression in Conflict Escalation

We have studied how people use IIs to deal with arguments as they escalate and eventually end up with object throwing, shoving, and pushing in the form of physical coercion. We examined how people judge the probability and advisability of aggressive versus conciliatory actions in an unfolding dispute within a married couple (Honeycutt et al., 2015).

The participants watched a five-scene video depicting an escalating marital conflict. Two videos were made in order to distinguish between male and female-initiated conflict. In one scenario, a man initiates the conflict. In the second scenario, a woman initiates the conflict. Both scenarios were identical. The only difference was reversed gender roles. After each scene, participants answered questions related to their expectations about their partners' future reactions, including violence and forgiveness. They were presented with a list of possible reactions, ranging from highly conciliatory actions (apologize, ask for forgiveness, discuss the issue calmly) to physical violence or aggression (push, grab, shove partner; slap partner; throw, smash, hit or kick something; hit or try to hit partner with something).

We also asked participants about their perceptions of the wife and husband having imagined interactions while engaging in the conflict. Items included were, "What is the probability that the wife will think about what to say next?" and "To what extent would you advise the wife to think about what to say next?" We also asked participants about their advice for the husband and wife to re-play the previous argument in their mind using imagined interactions. All items were measured on a 7-point Likert type scale with 1 indicating low probability or low advisability and 7 indicating high probability or high advisability of the behavior.

Individuals participated in a study employing two videotaped scenarios depicting martial conflict in which a spouse comes home after a long day at work only to criticize his/her partner for violating expectations of a good meal. One situation involved male-initiated conflict and female reactance, while another illustrated female-initiated conflict and male reactance. Participants were asked to predict the future reactions based on aggressive tactics (e.g., slapping the partner, insulting, swearing or cursing at the partner) or prosocial and forgiving communication (e.g., apologizing, discussing the issue calmly) as well as the use of online, imagined interaction rumination in which individuals replay arguments in their mind as well as thinking about what to say next during the argument. When we asked our participants what kind of conflict tactics they recommend for the wife and husband, both men and women agreed that the husband and the wife should use more apologizing and forgiving behavior and less physical violence. Over time, they advised more aggression and less conciliation. Some people believe that forgiveness is good, and retaliation is bad. However, at the moment when conflict reaches its peak, the forgiveness may seem impossible, and therefore, aggression is advised. It is interesting that our participants advised people to use IIs while the conflict unfolded. Figure 2.1 shows these results. However, there was a lower probability that they would actually be used. This reflects the old cliché; Do as I say, not as I do. It is often easier to give others practical advice, while not heeding it ourselves.

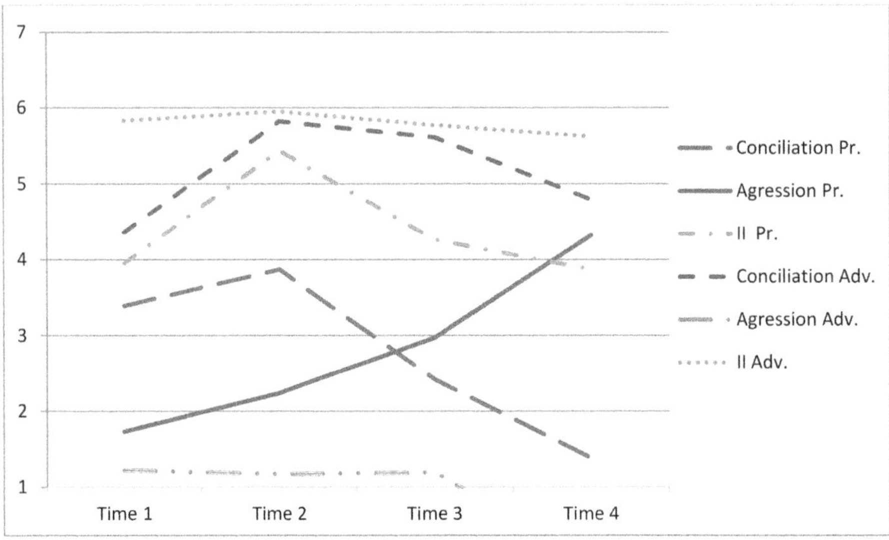

Figure 2.1. Conciliation, Aggression, and II Predictions across Conflict Escalation Legend: In descending order, the first line is II rumination advisability, Second line conciliatory advisability, Third line = II Rumination probabilities, Fourth line = Conciliatory probabilities, Fifth line = Aggression probabilities, Sixth line = Aggression advisability.

According to game theory, when people view an escalating conflict; they may have a cultural script for conflict resolution that involves "tit for tat" which is called, "quid-pro-quo." Tit for tat was first introduced by Rapoport (1966). Based on the English saying meaning "equivalent retaliation," a person using this strategy will initially cooperate, and then respond in kind to an opponent's previous action. If the opponent previously was cooperative, the person is cooperative and vice versa. According to Axelrod (1997) "tit for tat" is successful because it is "nice," "provoke-able" and "forgiving." Our findings reveal that a "tit for tat" strategy is both provocative and forgiving. When one partner defects, the other also defects. When one partners forgives; the other responds with forgiveness too. More research is needed to test the "forgiveness threshold"—how much hurt is too much, and at what point aggression becomes advisable. We believe that IIs have a mechanism in this decision, as the people access their memories of prior experiences with this person and implicitly, make a decision as to the probative value of forgiving. In order to use tit for tat as a negotiating strategy in escalating conflict, individuals use the proactive attribute of IIs and the rehearsal function in order to predict how the person might respond. Hence, as game theorists indicate, the actions and responses represent bids and rebids in successive iterations.

There are a number of methods that help manage daily conflict including "compensation" as individuals may not be in a position to enact revenge or retribution. Hence, they may feel catharsis by imagining discrepant scenarios that relieve tension or anxiety (Honeycutt, 2003). Additionally, heart disease is associated with remembering arguments (Honeycutt et al., 2014). Hence, people can use IIs in constructive ways to be resilient and overcome past trauma.

Participants in our sample advised the husband to replay the arguments in his mind before the next scene. We speculate that having retroactive IIs would help to relieve tension from the conflict in a previous scene, and potentially resolve the conflict. Managing conflict begins at the intrapersonal level of communication in terms of IIs (Honeycutt, 2015). Interestingly, the wife was not advised to have retroactive IIs about the previous argument, which indicates that men are taken as responsible for the conflict more than women. This supports gender role stereotypes.

In contrast though, there could a negative side to playing the 'game' with a significant other, which is difficult to escape from. Relational abuse (e.g., physical, psychological, or emotional) occurs when escalating conflict such as the one revealed in this study, results in reciprocating negative affect; recall the proverb of an "an eye for an eye." In these situations, individuals can choose from a few different strategies to deal with the past abuse. For example, victims from force can choose to use a self-negotiation strategy. By doing this, these individuals are choosing strategies, which can lessen the chances of themselves being the recipients of abuse. One way in which these individuals could choose to self-negotiate is by using IIs to mentally prepare for conversations with significant others and what they can say as well as envisioning how the other person might response. By using IIs these individuals could possibly use the rehearsal function to play out how to deal with their partner.

Excitation Transfer and Using IIs to Deal with Negative Affect

Replaying arguments in the mind while conflict is unfolding or escalating reflects what is called excitation transfer. Bryant and Miron (2003) suggests that the trace of negative affect left behind (perhaps revisited through the use of IIs) can combine additively with subsequent verbally aggressive acts. According to this idea, verbally aggressive behaviors produce negative emotional reactions, such as anger, and a covert verbal response which facilitates recall of the emotional experience. From this description, imagined interactions aid in the recollection process. Proactive and retroactive imagined interaction can perpetuate residual excitation. These features can be controlled in dealing with trauma as discussed in the studies of this book.

Aside from dwelling on past grievances, individuals unfortunately manage conflict through dysfunctional means because of an inability to effectively argue their points of view and emotions. Research reviewed by Honeycutt (2004; 2010) reflect Theorem 4 of imagined interaction conflict-linkage theory which states how suppressed rage is a result of the lack of opportunity or inability to articulate arguments with the target of conflict. Infante, Chandler, and Rudd (1989) explained verbal aggression in terms of the lack of communication skills rather than devising an argument that deals with the point of conflict. Hence, persons high in verbal aggression, attack the person with whom they are in conflict because they are frustrated in goal accomplishment and lack the communication skills to effectively espouse their views without alienating others. This has been labeled the Argumentative Skills Deficiency Model. As rage mounts, verbal aggression intensifies, possibly culminating in physical violence. Infante and Wigley (1986) note that not all verbal aggression leads to physical violence. If an individual experiences heightened arousal but stops short of physical violence, the result can be suppressed rage.

One of the functions of IIs is catharsis which helps people relieve pent-up or repressed feelings, hoping to alleviate anxiety and deal with stress. Emotions are released using this function. Imagined interactions can be a powerful tool in serving to create a sense of catharsis for an individual in a relationship by allowing one to relieve tension as well as to reduce uncertainty concerning another's actions (Honeycutt, 2015).

Using IIs to Deal with the Stress of Taking Conflict Personally

Some people are overly sensitive to criticisms while others are relatively calm. People who take conflict personally are likely to feel more daily stress due to the fact that the sympathetic nervous is aroused in the face of criticism. I will say that when someone says, "Don't take this personally, but …; you should in fact, take it personally. That is an inoculation preface before the criticism. Taking conflict personally (TCP) varies according to the context, though it can be seen as a personality trait (Wallfenfelsz & Hample, 2010).

TCP is "a feeling of being personally engaged in a punishing life event. [The person] feels threatened, anxious, damaged, devalued, insulted" (Hample & Dallinger, 1995, p. 206). It contains six dimensions: direct personalization (hurt feelings during conflict), persecution feelings (feeling attacked or abused during conflict), stress reactions (tension or pressure felt during conflict), positive relational outcomes (believing that conflict is good for a relationship), negative relational outcomes (believing that conflict is damaging to a relationship), and valence (the degree to which one enjoys arguing). The first three can be combined to form a measure called core TCP (Hample & Cionea, 2010).

People who score high on TCP are more likely to attempt to avoid conflict. Yet, when conflict is engaged in or cannot be avoided, they tend to be more aggressive than those who score low on TCP (Hample, 2018). Research has found that individuals who ruminate about conflicts are more likely to take conflict personally (Wallenfelsz & Hample, 2010). The longer a conflict continues, the more likely people will become aggressive, regardless of their tendency to take conflict personally. The aggressive tendency is partially based on imagined interaction conflict theory as previously noted in chapter one through retro and proactive IIs. Even after an argument is over, it is common for people to have flashbacks of conflict. Indeed, the purpose of much clinical counseling is to help clients deal with memories of painful experiences. Yet, IIs can be used as a type of self-therapy which is the premise of this volume.

We examined the effects of TCP on (II) conflict linkage rumination in terms of stress reactions as measured through blood pressure and heart rate (Honeycutt, Hample, & Hatcher, 2016). This study involved people watching the escalating conflict videos described earlier. Social learning theorist have demonstrated that watching emotionally charged movies affects heart rate and results in a small but significant increase in blood pressure (Child et al., 2014). Stress and empathic responses are activated when viewers watch others in a stressful situation as revealed in the release of cortisol (Engert, Plessow, Miller, Kirschbaum, & Singer, 2014). This occurs when viewing both strangers and romantic partners. The stress response was transmitted when observers watched the event live, through a one-way mirror, but also via video transmission in this study. About 24% of the viewers had increased cortisol levels when they watched a video version of the stressful event.

Taking conflict personally is associated with an increase in systolic and diastolic pressure while watching escalating conflict (Honeycutt et al., 2016). These findings reinforce the idea that high TCP levels make people more sensitive to conflicts, so that conflict watching/engagement results in various physiological effects. A major factor in the increase of blood pressure is stress or anxiety. Complementary research reveals that hostility is an independent correlate of increased low-frequency power of diastolic blood pressure and increased high-frequency power of systolic blood pressure (Virtanen et al., 2003). Correspondingly, using IIs to deal with conflict can be a constructive endeavor. As we ruminate about old grievances, we can envision more optimistic outcomes by having proactive IIs.

TCP is correlated with ruminating about conflict while watching conflict unfold. Additionally, TCP is associated with reports of victimization in the past year in terms of verbal or physical coercion. One explanation for this is that suffering physical or verbal abuse makes a person more sensitive to conflicts in general. Hence, the conflict linkage function of IIs can be used to heighten sensitivity to conflict (Hample, Richards, & Na, 2012). Having been victims of abuse, people may be weary of any type of conflict and are thus more likely to report taking conflict personally (as opposed to their non-abused counterparts). Another explanation might be that those who take conflict personally are more likely to report themselves as being abused, particularly those who score high on the persecution dimension of TCP. Because the victimization variable records both physical and verbal abuse, those who take conflict personally may be more likely to view themselves as the victims of verbal abuse.

The Trauma of Physical Abuse

In a series of studies, we have examined how IIs can mediate the association between verbal aggression and physical coercion (Honeycutt, 2003; 2010; Honeycutt & Sheldon, 2018). Verbal aggression reflects ridicule, yelling, profanity, taunts, and personal attacks on another person's self-concept. Verbal aggression chastises another's personality, skills, and physical appearance. (Infante & Wigley, 1986). A statistical technique known as path analyses that uses, what are called Beta (B) coefficients, reveals that the direct path between IIs and physical coercion is small (B = .17), while the direct path between verbal aggression and coercion is very strong (B = .59; see Honeycutt & Sheldon, p. 287 for more details). Indeed, "the potential for rehabilitation may lie in our discovery that imagined interactions mediate the direct link between verbal aggression and physical violence. Therefore, communication interventionists may attempt to create communication skills for more effective arguing and listening" (Honeycutt & Sheldon, 2018; p. 290).

Summary

IIs can be used constructively or destructively. A major means of dealing with the trauma of abuse is to use the catharsis function. We relive abuse in our minds. This is the whole point of cognitive behavioral therapy in order to deal with it through talk therapy. However, it is possible to use introspection as a form of emotional release. We reviewed studies on conflict escalation and how people advised the use of conciliatory and aggressive responses as conflict evolved. Under the presumption of game theory strategies, our participants advised the use of conciliatory strategies to a point, but then realize that rational reasoning is not operating and retaliate in kind (see Honeycutt, Keaton, Hatcher, & Hample, 2014 for more details).

Discussion Questions

1. *Provide examples of verbal, physical, and emotional abuse that you have witnessed. What was your reaction to this observation? Did you believe that is affected your momentary blood pressure?*
2. *A friend discloses to you that he/she is being verbally abused by their partner, but is afraid of leaving because of financially dependence on the partner. Your friend asks for advice on what they should do next. Would you advise them to do given their financial dependency?*
3. *Think of the last serious argument you had with someone. Did you or the interaction partner take the conflict personally? Is it a one-time argument or a serial, recurring disagreement? Did you use aggressive or conciliatory tactics during the argument?*

4. *To what extent do you use any of the functions of IIs (e.g., catharsis, rehearsal, compensation, understanding) to deal with recurring conflict?*

References

Alfred, C. (2014, August 03). These 20 countries have no law against domestic violence. *The Huffington Post*. Retrieved from https://www.huffingtonpost.com/2014/03/08/countries-no-domestic-violence-law_n_4918784.html

Axelrod, R. (1997). *The complexity of cooperation: Agent-based models of competition and collaboration*. Princeton, NJ: Princeton University.

Breiding, M. J., Black, M. C., & Ryan, G. W. (2008). Prevalence and Risk factors of intimate partner violence in eighteen U.S. states/territories, 2005. *American Journal of Preventive Medicine*, *34*(2), 112–118.

Bryant, J., & Miron, D. (2003). Excitation-transfer theory. In J. Bryant, D. Roskos-Ewoldsen, & J. Cantor (Eds.), *Communication and Emotion: Essays in Honor of Dolf Zillmann* (pp. 31–59). Mahwah, NJ: Erlbaum.

Child, N., Hanson, B., Bishop, M., Rinaldi, C. A., Bostock, J., Western, D., … Taggart, P. (2014). Effect of mental challenge induced by movie clips on action potential duration in normal human subjects independent of heart rate. *Circulation: Arrhythmia and Electrophysiology*, *7*(3), 518–523. doi: https://doi.org/10.1161/CIRCEP.113.000909

Engert, V., Plessow, F., Miller, R., Kirschbaum, C., & Singer, T. (2014). Cortisol increase in empathic stress is modulated by emotional closeness and observation modality. *Psychoneuroendocrinology*, *45*, 192–201. doi: 10.1016/j.psyneuen.2014.04.005

Hample, D. (2018). *Argumentation as interpersonal communication*. New York, NY: Peter Lang.

Hample, D., & Cionea, I. A. (2010). Taking conflict personally and its connections with aggressiveness. In T. A. Avtgis, & A. S. Rancer (Eds.), *Arguments, aggression, and conflict: New directions in theory and research* (pp. 372–387). New York, NY: Routledge, Taylor, and Francis.

Hample, D., & Dallinger, J. M. (1995). A Lewinian perspective on taking conflict personally: Revision, refinement, and validation of the instrument. *Communication Quarterly*, *43*(3), 297–319. doi: 10.1080/01463379509369978

Hample, D., Richards, A. S., & Na, L. (2012). A test of the conflict linkage model in the context of serial arguments. *Western Journal of Communication*, *76*(5), 459–479. doi: 10.1080/10570314.2012.703361

Honeycutt, J. M. (2003). *Imagined interactions: Daydreaming about communication*. Cresskill, NJ: Hampton.

Honeycutt, J. M. (2004). Imagined interaction conflict-linkage theory: Explaining the persistence and resolution of interpersonal conflict in everyday life. *Imagination, Cognition, and Personality*, *23*, 3–26. doi: 10.2190/240J-1VPK-K86D-1JL8

Honeycutt, J. M. (2010). Forgive but don't forget: Correlates of rumination about conflict. In J. M. Honeycutt (Ed.), *Imagine that: Studies in imagined interaction* (pp. 17–29). Cresskill, NJ: Hampton.

Honeycutt, J. M. (2015). Imagined interaction theory: Mental representations of interpersonal communication. In D. O. Braithwaite & P. Schrodt (Eds.), *Engaging theories in interpersonal communication* (2nd ed., pp. 75–87). Thousand Oaks, CA: Sage.

Honeycutt, J. M., & Eldredge, J. H. (2015). Applying game theory and signal detection theory to conflict escalation: A case study of a police investigator viewing a domestic argument. In K. Chapman (Ed.) *Decision and Game Theory: Perspectives, Applications and Challenges (pps. 17–30)*. NY: Nova Science.

Honeycutt, J. M., Hample, D. A., & Hatcher, L. C. (2016). A latent growth curve analysis of taking conflict personally as a consequence of sex, conflict initiation, victimization, conflict linkage, and cardiovascular reactivity. *Imagination, Cognition, and Personality*, *35*(4), 325–350. doi: 10.1177/0276236616636216

Honeycutt, J. M., Keaton, S. A., Hatcher, L. C., & Hample, D. (2014). Effects orumination and observing martial conflict on observers' heart rates as they advise and predict the use of conflict tactics. In J. M. Honeycutt, C. R. Sawyer, & S. A. Keaton (Eds.), *The Influence of Communication on Physiology and Health* (pp. 73–92). New York, NY: Peter Lang.

Honeycutt, J. M., & Sheldon, P. (2018). *Scripts and Communication for Relationships* (2nd ed.). New York, NY: Peter Lang.

Honeycutt, J. M., Sheldon, P., Pence, M. E., & Hatcher, L. C. (2015). Predicting aggression, conciliation, and concurrent rumination in escalating conflict. *Journal of Interpersonal Violence*, *30*, 133–151. doi: 10.1177/0886260514532717

Honeycutt, J. M., Vickery, A. J. & Hatcher, L. C. (2015). The daily use of imagined interaction features. *Communication Monographs*, *82*, *2*, 201–223. doi: 10.1080/03637751.2014.953965

Infante, D. A., Chandler, T. A., & Rudd, J. E. (1989). Test of an argumentative skill deficiency model of interpersonal violence. *Communication Monographs*, 56(2), 163–177. doi: 10.1080/03637758909390257

Infante, D. A., & Wigley, C. J. (1986). Verbal aggressiveness: An interpersonal model and measure. *Communication Monographs*, 53, 61–69. doi: 10.1080/03637758609376126

Rapoport, A. (1966). *Two-person game theory: The essential ideas*. Ann Arbor, MI: University of Michigan Press.

Virtanen, R., Jula, A., Salminen, J. K., Voipio-Pulkki, L. M., Helenius, H., Kuusela, T., & Airaksinen, J. (2003). Anxiety and hostility are associated with reduced baroreflex sensitivity and increased beat-to-beat blood pressure variability. *Psychosomatic Medicine*, *65*(5), 751–766. doi: 10.1097/01.PSY.0000088760.65046.CF

Wallenfelsz, K. P., & Hample, D. (2010). The role of taking conflict personally in imagined interactions about conflict. *Southern Communication Journal*, *75*(5), 471–487. doi: 10.1080/10417940903006057

· 3 ·

APPLYING IMAGINED INTERACTION TO AN EVOLUTIONARY VIEW OF JEALOUSY AND TRAUMA

Ryan D. Rasner

"What can I say? Is it in my head that their love is real, Or that ours isn't dead? Lord I try to keep my pride from making me insane. Is their song the silver lining for a cloud with so much rain?"

— Jamie Younkin, "Woman in gold" lyrics, 2018

History and popular culture provide cues to jealousy's omnipresence. Shakespeare's *Othello* portrayed the intense passions arising from suspicions of infidelity and *Moulin Rouge!* set forth a love triangle between a poet, actress/courtesan, and aristocrat wherein jealousy took center stage. In both *Othello* and *Moulin Rouge!*, the parties experiencing jealousy spent considerable time thinking about and imagining the situation; ruminating about what happened in the past and how the future should turn out. When individuals mention jealousy they are not, however, just referring to historical plays and box office movies, they are drawing upon their own personal encounters with the phenomenon. The cognitive appraisals individuals draw upon when thinking about jealousy evoke related feelings and subsequent behaviors. The communication elicited through feelings of jealousy plays a vital role in whether relationships survive or dissolve (Buss, 2000).

When people subsequently fail to address their feelings or cognitive appraisals, jealousy can cascade into cognitive rumination (Carson & Cupach, 2000), whereby the real or perceived relational threats play host to their imagined interactions. When individuals envision past experiences and the future consequences/outcomes associated with their feelings, they are participating in what is understood as imagined interactions (IIs). Jealousy, in turn, manifests itself cognitively and emerges behaviorally. Imagined interactions are commonly connected to intimate or romantic relationships (Edwards, Honeycutt, & Zagacki, 1988) and can aid researchers in understanding the link between cognition and communicative behaviors associated with jealousy. Honeycutt (2003) stated that individuals observe their relationship, then revisit those observations through IIs. One of the II functions is relational maintenance, which serves a meaningful role in sustaining romantic relationships (Honeycutt, 2003).Similarly, jealousy performs a maintenance role in intimate relationships often to maintain resources and prevent cuckoldry (Buss, 2000).

Jealousy, however, contains a darker traumatic side. Often referred to as the "green eyed monster" (Buss, 2000), jealousy can motivate significant others to violently attack and even murder their loved ones. Found in all cultures, jealousy remains among the main causes behind spousal homicides (Buss, 1995). According to Petrosky, Blair, Betz, Fowler, Jack, and Lyons (2017) in a Centers for Disease Control (CDC) report, between 2003 and 2014, 10,018 adult women were murdered due to intimate partner violence (IPV) and of those IPV related homicides 12% were reportedly associated with jealousy. This chapter's objective is to illuminate the understanding of jealousy in relation to imagined interactions through an evolutionary lens. First, this chapter reviews literature on imagined interactions to provide a foundational understanding of the concepts. The importance here is to understand jealousy through both communicative and evolutionary perspectives. The chapter will then tie together jealousy from an evolutionary stance and imagined interactions where the results from a current study are then reported. Specifically, the study investigated the predictability of jealousy through the functions and attributes of IIs. The preceding cognitive intrapersonal communication perspective could aid in predicting helpful versus harmful communicative acts of jealousy.

Imagined Interactions

As noted throughout this volume, imagined interactions are similar to daydreaming and serve a variety of functions (Honeycutt, 2003) including relationship maintenance, catharsis, conflict-linkage, and compensation. The explication of a new theoretical framework brought together communication and social cognition forming intrapersonal communication, or communication within an individual. Imagined interactions theory is based in symbolic interactionism and script theory (Honeycutt, 2003), positing that individuals build scripts for how to behave in interpersonal contexts. For example, individuals could learn from prior experiences of jealousy that it was good or bad for the relationship as a consequence of what was said and done. Hence, the next time the individual is feeling jealous they may choose alternative ways of expressing it. Imagined interactions take place in such a way that the communicator participates in cognitive portrayals of conversations complete with, both verbal and nonverbal characteristics (Honeycutt, 2003). Individuals imagine themselves in both anticipated encounters and those that previously took place (Honeycutt, Edwards, & Zagacki, 1989–1990) often because actual communication could lead to physical and/or emotional threats (Berkos, Allen, Kearney, & Plax, 2001). Therefore, individuals who have been on the receiving end of jealous acts by their significant other may choose to use IIs as a way to deal with the interactions internally, without fear of retaliation. Imagined interactions theory has been repeatedly employed to operationalize investigations of interpersonal communication (Honeycutt, 2015) with great success through its functions and attributes.

Honeycutt (2003) articulated the variety of functions and attributes associated with IIs, To begin with, *frequency* refers to how often IIs occur in individuals' minds. *Valence* describes the positive or negative quality of the imagined interaction. Explaining if the imagined interaction turned out similar to the way it was imagined refers to *discrepancy*. The *self-dominance* attribute indicates how prominent of a role the person having the imagined interaction has versus the other person. Characterizing the interaction as having previously occurred and the person is thinking back on it denotes *retroactivity*. Conversely, *proactivity* references an imagined interaction that has not yet taken place, but the individual imagines the scenario playing out in the future. *Specificity* signifies the amount of detail described in the imagined interaction. Finally, the number of partners and topics experienced within each imagined interaction distinguishes the *variety* attribute of imagined interactions.

Along with the attributes previously explained, IIs contain six functions. The *relational maintenance* function helps individuals in shaping relationships during development through IIs. *Conflict linkage* is used in maintaining conflict in the relationship. The *rehearsal* function of IIs is used when planning future communication encounters. Individuals reflecting on desires and fears alike, clarifying thoughts and feelings, use the *self-understanding* function of IIs. *Catharsis* refers to the function of relieving tension and anxiety within the relationship. Finally, *compensation* is used to compensate for the lack of communication or lack of ability to communicate.

Imagined interactions theory developed along multiple dimensions, one of which employs a trait-based approach to understanding human communicative behavior (Honeycutt, Pence, & Gearhart, 2013). Scholars have provided valuable support for imagined interactions over the past few decades through the contexts of gender differences (e.g., Edwards, Honeycutt, & Zagacki, 1989; Honeycutt, 1991; Honeycutt & Patterson, 1997), relationships (e.g., Honeycutt, 1991; Honeycutt, 2009; Van Kelegom & Wright, 2013), dreams (Eldredge, Honeycutt, White, & Standige, 2016); personality (e.g., Eldredge, 2016; Honeycutt & Keaton, 2013; Honeycutt et al., 2013; Honeycutt, Pence, & Gearhart, 2012), and emotion (e.g., Allen, 1990; Trammell, 2009; Zagacki, Edwards, & Honeycutt, 1992). Utilizing imagined interaction theory (II: Edwards et al., 1988) researchers found that certain II attributes and functions are associated with specific personality traits such as narcissism through which narcissistic profiles emerge for scholars to better understand these individuals (Honeycutt et al., 2013). Furthermore, Zagacki, Edwards, and Honeycutt (1992) discovered that individuals harboring negative emotions did so with less pleasantness, increased discrepancy, and significantly more self-dominated IIs.

Gender differences also appeared present in the characteristics of imagined interactions. Women have been found to report higher occurrences of IIs than men (Edwards, Honeycutt, & Zagacki, 1989). Furthermore, Edwards et al., (1989) found that females reported higher levels of pleasantness (positive valence) in their imagined interactions than males. Honeycutt, Vickery, and Hatcher (2015) reported that proactivity was the most abundant characteristic reported by participants, while specificity was the least routinely stated characteristic.

One way to facilitate more productive communication of jealousy is to understand how jealousy is operating in terms of IIs. The functions and attributes associated with IIs illuminate the intrapersonal communication associated with jealousy in relationships. Past experiences with jealousy provide individuals a script from which they draw upon in future communication, thus allowing them to learn how to express their jealousy. Therefore, applying IIs to an evolutionary view of jealousy remains important and relevant for current and future research.

Jealousy

"Jealousy channels attention, calls up relevant memories, and channels thought in particular directions" (Buss, 1995, p. 14). Jealousy is an evolutionary attribute used to maintain relationships, but it can also destroy them (Buss, 2000). Among other psychological mechanisms, jealousy serves as an alert system to interferences in individuals' mating strategies (Buss, 1994). Jealousy may arise out of observed sexual threats from a partner's friends, or perceived emotional intimacy with another person (Worley & Samp, 2014). Men and women, however, differ in the type of jealousy experienced; men often report more cognitive jealousy and women express more behavioral jealousy (Goodboy, Horan, & Booth-Butterfield, 2012). Furthermore, a man will perceive physical sexual threats as more severe, while women will perceive emotional intimacy as a more severe threat (Buss, 1994; Buss, 2000; Metson & Buss, 2009).

Elphinston, Feeney, Noller, Connor, and Fitzgerald (2013) found that cognitive jealously and surveillance behaviors were related to relational dissatisfaction through the mediator of rumination. They defined rumination as repetitive thoughts about a current relationship. When jealousy arises in individuals, it is often a reaction to a perceived threat wherein people experience a wide range of emotions (Buss, 2000; Carson & Cupach, 2000). How individuals cope with the emotions is cognitively driven and chronic jealousy often leads to rumination, or conscious and reoccurring thoughts (Carson & Cupach, 2000). Honeycutt (2004; 2011) discussed how IIs through the conflict-linkage function are characterized by ruminating about unresolved arguments as some people become obsessed with an argument that they cannot forget. Therefore, the following hypotheses are set forth in the current study:

H1: Jealousy will be predicted by IIs involving rumination.

Personality traits play a vital role in predicting jealousy within relationships. Chin, Atkinson, Raheb, Harris, and Vernon (2017) found that cognitive, emotional, and behavioral jealousy positively correlated with traits of the dark triad (Machiavellianism, narcissism, and psychopathy). These traits also indicate deceptive behaviors, which lead to conflict within the relationship. Sexual conflict is inescapable when discussing human relationships. Humans mate long-term and within that there are explicit and implied rules regarding distribution of sexual and emotional resources (Buss, 2017). Defending against infidelity is paramount to securing sexual and emotional resources and jealousy is one such tactic (Buss, 1994). Some individuals, such as those displaying traits associated with the dark triad may purposely induce feelings of jealousy in their partner. Therefore, partners of individuals displaying dark triadic traits may take the conflict personally, unknowingly stroking the ego of their partner. It may be difficult for a person who has a tendency to take conflict personally to imagine a conflict that is not personal (Wallenfelsz & Hample, 2010). Theorem 3 of II conflict-linkage theory stated that negative IIs are invasive when people attempt to purposely create positive IIs as a therapy for conflict. A reason for this may be the tendency to take conflict personally. Therefore, the following hypotheses were posited:

H2: Jealousy will be predicted by IIs involved in conflict

H3: Jealousy will be predicted by the catharsis function of II

Jealousy may also arise from a lack of physical and/or emotional resources (Buss, 2017). The compensation function of IIs allows individuals an outlet for a lack of communication. Many individuals may feel like they are unable to communicate with their partner for fear of retaliation or other negative consequences. Conversely, individuals who are unfaithful to their partner may elicit the compensation function to intrapersonally communicate their shortcomings without any consequences, since telling their partner about their infidelities would destroy the relationship and emotionally harm the other person. Therefore, the following hypotheses were set forth:

H4: The frequency of IIs will be a predictor of jealousy.

Current Study

Procedures

A collegiate sample (N = 442) was drawn from a large southern university. Undergraduate students enrolled in introductory courses earned credit for participating in the survey through a research participation system. Participants were included based on the following criteria: 18 years or older, currently or in the last six months been in a relationship, literate in English, and enrolled in coursework at the university. Each participant signed up for a timeslot wherein they received an anonymous link where they were directed to Qualtrics for survey completion. Upon clicking the link, participants read a consent form and acknowledged their agreement or disagreement to participate in the survey.

Participants

Participants' (N = 442) age ranged from 18 to 36 (M = 19.81, *SD* = 1.673) and their ethnicities included: 77.8% Caucasian, 13.6% Black or African American, 2.7% Asian, 4.3% Hispanic, and 1.6% Other. Participants' biological sex included: 52.4% Female and 47.6% Male. Participants characterized their current relationship status as: 49.9% Single, 42.9% In a relationship, 0.7% Engaged, 0.2% Married, 1.4% In an open relationship, 4.8% It's complicated, and 0.2% Other.

Measurements

The survey consisted of multiple measurement sections that included demographics (e.g., age, education, ethnicity, sexual orientation, relationship status). Following the demographic section, participants were asked to indicate how long they identified with their current relationship status. Following this question, they were directed to think about the last argument or disagreement they had with their partner and report a general description and how long ago it occurred. This question primed their memory for the remaining questions.

Imagined interactions

The scale of imagined interactions (SII; Honeycutt, 2003) was implemented to address the functions and attributes associated with jealousy. This scale measures participants' use of imagined interactions on a 7-point Likert type scale (1 = *Strongly agree*; 7 = *Strongly disagree*). Participants were asked to answer questions pertaining to the eight attributes of IIs: frequency (e.g., I frequently have imagined interactions), proactivity (e.g., I often have imagined interactions *before* interacting with someone of importance), retroactivity (e.g., After important meetings, I frequently imagine them), variety (e.g., Many of my imagined interactions are with different people), discrepancy (e.g., I usually say in real life what I thought I would say), valence (e.g., I enjoy most of my imagined interactions), specificity (e.g., It is hard recalling the details of imagined interactions), and self-dominance (e.g., I talk a lot in my imagined interactions). Participants then answered questions in response to the six II functions: self-understanding (e.g., Imagined interaction helps me understand myself better), rehearsal (e.g., Imagined interactions help me plan what I am going to say for an anticipated encounter), catharsis (e.g., Imagined interactions help me relieve tension and stress), conflict linkage (e.g., Imagined interactions help me manage conflict), compensation (e.g., Imagining talking to someone substitutes for the absence of real communication), and relational maintenance (e.g., Imagined interactions help keep relationships alive). The scales were very reliable with an average reliability of .80.

Jealousy Scale

The Multidimensional Jealousy Scale created and validated by Pfeiffer and Wong (1989) was used to measure jealousy in the relationships and investigate the connection between IIs and jealousy communication in interpersonal relationships. Participants were asked questions pertaining to cognitive jealousy and they have certain thoughts about their partner (e.g., I suspect that my partner is secretly seeing someone behind my back) on a 7-point Likert scale (1 = *Always*; 7 = *never)*. Participants were then asked how they would emotionally react to a series of questions pertaining to emotional jealousy (e.g., my partner is flirting with someone of the opposite sex) on a 7-point likert scale (1 = *Very pleased*; 7 = *Very upset*). Finally, participants were asked to rate how often they engage in a number of behaviors on a 7-point likert scale (1 = *Never*; 7 = *Always*), which measured behavioral jealousy (e.g., I call my significant other unexpectedly, just to see if s/he is there). The subscales all had significantly strong alpha reliabilities and the combined sub-scales reliability was .90.

Results

The hypotheses were initially tested using one-tailed Pearson correlation (see Table 3.1). For those of you are interested in statistics, you can google the statistics to see what they mean. Probability levels of both 0.05 and 0.01 were retained and adopted as noted. Correlations range from −1 to 1 with absolute vales of .25 indicating a medium sized effect while values above .50 are large. Table 3.2 presents the standardized regression coefficients for cognitive jealousy predicted by the attributes (block 1) and functions (block 2) of imagined interactions. Again, the values range from −1 to 1 and values with increasing magnitude are important. Table 3.3 presents the standardized regression

Table 3.1. Correlations.

Attributes	*Cognitive*	*Emotional*	*Behavioral*
Frequency	–.29**	.04	.15**
Proactivity	–.13**	.02	.02
Retroactivity	–.18**	.02	.09*
Variety	–.14**	–.05	–.02
Discrepancy	–.11**	.15**	.09*
Valence	.001	.01	–.07
Specificity	–.20**	.09*	.09*
Self-Dominance	–.03	.04	.02
Functions			
Self-Understanding	–.14**	.01	.11*
Rehearsal	–.10*	.001	.04
Catharsis	.14**	–.06	–.10*
Conflict-Linkage	–.29**	.18**	.28**
Compensation	–.09*	.13**	.17**
Relational Maintenance	–.08	.04	.11**

Note: ** Indicates significance at the 0.01 level. * Indicates significance at the 0.05 level.

Table 3.2. Predictors of Cognitive Jealousy.

Attributes	ß	t
Frequency	–.66	–4.58**
Proactivity	.08	1.23
Retroactivity	–.06	–.93
Variety	–.001	–.02
Discrepancy	–.06	–1.28
Valence	.104	2.14*
Specificity	–.134	–2.62**
Self-Dominance	–.001	-.03
Functions		
Self-Understanding	.07	–1.20
Rehearsal	–.07	–1.09
Catharsis	.13	2.53**
Conflict-Linkage	–.23	–4.40**
Compensation	-.04	–.72
Relational Maintenance	.03	.63

Note: N = 442. Block 1: r^2 = .110; Adjusted r^2 = .093. Block 2: r^2 = .104; Adjusted r^2 = .092.
** Indicates significance at the 0.01 level. * Indicates significance at the 0.05 level.

Table 3.3. Predictors of Emotional Jealousy.

Attributes	ß	t
Frequency	.20	.40
Proactivity	.01	.21
Retroactivity	–.01	–.17
Variety	–.11	–1.85
Discrepancy	–.15	3.00*
Valence	.001	.02
Specificity	.12	2.10*
Self-Dominance	.022	.45
Functions		
Self-Understanding	.03	–.41
Rehearsal	.001	.01
Catharsis	–.01	–.17
Conflict-Linkage	.17	3.06**
Compensation	.09	1.78
Relational Maintenance	–.02	–.30

Note: N = 442. Block 1: r^2 = .039; Adjusted r^2 = .021. Block 2: r^2 = .041; Adjusted r^2 = .028.
** Indicates significance at the 0.01 level. * Indicates significance at the 0.05 level.

coefficients for emotional jealousy predicted by the functions (block 1) and attributes (block 2) of imagined interactions; and Table 3.4 presents the standardized regression coefficients for behavioral jealousy predicted by the functions (block 1) and attributes (block 2) of imagined interactions. The results provide moderate support for the hypotheses: (H1) jealousy will be predicted by IIs involving rumination, (H2) jealousy will be predicted by IIs involving conflict, (H3) jealousy will be predicted through the catharsis function of IIs, and (H4) the frequency of IIs is a predictor of jealousy. Both blocks of cognitive, emotional, and behavioral jealousy predicted by IIs were significant. As revealed in tables one through three, there was support for the first and second hypotheses about jealousy's prediction by IIs involving rumination and jealousy associated with IIs involving conflict. The conflict-linkage function of IIs had a strong effect across all three indicating that levels of cognitive, emotional, and behavioral jealousy can be predicted by the conflict-linkage function of IIs. Additionally, support was found for the third hypothesis, revealing that cognitive jealousy is predicted by the catharsis function of IIs. Finally,

Table 3.4. Predictors of Behavioral Jealousy.

Attributes	ß	t
Frequency	.18	3.01*
Proactivity	–.09	–1.37
Retroactivity	.09	1.46
Variety	–.11	–1.88
Discrepancy	.06	1.25
Valence	–.11	–2.19*
Specificity	.09	1.63
Self-Dominance	.01	.11
Functions		
Self-Understanding	.06	.91
Rehearsal	–.01	–.20
Catharsis	–.06	–1.08
Conflict-Linkage	.23	4.25**
Compensation	.11	2.16*
Relational Maintenance	.01	.14

Note: N = 442. Block 1: r^2 = .055; Adjusted r^2 = .037. Block 2: r^2 = .093; Adjusted r^2 = .081.
** Indicates significance at the 0.01 level. * Indicates significance at the 0.05 level.

the fourth hypothesis was supported in that cognitive jealousy and behavioral jealousy are predicted by the frequency attribute of IIs.

Furthermore, the models provided additional predictors of jealousy. A strong negative effect is discrepancy and cognitive jealousy which indicates that the more cognitively jealous an individual is, the less discrepant their IIs become. In other words, what they imagine happening in a conversation does not play out in a similar fashion and the more cognitively jealous they become the less likely their IIs will match the conversational outcome. Discrepancy is also moderately predictive of emotional jealousy. The valence attribute also had moderate effects on cognitive and behavioral jealousy. These effects indicate that the more cognitively jealous a person is, the more positive their IIs are. Conversely, the more behaviorally jealous an individual is, the more negative their IIs become. Specificity moderately predicted emotional jealousy and compensation predicted behavioral jealousy. Hence, individuals become more emotionally jealous as their IIs increase in specificity and they sue the compensation function of IIs as their behavioral jealousy increases.

Summary and Applications to Mental Health

The purpose of the current study was to extend the literature on imagined interactions theory in understanding how the attributes and functions operate with respect to jealousy in romantic relationships. Particular imagined interaction attributes and functions emerged as strong and moderate predictors of jealousy. Therefore, insight into some attributes of jealous individuals surfaced through this investigation. As such, forms of cognitive, emotional, and behavioral jealousy appear to be predicted by certain attributes and functions of imagined interactions.

Extending the II literature, this investigation provided continued support for II theory's predictive power in interpersonal contexts. Specifically, IIs involving rumination and conflict are strong predictors of jealousy across all three categories through the conflict-linkage function or keeping conflict alive through imagined interactions. The strong negative effect between cognitive jealousy and conflict-linkage suggests that individuals may not be trying to keep conflict alive in their relationship through imagined interactions. Rather, they may be replaying the conflict in an effort to decrease their jealousy. Conversely, the strong positive effects found between conflict-linkage and emotional and behavioral jealousy indicates that increased rumination about jealousy evoking circumstances increases how they feel about and express their jealousy. Individuals might continue thinking about the circumstances in an effort to decrease their jealousy just to have the feeling and behaviors increase as a result. This leads people to the catharsis function of their imagined interactions. As results indicated, the catharsis function adequately predicts jealousy. Thinking more about why they are jealous or the situation that lead to jealousy might actually increase an individual's jealousy inadvertently. Thus, these findings show that thinking a lot about the jealous enticing circumstances may be detrimental to the actual amelioration of the feelings.

Imagine this scenario: Think about the thoughts that you have when you feel jealous. Lurking behind the paranoia toward our partners, or the criticisms toward a perceived third-party threat, are often critical thoughts toward others. Thoughts like, "What does he/she see in them?" can quickly reflect social comparison theory in which we compare ourselves to others (e.g., "They are more attractive or successful than me!"). Yet, if cognitive jealousy turns into behavioral jealousy, when you learn of a partner's infidelity, then you may react by directing anger at yourself for being "foolish, unlovable, ruined or rejected." Hence, conflict-linkage and rumination is used which is directed toward you or the partner. Hence, you can use self-therapy in the form of imagined interactions to deal with your jealousy emotion.

As Parrott (2001) notes, "jealousy involves an entire "emotional episode," including a complex "narrative": the circumstances that lead up to jealousy, jealousy itself as emotion, any attempt at self-regulation, subsequent actions and events and the resolution of the episode" (p. 306). The narrative can originate from experienced facts, thoughts, perceptions, memories, but also imagination, guess and assumptions. The more society and culture matter in the formation of these factors, the more jealousy can have a social and cultural origin, which reflects an evolutionary view. Hence, introspection and imagined interactions about jealousy can help with the trauma of jealousy if done constructively; which means use of the catharsis (e.g., I feel about this and need to move on) and the, self-understanding (e.g., why I am jealous) functions. Yet, avoid destructive uses including continual rumination over the jealousy incidents. They there is research on catastrophizing in which individuals continually imagine, the worst possible outcomes which results in depression (Honeycutt, 2000).

This study also found effects that were not initially hypothesized. Discrepancy, or the similarity between the imagined interaction and the actual outcome, moderately predicted cognitive jealousy. An individual may be doing more harm than good when thinking about the jealousy-evoking situation instead of addressing in through verbal communication. This also plays into an individual keeping the conflict alive through the conflict-linkage function. Furthermore, the positive/negative valanced imagined interactions had a positive effect on cognitive jealousy and a negative effect on behavioral jealousy. The more negatively an individual imagines a situation the more cognitively jealous they become. Also, as one would believe, the more specific the imagined interaction is, the more emotionally and behaviorally jealous they become.

In sum, this current study contributed to the line of jealousy in close relationships and the predictive power of imagined interactions theory. These findings point to the need for further investigation into this phenomenon. This study may result in important practical implications for therapists, psychiatrists, and psychologists when dealing with jealousy in romantic relationships. The predictive nature could help combat violent behaviors and outcomes before they occur.

Discussion Questions

1. *When was the last time you were jealous of someone or something? Did you have an inner voice in the form of imagined interactions in which you confronted the person? Was it beneficial or destructive? Why or why not?*
2. *What types of jealousy (cognitive, behavioral, or emotional) do you most often have? How do you deal with your jealousy in constructive and destructive ways?*
3. *Have you ever felt depressed by dealing with jealousy? Can you provide examples of imagined interactions in which you discussed why you felt jealous with the person who made you feel jealous? Did this help you?*

References

Allen, T. H. (1990). An investigation of Machiavellianism and imagined interaction. *Communication Research Reports*, *7*(2), 116–120. doi: http://dx.doi.org/10.1080/08824099009359864

Berkos, K. M., Allen, T. H., Kearney, P., & Plax, T. G. (2001). When norms are violated: Imagined interactions as processing and coping mechanisms. *Communication Monographs*, 68(3), 289–300.

Buss, D. M. (1994). *The evolution of desire: Strategies of human mating*. New York, NY: Harper Collins.

Buss, D. M. (1995). Evolutionary psychology: A new paradigm for psychological science. *Psychological Inquiry*, 6, 1–30.

Buss, D. M. (2000). *The dangerous passion: Why jealousy is as necessary as love and sex*. New York, NY: The Free Press.

Buss, D. M. (2017). Sexual conflict in human mating. *Current Directions in Psychological Science*, 26(4), 307–313. doi: 10.1177/0963721417695559

Carson, C. L. & Cupach, W. R. (2000). Fueling the flames of the green-eyed monster: The role of ruminative thought in reaction to romantic jealousy. *Western Journal of Communication*, 64(3), 308–329.

Chin, K., Atkinson, B. E., Rahebh, H. Harris, E., & Verson, P. A. (2017). The dark side of romantic jealousy. *Personality and Individual Differences 115(1)*, 23–29. doi: 10.1016/j.paid.2016.10.003

Edwards, R., Honeycutt, J. M., & Zagacki, K. S. (1988). Imagined interaction as an element of social cognition. *Western Journal of Speech Communication*, *52(1)*, 23–45.

Edwards, R., Honeycutt, J. M., & Zagacki, K. S. (1989). Sex differences in imagined interactions. *Sex Roles*, *21*, 263–272. doi: http://dx.doi.org/10.1007/BF00289906

Eldredge, J. H. (2016). Imagined interaction frequency and the five-factor model of personality. *Imagination, Cognition, and Personality*, 35(4), 351–358. doi:10.1177/0276236616636215

Eldredge, J. H., Honeycutt, J. M., White, R. C., & Standige, M. (2016). On the functions of imagined interactions in night dreams. *Imagination, Cognition, and Personality*, *35(3)*, doi:10.1177/0276236615595231

Elphinston, R. A., Feeney, J. A., Noller, P., Connor, J. P., & Fitzgerald, J. (2013). Romantic jealousy and relationship satisfaction: The cost of rumination. Western Journal of Communication, 77(3), 293–304. doi: 10.1080/10570314.2013.770161

Goodboy, A. K., Horan, S. M., & Booth-Butterfield, M. (2012). Intentional jealousy-evoking behavior in romantic relationships as a function of received partner affection and love styles. *Communication Quarterly*, 60(3), 370–385. doi: 10.1080/01463373.2012.688792

Honeycutt, J. M. (1991). The endorsement of myths about marriage as a function of gender, age, religious denomination, and educational level. *Communication Research Reports*, 8(2), 101–111. doi: 10.1080/08824099109359881

Honeycutt, J. M. (2000). It's the thought that counts. In C. G. Waugh (Ed.), *Let's talk: A cognitive-skills approach to interpersonal communication* (pp. 18–20). Newark, DE: Kendall-Hunt.

Honeycutt, J. M. (2003). *Imagined interactions: Daydreaming about communication*. Cresskill, NJ: Hampton Press.

Honeycutt, J. M. (2009). Symbolic interdependence, imagined interaction, and relationship quality. *Imagination, Cognition, and Personality*, 28, 303–320. doi: 10.2190/IC.28.4.b

Honeycutt, J. M. (2015). Imagined interaction theory: Mental representations of interpersonal communication. In D. O. Braithwaite & P. Schrodt (Eds.), *Engaging Theories in Interpersonal Communication* (2nd ed., pp. 75–87). Thousand Oaks, CA: Sage.

Honeycutt, J. M. (2015). Imagined interactions theory: Mental representations of interpersonal communication. In L. A. Baxter, & D. O. Braithwaite (Eds.), *Engaging theories in interpersonal communication* (pp. 77–87). Thousand Oaks, CA: Sage.

Honeycutt, J. M., Edwards, R., & Zagacki, K. S. (1989–1990). Using imagined interaction features to predict self-awareness: Loneliness, locus of control, self-dominance and emotional intensity. *Imagination, Cognition, and Personality*, *9(1)*, 17–31.

Honeycutt, J. M., & Keaton, S. A. (2013). Imagined interactions and personality preferences as predictors of relationship quality. *Imagination, Cognition, and Personality*, *32*, 3–21. doi: http://dx.doi.org/10.2190/IC.32.1.b

Honeycutt, J. M., & Patterson, J. (1997). Affinity strategies in relationships: The role of gender and imagined interactions in maintaining liking among college roommates. *Personal Relationships*, 4, 35–46. doi: 10.1111/j.1475-6811.1997.tb00129.x

Honeycutt, J. M., Pence, M. E., & Gearhart, C. C. (2013). Using imagined interactions to predict covert narcissism. *Communication Reports*, 26, 26–38. doi: 10.1080/08934215.2013.77305115

Honeycutt, J. M., Pence, M. E., & Gearhart, C. C. (2012). Associations between imagined interactions and the "big five" personality traits. *Imagination, Cognition, and Personality*, 32(3), 273–289. doi: http://dx.doi.org/10.2190/IC.32.3.d

Honeycutt, J. M., Vickery, A. J. & Hatcher, L. C. (2015). The daily use of imagined interaction features. *Communication Monographs*, 82, 2, 201–223.doi: 10.1080/03637751.2014.953965

Metson, C. M., & Buss, D. M. (2009). *Why women have sex: Understanding sexual motivations–from adventure to revenge (and everything in between)*. New York, NY: Henry Holt and Company.

Parrott, W. G. (2001). *Emotions in social psychology: Essential readings*. Philadelphia, PA: Hove Psychology Press.

Petrosky, E., Blair, J. M., Betz, C. J., Fowler, K. A., Jack, S. P., & Lyons, B. H. (2017). Racial and ethnic differences in homicides of adult women and the role of intimate partner violence—United States, 2003–2014. *Morbidity and Mortality Weekly Report*, 66(28), 741–746. doi: http://dx.doi.org/10.15585/mmwr.mm6628a1

Pfeiffer, S. M., & Wong, P. T. P. (1989). Multidimensional jealousy. *Journal of Social and Personal Relationships*, *6(2)*, 181–196.

Trammell, E. S. (2009). Forgiving self: The role of imagined interaction in forgiveness. *LOGOS: A Journal of Undergraduate Research*, *2*, 92.

Van Kelegom, M. J., & Wright, C. N. (2013). The use of imagined interactions to manage relational uncertainty. *Southern Journal of Communication*, *78(2)*, 91–106. doi: 10.1080/104179X.2012.726688

Worley, T. R., & Samp, J. A. (2014). Exploring the associations between relational uncertainty, jealousy about partner's friendships, and jealousy expression in dating relationships. *Communication Studies*, 65(4), 370–388. doi: 10.1080/10510974.2013.833529

Younkin, J. (2018). Woman in gold. *On Did it anyway* [Compact Disc]. Florida: Jamie Younkin.

Zagacki, K. S., Edwards, R., & Honeycutt, J. M. (1992). The role of mental imagery and emotion in imagined interaction. *Communication Quarterly*, 40, 56–68. doi: 10.1080/01463379209369820

SECTION 2

DEALING WITH PHYSICAL, EMOTIONAL, AND MATERIAL LOSS

· 4 ·

THE ROLE OF MENTAL IMAGERY AND IMAGINED INTERACTIONS IN COPING WITH BEREAVEMENT AND LOSS

Jonathon K. Frost

It is no mystery that the death of a loved one is one of the single most challenging events a person will face in a lifetime, and it is something that nearly everyone will face at some point. The death of a significant other is viewed as one of life's greatest stresses, with reports of increased mortality and morbidity for the surviving spouse or parent, especially in the early months of bereavement (Buckley et al., 2012). How we grieve, however, varies drastically, depending on a considerably large list of factors including personality, socialization, experience with loss, or emotional intelligence. Consider the following passage:

> … my father, although he was a very ordinary man, had 300 or 400 people who came to his funeral, who were also under a moral obligation to shake the hand of the principal bereaved. So, it wasn't just enough for them to be there in the crowd. They all came up to you and shook your hands, and as they shook your hands they say it like a cliché, they say "sorry for your trouble." In fact, they shake your hands so many times that the bones in your hand begin to ache. This is a way of countering death denial. Because these individuals are shaking your hand, pressing into your flesh and they're saying—it's not just sorry for your trouble, but: "they're dead. They're dead. They're dead. They're dead. They're dead." So you, at the end of that existential experience, it's very hard to think they're coming back, which again is a very normal reaction to grief. (BBC, 2018)

The preceding passage is a reflection from Kevin Toolis, author of *My Father's Wake*, on the power of bereavement rituals (specifically an Irish funeral) in helping us come to terms with mortality—not only with our own mortality, but also with the mortality of those we love. However, the passage also reflects something fundamental about the nature of bereavement—the power of the mind in shaping how we grieve. In the aforementioned case, the interactions of mourners with the principle bereaved serve not simply as a form of social support, but also to convey and cement a very specific message: your loved one is dead, and is not returning. The message serves to combat the mental imagery that a loved one is still alive, or will be returning, something which is quite common among the bereaved, especially individuals suffering from pathological bereavement (Fidaleo, Proano, & Friedberg, 1999). Such individuals might imagine scenarios in their head in which their deceased loved one is still alive, which can become so vivid that the individual actually begins to believe they are interacting with the deceased. This is a prime example of how mental imagery influences the bereavement process. The purpose of this chapter is to examine just that, to explore ways that individuals and therapist use mental imagery—specifically imagined interactions (referenced throughout this volume; see also Honeycutt, 2003, 2010; Zagacki, Edwards, & Honeycutt, 1992)—to navigate the bereavement process and to cope with their loss.

Examining the Bereavement Process

In order to understand the role of mental imagery in bereavement, it is important to first understand the phenomenon itself. Death has a profound effect on the human psyche. Take a moment to consider a person you care deeply about, someone who instantly comes to your mind when you think of the phrase "loved ones." Even as you read these lines, you are likely having an instinctual unpleasant reaction to the thought of that person dying. If you do have an emotional reaction to the thought, what is it? Anger? Anxiety? Sadness? Or simply an acute feeling of emptiness? The truth is, all of these are regular, normal, and potentially even healthy responses to grief. In fact, bereavement has been associated with over 15 different emotional responses (Nesse, 2005).

Bereavement is a very unique phenomenon. During bereavement, every individual will grieve in different ways, varying across emotion type, frequency, intensity, and duration. Accordingly, there is no single model that perfectly encapsulates the act of bereavement. There are, however, a variety of approaches that help us better understand the experiences of a bereaved individual, the most serialized of which being the Kübler-Ross (1969; Kübler-Ross & Kessler, 2005) model. Even if you have never formally studied bereavement, you are likely already somewhat familiar with the model, due to its prolific use in television and film. The model describes 5 different emotional responses that are considered to universally apply to grief, although it is not assumed that everyone will grieve the exact same way, or that each person will experience all five stages. The five stages are denial, anger, bargaining, depression, and acceptance. While the model has received a great deal of criticism for its linearity (see Konisberg, 2011), upon initial construction the model was not intended to describe a linear progression, but rather to represent fundamental grief responses in the wake of death. It is not expected that each individual will experience all stages, or that they will experience each stage only once. Instead, individuals may move back and forth through the stages numerous times, or may linger in a single stage for long periods of time. For example, during complicated grief, in which the bereavement process endures for an excessive period of time (Physician Data Query, 2013), individuals may fluctuate between anger and depression for years without ever reaching a place of acceptance.

Maciejewski, Zhang, Block, and Prigerson (2007) obtained findings consistent with the five stage model, although some of their other findings were inconsistent, suggesting that it is not a perfect model. The model is most useful when considered as a representation of the basic human emotions that are likely occur following the death of a loved one. While each person will experience variations in the bereavement process, the truth is that there are a great deal of similarities in the ways people grieve. We may not be able to predict with accuracy the way that a single individual will grieve, but we can identify patterns among groups of individuals and learn to identify emotional responses when they occur.

We can think of the Kübler-Ross model as an emotional model to understanding bereavement. Bereavement, however, is not strictly an emotional response. Bereavement encompasses not only the emotional challenges that a person faces after a loved one dies, but also the practical challenges of everyday life. Indeed, the Kübler-Ross model might be better characterized as a model of grief, rather than a model of bereavement (as Kübler-Ross herself characterized it in later years; see Kübler-Ross & Kessler, 2005). Conversely, the dual-process model of bereavement (Stroebe & Schut, 1999) was designed to encompass both the emotional and practical challenges of bereavement. According to the model, when a loved one dies, we experience not only emotional turmoil, as articulated by the Kübler-Ross model, but also disruption to our daily routine and potential threats to our very identity. Depending on how intertwined an individual's life was with the deceased, the survivor could suffer extreme disruption to their daily life. When two people's lives are closely connected, financial burdens, daily routines, and other responsibilities are often shared between the two individuals, sometimes disproportionately. For example, a married individual may tend to nearly all of the financial responsibilities, while their spouse assumes more of other responsibilities. When one of them dies, the survivor is then solely responsible for tending to all of those issues (Caron, Lafontaine, Bureau, Levesque, & Johnson, 2012). Depending on the duration of the relationship, the surviving partner may be wholly unprepared to deal with those responsibilities, lacking the toolsets required to navigate the practical challenges, all the while dealing with the emotional weight of their loved one's death.

Adding to the practical challenges of bereavement are the external relationships and internal roles that a person possesses. For example, a married individual's external relationships often exists only within the context of that person's marriage. When the spouse dies, the dynamics of the surviving individual's external relationships are forever changed, because the role that the surviving individual plays, and thus his or her very identity, has changed (Ford, 2010). For example, if a woman's husband dies, she no longer possesses the role of "wife," which is then supplanted by the role "grieving widow." People interacting with her will therefore adjust their patterns of behavior to adapt to this new role. Thus, in a way, the wife has not only lost her husband, but has also lost the stability of various other relationships within her life. The relationships may not disappear entirely, of course, and may return to normal given a period of time, but at least temporarily those relationships are drastically changed. In extreme circumstances, those relationships can serve as a constant reminder of the bereaved individual's loss, inhibiting their ability to heal (Rossetto, Lannutti, & Strauman, 2015).

A third way of examining bereavement is to distinguish between grieving patterns deemed as normal or healthy, and those deemed as disruptive or unhealthy. The National Cancer Institute (Physician Data Query, 2013) has identified three different types of grief that individuals experience, based on the chronology of death and the duration of grief: anticipatory grief, normal grief, and complicated or chronic grief. Anticipatory grief occurs before an individual passes, but after the possibility or inevitability of death is known, and can be both healthy or unhealthy. Normal grief is the process that most people go through, is considered to be a healthy and necessary process, and generally continues for a period of time ranging from 6 months 2 to years. Finally, complicated or chronic grief mirrors the patterns of normal grief, but is extremely severe in intensity and duration, to the point that it is considered debilitating.

Of the three types, anticipatory grief only applies to individuals who have knowledge of impending death prior to the actual event. During anticipatory grief, individuals attempt to process the difficult emotions surrounding an individual's death. Proactive imagined interactions are often common during anticipatory grief, as individuals imagine the moment of the person's passing, as well as imagining future life without the person (PDQ, 2013). Anticipatory grief can serve to help aid the healing process in surviving family members, and can decrease the intensity and duration of bereavement, but not erase it entirely (Overton & Cottone, 2016). Anticipatory grief is rare, however, as people often refuse to confront their emotions prior to a person's passing, even if death is expected (PDQ, 2013). Dealing with those emotions is not only incredibly challenging, but it can also feel like an act of abandonment towards the person who is still alive. Furthermore, while anticipatory grief can be beneficial to survivors, it can be incredibly emotionally taxing to dying patients. Being surrounded by mourners can force the individuals to feel emotionally overwhelmed and withdraw from others, and can also deprive them of positive emotions in the waning moments of their lives (PDQ, 2013). Accordingly, it is important that a trained grief councilor or medical professional supervise the process, and that mourners dedicate time and energy into making the person's final moments happy as well as attempting to find closure.

Survivors of the deceased experience normal grief or complicated grief in the aftermath of death, and they share similar characteristics. People experiencing normal grief still experience the same negative emotions typically associated with bereavement. Regardless of the mental health of the bereaved individual, the death of a loved one is extremely taxing, and requires a great deal of time to recover from. The most intense symptoms of grief dissipate, however, typically somewhere between six months to two years after the death (PDQ, 2013). Research suggests that the majority (80%–90%) of people experience normal grief (Lobb et al., 2010). In general, a period of denial or avoidance is common shortly following the incident. Shortly after, the bereaved individual experiences intense emotional reactions, including anger, resentment, frustration, sadness, despair, fear, etc., coupled with declining appetites for food, social interaction, and sexual activity. Bereavement may interfere with the individual's daily routine, and many bereaved individuals suffer from a loss of motivation and extreme fatigue. Eventually, given enough time to deal with the emotional challenges and practical realities that follow death, people begin to recover, and appetites start to return. Typically, the appetite for food is the first to recover, followed shortly after by social and sexual appetites. People begin planning for the future, and adjusting to their new reality without their deceased loved one. By the two year mark, most people have recovered from the most severe symptoms of grief and are able to lead a normal life free of bereavement-related disruption (PDQ, 2013).

While most people experience a normal bereavement process, for a portion of the bereaved population (10%–20%), grief develops into a maladaptive pattern that lasts for far longer and is extremely detrimental to the health and wellbeing of the bereaved individual (PDQ, 2013). Complicated grief is "a pattern of adaptation to bereavement that involves the presentation of certain grief-related symptoms at a time beyond that which is considered adaptive" (Lobb et al., 2010, p. 674). While the experiences of a bereaved individual suffering from complicated grief mirror the symptoms of normal grief, the symptoms are more acute and last far longer, and can be debilitating to daily functioning. If there is no intervention, the grief can develop into a pathological state that controls nearly every component of the bereaved individual's life (Fidaleo et al., 1999).

There are a variety of factors that influence an individual's risk of developing complicated grief. In general, 58% of individuals are at low risk of developing complicated grief, 36% are at moderate risk, and 6% are high risk (Aoun et al., 2015). Relationship intensity and duration, a lack of social support following death, sudden unexpected deaths, low self-esteem or self-efficacy, certain religious beliefs, and a lack of an opportunity to speak with the deceased prior to their passing are all factors that increase an individual's chances of developing complicated grief (Aoun et al., 2015; Lobb et al., 2010; PDQ, 2013). Additionally, recent research suggests that mental imagery, including imagined interactions with the deceased, may play a role in shaping how individuals bereave, and could in fact be a determining factor in whether or not the individual suffers from complicated grief (Fidaleo et al., 1999; Foa, Ikeda-Hearst, & Perry, 1995; Ford, 2010). This chapter now turns to an examination of how mental imagery can be used to both the benefit and detriment of bereaving individuals.

The Role of Mental Imagery in the Bereavement Process

Mental imagery associated with the bereavement process can be both positive and negative. On the one hand, imagined interactions can be used to gain a sense of catharsis and relive positive past experiences with the deceased (Ford, 2010). However, in extreme situations mental imagery can be downright debilitating, forcing individuals to relive traumatic moments over and over again or preventing them from gaining closure and moving on with their life. Indeed, in many situations of complicated bereavement, bereaved individuals demonstrate symptoms similar in form to symptoms of post traumatic stress disorder, or PTSD (Foa et al., 1995; Kavanaugh, 1990; Rynearson, 1994). Intrusive images, a hallmark symptom of PTSD, similarly characterize pathological grief reactions (Horowitz, Bonanno, & Holen, 1993). Individuals experiencing bereavement stemming from violent and unexpected death are particularly susceptible to negative mental imagery. It is not uncommon for such individuals to experience intrusive reenactment (even if they did not witness the death first hand), nightmares, concentration issues, and pervasive fear surrounding the circumstances of their deceased loved one's demise (Rynearson, 1994). Similarly, individuals suffering from pathological bereavement experience physiological arousal, phobic avoidance, and emotional numbing in ways that mirror individuals suffering from PTSD (Foa et al., 1995).

Imagined interactions are extremely common for a person experiencing pathological grief, are extremely negative in valence, and can disrupt a healthy grieving process. Individuals replay the final moments of their loved one over and over again in their mind. As Fidaleo et al., (1999) note, "Bereaved individuals may repeatedly imagine the lost loved one's final moments before death. These last painful images are repeatedly elicited and consequently, the bereaved individual holds onto only a partial memory wherein the loved one is seen as injured, damaged, vulnerable, and/or impaired. The bereaved individual is then left with an incomplete image which does not reflect the deceased's entire life" (p. 117). This incomplete picture of a lost loved one leaves a deep emotional scar that may prevent the bereaved individual from benefiting from positive reflection, instead forcing them into a pattern of negative rumination. Accordingly, the individual develops a pattern of phobic avoidance towards anything that reminds them of the deceased, which can be incredibly disruptive to that individual's daily routine, and prevent them from adequately emotionally processing their grief in a healthy way. Such cycles can last years, even decades, without proper intervention.

Clinical psychologists have dedicated a great deal of time into researching how positive mental imagery can be used in psychotherapy as a way of treating the negative mental imagery characteristic of pathological bereavement (Fidaleo et al., 1999). The role of imagery work in psychotherapy is to increase personal empowerment and to combat false or incomplete mental narratives that dominate bereaved individuals' thoughts. Individuals suffering from traumatic grief reactions likely possess damaged perceptions of self-efficacy and a greater sense of vulnerability (Gluhoski, 1995). Through increasing the individual's perception of self-control and decreasing feelings of vulnerability, mental imagery work serves to help individuals feel more capable of confronting the negative emotions eroding their day-to-day lives, in order to eventually positively reframe the negative cycles of rumination, leading to a more healthy bereavement process. While there are a variety of mental imagery techniques used by clinical psychologists to treat pathological bereavement, they typically around these two basic notions.

Examples of mental imagery work in psychotherapy include writing a goodbye letter to a deceased loved one, visiting the loved one's grave and having a conversation with them, or an imagined interaction with the bereaved loved one in a positive environment in order to combat negative thoughts about the individuals death (Fidaleo et al., 1999). All three examples illustrate the therapeutic role of imagined interactions in the bereavement process. While negatively valenced imagined interactions can lead to rumination cycles that disrupt individuals lives, positive imagined interactions can be used to counteract negative mental imagery and to bolster the healing process.

Imagined Interactions as a Form of Relational Maintenance Following Sudden Death

So far, this chapter has detailed a variety of potential negative outcomes associated with mental imagery in the aftermath of death. The use of imagined interactions, however, is quite normal during the bereavement process (Frost, Honeycutt, & Heath, 2017), and can be a healthy coping mechanism. Imagined interactions have been noted for their therapeutic uses when real interactions cannot take place (Honeycutt, 2003). As noted by clinical psychologists (Fidaleo et al., 1999; Foa et al., 1995), imagined interactions with the deceased can be used to positively reframe the person's death as well as the relationship between the survivor and the deceased. Imagined interactions can also be useful for obtaining catharsis and self-understanding (Honeycutt, 2010), by allowing individuals to explore any lingering unfinished business with the deceased and to examine the nature of their relationship.

Research suggests that grief is exacerbated when a bereaved individual is incapable of speaking to a dying loved one prior to death (Parkes, 1975). In such an event, individuals are left ruminating on all the things they never got a chance to say to their deceased loved ones (Costello, 1999; Parkes & Weiss, 1983). Accordingly, they may have more imagined interactions with the deceased than individuals who were able to achieve some sense of catharsis prior to the death incident. Ford (2010) identified an inverse relationship between psychological adjustment to bereavement and the use of imagined interactions with the deceased loved one. There are two possible explanations for the inverse relationship. The first explanation is that imagined interactions are simply damaging to the healing process. As previously outlined, improper use of imagined interactions can lead to an unhealthy rumination cycle that can be extremely disruptive. Nevertheless, there are also well-documented positive outcomes for the use of imagined interactions. It is possible that social stigma associated with holding onto the deceased (Klass, Silverman, & Nickman, 2014) damages the bereaved individual's perception of using imagined interactions, even if they are used in a positive manner.

The second explanation is a reverse causal relationship, in that individuals who are suffering more are then more likely to turn to imagined interactions to alleviate their suffering, for better or worse. Frost et al., (2017) explored this relationship by examining the relationship between the nature of death and the use of imagined interactions. Because individuals are unable to speak to the deceased prior to passing, and because they are unable to emotionally prepare themselves for their impending loss, individuals bereaving from a sudden, unexpected death suffer more than individuals bereaving from an expected death. While both situations are challenging, the damaging impact of sudden death is well documented, resulting in severe psychological and physiological trauma that can potentially even lead to death (; Lundin, 1984; Parkes, 1975; Parkes & Weiss, 1983; Tsai et al., 2016).

Frost et al., (2017) argued that individuals experiencing sudden death bereavement would be more likely to turn to imagined interactions and social media to maintain their relationship with the deceased following his or her death. Because the survivor is unable to speak to the deceased directly, they may post on social media memoriums as a way to communicate final thoughts directly to the deceased, or to send and receive social support (Rossetto et al., 2015). Additionally, survivors should be more likely to use imagined interactions to attempt to relive past encounters with the deceased or imagine new conversations with the deceased (Frost et al., 2017). In order to test the hypothesis, the authors conducted a survey of bereaving individuals consisting of both those experiencing sudden death bereavement and those experiencing expected death bereavement. Correlation analysis results are shown in Table 4.1.

Table 4.1. Correlations and Mean Patterns for Bereaving Behaviors and Perceptions in SDB and EDB Conditions.

	1	2	3	M	SD	SDB M	EDB M	*t*	*p*
1. Type of Bereavement									
2. Social Support	.16*			5.31	.90	5.14	5.43	5.40*	.02*
3. Relational Maintenance via IIs	–.16*	.08		3.68	1.27	3.86	3.45	4.54*	.03*
4. Social Media Use	–.17*	.08	.28**	1.90	1.12	2.11	1.70	4.22*	.04*

Note: N = 201. A point-biserial correlation is reported between bereavement type and continuous variables.
* Correlation/t-test is significant at the 0.05 level (2-tailed).
** Correlation/t-test is significant at the 0.01 level (2-tailed).

A significant relationship was identified between bereavement type and the use of imagined interactions and social media for relational maintenance, such that individuals suffering sudden death bereavement were more likely to use both than individuals suffering expected death bereavement. The pattern was replicated using a multiple discriminant analysis. This statistical technique is used to find a linear combination of that characterizes or separates two or more classes of objects or events. Hence, people with sudden death bereavement maybe classified by a combination of certain characteristics. The standardized canonical coefficients range from −1 to 1 with higher magnitudes indicating more discriminatory power on behalf of the variable.As shown in Table 4.2, the coefficients reveal that sudden death bereavement is associated with an increased use of imagined interactions and social media for relational maintenance and a decreased perception of social support compared to expected death bereavement.

Table 4.2. Multiple Discriminant Analysis of Sudden Death vs. Expected Death on Bereaving Behavior and Perception.

Bereaving Behaviors/Perceptions	*Standardized Function Coefficient*
Social Support	–.65
Relational Maintenance with Deceased via II's	.36
Psychological Distress	.09
Social Environment	–.10
Relationship with Family	–.25
Social Media Use	.64
Bereavement Self-Efficacy	.01

Bereavement expectancy function: χ^2 (2) = 13.97, p = .05, canonical r = .30
Group centroids: Sudden Death Bereavement = .28, Expected Death Bereavement = –.34

When a loved one dies suddenly, survivors are left desperately wishing for an opportunity to speak to the deceased one final time (Costello, 1999). Accordingly, they turn to imagined interactions and social media to facilitate final conversations, even if they are only imagined. While this can be a healthy coping mechanism, it can also be detrimental if the process becomes a negative rumination cycle. It is vitally important that individuals suffering sudden death bereavement have a strong social support structure, as they tend to feel less supported on average than individuals experiencing expected death bereavement.

Summary

Bereavement is a natural process, and one that everyone will likely experience at some point throughout their life. Mental imagery and imagined interactions play an important role in determining how people cope while bereaving, and whether or not they will suffer from complicated grief or pathological bereavement. Mental imagery plays a role in both healthy and unhealthy bereavement. Due to the inability to communicate with the deceased directly, imagined interactions can serve a therapeutic function by allowing individuals to relive positive past experiences with the deceased or to communicate final thoughts to the deceased in order to achieve catharsis and self-understanding. If left unchecked, however, mental imagery surrounding the individuals death and imagined interactions with the deceased can monopolize the bereaved individual's mind and cause severe disruption to the survivor's life and increase the individual's risk of developing complicated or pathological grief. At the same time, however, cognitive behavioral therapists use mental imagery and imagined interactions to combat complicated or pathological grief.

Individuals bereaving from sudden or unexpected deaths are more likely to use imagined interactions to relive past experiences with the deceased or to imagine new conversations with the deceased. As individuals experiencing sudden death bereavement are already more susceptible to complicated grief, it is likely that they are more susceptible to falling into an unhealthy rumination pattern in which imagined interactions could become detrimental. This is an important implication from both a theoretical and clinical perspective. Future research should seek to better explore the relationship between imagined interactions, mental imagery and patterns of grief.

Discussion Questions

1. *Think of someone in your life who you are close to but are currently in some sort of conflict with. If that person were to pass away suddenly, without any warning, what effect would it have on you? Would you feel like you had unfinished business with that person? How would you manage those emotions?*
2. *Have you ever wished that you could speak to someone who is no longer alive? Do you ever replay interactions with that person in your mind, or imagine new interactions with that person as if you were able to speak to them?*
3. *This chapter discussed both positive and negative uses of mental imagery during the bereavement process. Based on what you know so far, do you believe that imagined interactions with a deceased relative are healthy, or unhealthy? Why do you feel that way?*
4. *How might the use of IIs as a type of therapeutic intervention be applied to other forms of grief outside of bereavement?*

References

Aoun, S. M., Breen, L. J., Howting, D. A., Rumbold, B., McNamara, B., & Hegney, D. (2015). Who needs bereavement support? A population based survey of bereavement risk and support need. *Plos One*, *10*(3), e0121101. doi:10.1371/journal.pone.0121101

BBC (Producer). (2018, April 26). *Why we need to face our own mortality* [Video File]. Retrieved from https://www.bbc.com/ideas/videos/why-we-need-to-face-our-mortality/p065dm7f?playlist=dying-thoughts

Buckley, T., Sunari, D., Marshall, A., Bartrop, R., McKinley, S., & Tofler, G. (2012). Physiological correlates of bereavement and the impact of bereavement interventions. *Dialogues in Clinical Neuroscience, 14*(2), 129–139.

Caron, A., Lafontaine, M. F., Bureau, J. F., Levesque, C., & Johnson, S. M. (2012). Comparisons of attachment in close relationships: An evaluation of attachment to parents, peers, and romantic partners in young adults. *Canadian Journal of Behavioral Science, 44*(4), 245–256. doi: 10.1037/a0028013

Costello, J. (1999). "Filling the void": Grief and loneliness in older adults. *Illness, Crisis & Loss, 7*(3), 218–232. doi: 10.1177/105413739900700302

Fidaleo, R. A., Proano, T., & Friedberg, R. D. (1999). Using imagery techniques to treat PTSD symptoms in bereaved individuals. *Journal of Contemporary Psychotherapy, 29*(2), 115–126.

Foa, E. B., Ikeda-Hearst, D., & Perry, K. J. (1995). Evaluation of a brief cognitive-behavioral program for the prevention of chronic PTSD in recent assault victims. *Journal of Consulting and Clinical Psychology, 63*(6), 948–955.

Ford, S. G. (2010). Retroactive imagined interactions, compensation, and bereavement. In J. M. Honeycutt (Eds.), *Imagine that: Studies in imagined interaction* (pp. 67–82). Cresskill, NJ: Hampton.

Frost, J. K., Honeycutt, J. M., & Heath, S. K. (2017). Relational maintenance and social support in the aftermath of sudden and expected death. *Communication Research Reports, 34*(4), 326–334. doi: 10.1080/08824096.2017.1350573

Gluhoski, V. L. (1995). A cognitive perspective on bereavement: Mechanisms and treatment. *Journal of Cognitive Psychotherapy, 9*(2), 75–84.

Honeycutt, J. M. (2003). *Imagined interactions*. Cresskill, NJ: Hampton.

Honeycutt, J. M. (2010). Introduction to imagined interactions. In J. M. Honeycutt (Ed.), *Imagine that: Studies in imagined interaction* (pp. 1–14). Cresskill, NJ: Hampton.

Horowitz, M. J., Bonanno, G. A., & Holen, A. (1993). Pathological grief: Diagnosis and explanation. *Psychosomatic Medicine, 55*(3), 260–273.

Kavanaugh, D. J. (1990). Towards a cognitive-behavioural intervention for adult grief reactions. *British Journal of Psychiatry, 157*(3), 373–383.

Klass, D., Silverman, P. R., & Nickman, S. (Eds.). (2014). *Continuing bonds: New understandings of grief*. New York, NY: Routledge.

Konisberg, R. D. (2011). *The truth about grief: The myth of its five stages and the new science of loss*. New York, NY: Simon & Schuster.

Kübler-Ross, E. (1969). *On death & dying*. New York, NY: Simon & Schuster/Touchstone.

Kübler-Ross, E., & Kessler, D. (2005). *On grief and grieving: Finding the meaning of grief through the five stages of loss*. New York, NY: Simon & Schuster.

Lobb, E. A., Kristjanson, L. J., Aoun, S. M., Monterosso, L., Halkett, G. B., & Davies, A. (2010). Predictors of complicated grief: a systematic review of empirical studies. *Death Studies, 34*(8), 673–698.

Lundin, T. (1984). Morbidity following sudden and unexpected bereavement. *British Journal of Psychiatry*, *144*, 84–88.

Maciejewski, P. K., Zhang, B., Block, S., & Prigerson, H. G. (2007). An empirical examination of the stage theory of grief. *Journal of the American Medical Association*, *297*, 716–723. doi: 10.1001/jama.297.7.716. PMID 17312

Nesse, R. M. (2005). An evolutionary framework for understanding grief. In D. Carr, R. M. Nesse, & C. B. Wortman (Eds.), *Spousal Bereavement in Late Life* (pp. 195–226). New York, NY: Springer.

Overton, B. L., & Cottone, R. R. (2016). Anticipatory grief. *Family Journal*, *24*(4), 430–432. doi: 10.1177/1066480716663490

Parkes, C. M. (1975). Determinants of outcome following bereavement. *Omega— Journal of Death and Dying*, 6(4), 303–323. doi: 10.2190/PR0R-GLPD-5FPB-422L

Parkes, C. M., & Weiss, R. S. (1983). *Recovery from bereavement*. New York, NY: Basic Books.

Physician Data Query (PDQ®). (2013). *Supportive and Palliative Care Editorial Board. PDQ grief, bereavement, and coping with loss*. Bethesda, MD: National Cancer Institute. Retrieved from http://www.cancer.gov/about-cancer/advanced-cancer/caregivers/planning/bereavement-pdq

Rossetto, K. R., Lannutti, P. J., & Strauman, E. C. (2015). Death on facebook: Examining the roles of social media communication for the bereaved. *Journal of Social and Personal Relationships*, *32*(7), 974–994. doi: 10.1177/0265407514555272

Rynearson, T. (1994). Psychotherapy of bereavement after homicide. *Journal of Psychotherapy Practice and Research*, 3(4), 341–347.

Stroebe, M. S., & Schut, H. (1999). The dual process model of coping with bereavement: Rationale and description. *Death Studies*, *23*(3), 197–224.

Tsai, W., Prigerson, H. G., Li, C., Chou, W., Kuo, S., & Tang, S. T. (2016). Longitudinal changes and predictors of prolonged grief for bereaved family caregivers over the first 2 years after the terminally ill cancer patient's death. *Palliative Medicine*, 30(5), 495–503.

Zagacki, K. S., Edwards, R., & Honeycutt, J. M. (1992). The role of mental imagery and emotion in imagined interaction. *Communication Quarterly*, 40, 56–68. doi: 10.1080/01463379209369820

· 5 ·

USING MUSIC THERAPY AND IMAGINED INTERACTION TO COPE WITH STRESS

James M. Honeycutt and Jake Harwood

Music has been called the universal language due to its rhythm and tonality, and because it (at least on the surface) transcends group-based language barriers. It is a pervasive part of human culture that predates our recorded history (Darwin, 1871); the earliest musical artefacts date back over 30 thousand years (Conard, Malina, & Münzel, 2009). People sing to babies because infants are altricial and need parental attention to survive (Mehr, Kotler, Howard, Haig, & Krasnow, 2017). Music can inspire people as well as depress them. It can be a soothing balm for many people. For example, the late Tom Petty, the classic rock n roll Hall of Famer who died at age 66 in October of 2017, said in his biography that music became a "safe place" where he was free from worrying about his abusive and alcoholic father who would physically him, his mother and younger brother (Zane, 2015). In fact, music can be so soothing for emotional control and release similar to the catharsis function of IIs, that there are songs of tribute. One of most famous tribute songs, the eight-and-a-half-minute "American Pie" by Don MacLean, is about the airplane deaths of early rock n rollers, Buddy Holly, Ritchie Valens, and J. P. "The Big Bopper" Richardson. The famous chorus is "the day the music died." In 2017, McLean's original recording was selected for preservation in the National Recording Registry by the Library of Congress as being "culturally, historically, or artistically significant" (see https://www.loc.gov/item/prn-17-029/). National anthems serve a similar function of praise (e.g., The Star-Spangled Banner, US; God Save the Queen, UK; the State Anthem of the Russian Federation, Russia; Oh Canada, Canada; La Marseillaise, France; Wilhelmus, The Netherlands—oldest in the world). In this chapter, we discuss how music along with IIs can be used to cope with trauma. Indeed, when people listen to music, they often can be taken back to time and place as well as seek escape from the daily hassles of life.

Relational Maintenance

One of the major functions of IIs is the psychic ability to retain human relationships within the mind. People imagined encounters with relational partners and relive positive or negative moments. Bodie, Honeycutt and Vickery (2013) showed that lower usage of IIs for relational maintenance and conflict management and higher usage of IIs for catharsis is associated with higher frequency and lower self-dominance. On the one hand, Honeycutt and Sheldon (2018) discuss the classic maxim of "absence makes the heart fonder" in terms of IIs for relational maintenance. They report how engaged partners had more IIs, IIs that were positively valenced, and IIs that were used to compensate for the lack of real interaction than did marital partners. They speculated that there also may be less rehearsal among the engaged partners due to less conflict in the honeymoon phase of their relational development.

A real-life example of the relational maintenance function of IIs comes from the account of Sir Paul McCartney of the number one ranked classic rock and roll band (according to *Rolling Stone* polls: https://www.rollingstone.com/music/lists/100-greatest-artists-of-all-time-19691231/the-beatles-20110420), The Beatles. They had the most number one songs in at least one chart (n = 103), followed by Elvis Presley (n = 75), and the Rolling Stones (n = 64) (https://tsort.info/music/faq_num1.htm). They are the only band to have an entire *Cirque de Soleil* show covering their music (*Love*).

In a Rolling Stone interview, Sir Paul discusses how he has imagined interactions with John Lennon, founder of the band and George Harrison, who was a guitarist. Lennon was brutally assassinated in December of 1980 when he was shot at point blank range in New York while George Harrison died of lung cancer that spread to his brain in 2001. In 1999, he warded off an intruder in his home who stabbed him in the lung and causing head injuries before his wife incapacitated the assailant by striking him repeatedly with a fireplace poker and a lamp.

Anyone can google the trauma of Lennon's assassination. Sir Paul has discussed his contempt for the assassin. However, he has imagined interactions with John in the recording studio that reveals how he is using the relational maintenance function and catharsis as a way to continually deal with this trauma. He said the following about imagining John Lennon being in the recording studio with him.

There was another collaborate in the room, who's been there for decades. If I'm at a point where I'm not sure about this, I'll throw it across the room to John. Following are the literal lines of imaginary dialogue:

John: You can't go there, man
Paul: You're quite right. How about this?
John: Yeah, that's better.

Forgiveness

In the interview, McCartney says, "We'll have a conversation. I use that; it's a very valuable thing. I don't want to lose that." (Weiner, 2013; p. 44) McCartney also describes how he uses IIs to deal with conflict. The Beatles broke up with John Lennon spent more time with artist, Yoko Ono. McCartney discussed how when he thinks about the end of the Beatles as a band and forgiveness with Ono and Lennon; George Harrison encouraged him. He tells a retroactive II in which George said, "You don't want stuff like that hanging around in your life" (Weiner, 2013; p. 46). Sir Paul said the following in terms of forgiveness about how the band broke up:

George would say to me: "You don't want stuff like that hanging around in your life."

Catharsis and Music Therapy

As shown throughout this volume, catharsis is a major function of IIs in order to alleviate stress. Background music can facilitate recall of pleasant and unpleasant memories as the music triggers endorphins in the brain (Salimpoor, Benovoy, Larcher, Dagher, & Zatorre, 2011). While listening to music, people often have imagined interactions as they experience of a range of emotions depending on the key and tempo of the song. Background music is prevalent in our society with the use of smart phones with streaming services and muzak, and it can act as a type of implicit music therapy that can relax or energize people. Even, Ancient Greek philosopher, Plato (428–347 BC), quoted "music gives wings to mind" and believed that music played in different modes would arouse different emotions (Cooke, 1959). Indeed, the emotional processing of music occurs in the amygdala, cingulate gyrus and medial orbitofrontal cortex of the brain (Nizamie & Tikka, 2014).

Music is linked with physiological responses including heart rate and blood pressure. The relationship between music and heart rate is complex and can be beneficial to health (Honeycutt, 2019). The sentimentality of music on listener increases in conjunction with a fast, loud, jumpy rhythm, which sounds happy because it reflects the way an excited person behaves. Conversely, slow, quiet music with a regular beat mimics a mournful emotional state due to brain hardwiring and activation of the amygdala. Songs in major keys tend to sound cheerful, while those in minor keys sound sad (Bowling, Gill, Choi, Prinz, & Purves, 2010). The pattern of pitches in excited speech mimics music played in major keys, while those of dejected speech matched minor music (Honeycutt, 2019). Hence, happy music tends to be faster while sad music is slower. Bowling and his associate found the same association for Mandarin Chinese speakers, suggesting the link is cross cultural, thus enhancing universal similarity. People who listened to music for 20 to 30 minutes each day had lower blood pressure and a slowed heart rate compared with those who did not listen to music with a faster rhythm, such as rap, increases a person's heart rate, instead of providing a relaxing effect. Studies have shown that adding vocals to instrumental music activates different regions in the brain and may lead to different sensations. Adding vocals to sad music intensifies its emotional impact; cheerful music has a greater emotional impact without words (Trappe, 2010; 2014).

Prior research has shown that listening to music that people considered pleasurable increased the release of dopamine in the brain, and dopamine is well known as a "feel good" neurotransmitter (Gold, Frank, Bogert, & Brattico, 2013). Additionally, listening to classical, symphonic music (Mozart) and Romantic symphonic music (Straus) as well as pop music (Abba) lowered subjects' heart rate compared to the baseline as well as lowering serum cortisol (Trappe & Voit, 2016). Interestingly, Rickard (2004) reported how skin conductance increased for subjects who were exposed to an emotionally powerful film scene that was accompanied by emotionally powerful music from a piece selected by the subjects compared to relaxing and arousing music conditions.

Relational maintenance and conflict linkage are two common functions of IIs that are easily referenced in music. When people listening to sad music, that they self-select as making them feel sad; people relive conflict which creates a closed, reciprocal cycle of negativity leading to sad memories which reinforces depressive feelings (Garrido & Schubert, 2013). Conversely, when listen to music that they believed selected as making them feel happy, even those with high levels of depression felt much better. Garrido and Shubert (2013) provide an example of a person who suffered from a negative body image and esteem who reported that found that listening to the song "What Makes You Beautiful" by One Direction, made her focus on positive aspects of herself. Their study show that when people reported feeling more depressed after listening to sad music, they still tended to report that the music had helped them. Other studies too have shown that some people persist in listening to music that is actually making them feel worse. Next, we compare the functions of music and how they resemble some various features of IIs.

Functions of Music

The question of why people listen to music has been reviewed in numerous studies. Schäfer, Sedlmeier, Städtler, and Huron (2013) surveyed the literature from the past 50 years and identified more than 500 functions for music. From their analysis, they assembled a list of 129 non-redundant musical functions. They tested the reliability of these functions by collecting survey responses from a comparatively large sample. A factor analysis revealed just three distinct dimensions that they refer to as the Big Three of music listening: People listen to music to (1) achieve self-awareness,(2) expressing social relatedness, and (3) regulate arousal and mood. Respectively, these functions are similar to the II features of valence, self-understanding, and relational maintenance.

In terms of expressing social relatedness, evolutionary psychologist that cohesion and social action can be motivated by music. Work and war songs, lullabies, and national anthems have bound together families, groups, or whole nations. Relatedly, music provides a means to reduce social stress and temper aggression in others. The idea that music may function as a social cement has many proponents (see Bicknell, 2007; Huron, 2001; Mithen, 2006).

Empirical studies of musical functions have been very heterogeneous (see Schäfer et al., 2013 for a review). Various studies were motivated by questions related to development, social identity, cognitive psychology, aesthetics, cultural psychology, or personality psychology. Studies differ according to the sample. Table 5.1 summarizes the major functions of music identified by Schäfer and his associates. Column 1 presents one the underlying basic music functions in terms of the robust, tripartite dimensions. Column 2 represents 17 functions identified by Schäfer and Sedlmeier (2009). Column 3 represents the corresponding II feature equivalent. The horizontal line in the middle of the table represents the cutoff point for the top seven functions which are rank ordered by Schäfer on the basis of importance in predicting musical preference that reflects many listeners liked and needed music (e.g., I like this music. I am a passionate listener of this music. I couldn't live without this music). Table 5.1 reveals that self-understanding is the most used function of IIs when listening to music. It reflects achieving self-identity. These functions occur across all music genres (e.g., symphonic, electronic, rock, rap, pop, country) that were sampled.

A novel evolutionary theory is offered by Falk (2004a, b) who has proposed that music arose from humming or singing intended to maintain infant-mother attachment. The "putting-down-the-baby hypothesis" suggests that

Table 5.1. Functions of Music Compared to Imagined Interaction Features.

Big Three Music Function	*More Specific Music Function*	*II Feature Equivalent*
Achieve self-awareness	Express self-identity	Self-understanding
Social Relatedness	Helps me meet people	Relational maintenance
Regulate arousal/mood	Makes me feel ecstatic	Valence
Achieve self-awareness	Express my values	Self-understanding
	Lets me appreciate as art	
Regulate arousal/mood	Puts me in a good mood	Valence
	Gives me information	
Regulate arousal/mood	Helps me chill and time out	Catharsis
	Energizes me	
	Enables me to reminisce	Retroactivity
Achieve self-awareness	Enables me to better understand my thoughts and feelings	Self-understanding
	What I listen to as background music	
	Is what I like to dance to	
	Lets me forget my problems	Catharsis
Express social relatedness	Helps me feel close to others	Relational maintenance
Achieve self-awareness	Lets me experiment with different sides of my personality	Rehearsal
	Makes me identify with the artists	

mothers would have profited from putting down their infants in order to make their hands free for other activities. Humming or singing consequently arose as a consoling signal indicating caretaker proximity in the absence of physical touch.

Recall chapter four on using IIs to deal with the trauma of loss through bereavement. An evolutionary view espouses that music helps deal with the anxiety related to death, and the consequent quest for meaning. Dissanayake (2009) has argued that people have used music to deal with awareness of life's transitoriness. In a manner similar to religious beliefs about the hereafter or a higher transcendental purpose, music can help assuage human anxiety concerning mortality (Newberg, D'Aquili, & Rause, 2001).

A non-evolutionary view of music is the "uses-and-gratifications" approach (Arnett, 1995). This approach focuses on the needs and concerns of the listeners and tries to explain how people actively select and use music to serve these needs. Arnett (1995) provides a list of potential uses of music such as entertainment, identity formation, sensation seeking, or culture identification.

Music and Group Connectedness

As hinted above, theories of the origins of human music often reference intergroup processes. Music could have emerged as a form of coalition signaling (Hagen & Bryant, 2003): by using music in groups, we signal to others that our group is organized, resource-rich, synchronized, and "in tune" (both literally and metaphorically) with one another. Such coalition signaling is functional in the animal world for signaling a joint ability to respond to threat (e.g., in coordinated singing of duets in birds to protect territory: Hall & Magrath, 2007). As such, music can be seen as encouraging intergroup divisiveness, and indeed it can emphasize group boundaries (Harwood, 2017, 2018). As is clear from the earlier discussion of national anthems, music can mark group memberships and differentiate ingroup from outgroup. Outgroup music often sounds unusual, and while we can sometimes enjoy it for its exotic qualities, full understanding of non-native music can be difficult and require extensive study (e.g., consider most Westerners' responses to Indian ragas: they might appreciate the overall "sound" but have virtually no understanding of the music's tonality or structure (Laukka, Eerola, Thingujam, Yamasaki, & Beller, 2013). At extremes, music can enact direct intergroup provocation (e.g., Irish Protestant bands playing "The Sash" while marching through Catholic areas of Ulster), stimulate intergroup hostility (e.g., white supremacist rock), or can even be directly involved in intergroup violence (e.g., the uses of music in torture, or in conflict—the use of drummers in battle, for instance, goes back many centuries: Norris, 2012).

However, this somewhat pessimistic take on music conceals two important points. First, of course, while the music is separating some people, it is also bringing people together. The reason that music can be effective in separating groups is that within groups it is incredibly effective at connecting individuals, bringing them together with a unique combination of temporal synchronization and emotional connection (Wallace & Harwood, 2018). Its intergroup strength derives from its powers to connect people interpersonally. Wallace and Harwood, for instance, demonstrate that emerging adults who engaged in joint musical activities with their parents during their childhood and adolescence, experience more positive relationships with their parents when the emerging adults are in college. Those effects are mediated through perceptions of empathy with the parents, and even more strongly through feelings of being coordinated or synchronized with the parents. Notably, the effects persist when other forms of (non-musical) joint activity are controlled statistically. Such effects mirror nicely the description earlier of music building connections between mothers and their infants and suggest that the bonding power of music does not stop with very early mother-child interaction.

Second, therefore, the same strategies by which music separates groups of people can, in the correct circumstances, be used to bring those groups together. As demonstrated repeatedly, contact between individuals from different social groups has the potential to reduce intergroup conflict and prejudice (Allport, 1954; Pettigrew & Tropp, 2006). Just by spending time with one another, people from different groups come to understand one another more, and perhaps even to like and appreciate their mutual differences. Music offers some unique tools to facilitate such intergroup contact. Specifically, it allows contact between members of different groups that is:

- Equal status: While status differences might emerge in some fairly specific musical circumstances (e.g., a conductor of an orchestra relative to a second violinist), musical contact is for the most part an equal status activity (e.g., members of a crowd dancing to a band);
- Low conflict: While some forms of intergroup interaction offer the possibility for disagreement (e.g., any form of verbal communication offers up the possibility for alternate viewpoints), music is largely free of semantic content. It has, to use Cross and Morley's (2009) term, *floating intentionality*. A lack of semantic meaning reduces the possibility for

disagreement, and thus enhances the possibilities for positive and conflict-free interaction.

- Physically synchronized: The potential for music to synchronize people in time is almost uniquely human and offers tremendous possibilities for interpersonal harmony. We like people more when we are physically coordinated with them. Simply moving in time with another person stimulates feelings that we are somehow similar to one another and may suggest that our selves "overlap" (Lumsden, Miles, & Macrae, 2014).
- Emotionally involving: While language can clearly express emotion, music is uniquely emotionally expressive—even "super-expressive" (Juslin & Timmers, 2010)—and thus intergroup musical experiences offer opportunities for shared emotional experiences that go beyond what might be experienced in non-musical interaction. Shared emotional experiences, and the sensation of sharing emotion with another (empathy) are very closely tied to interpersonal closeness and relational development.
- Positively group-salient: One challenge in intergroup contact is maintaining positivity and enjoyable interaction, while also maintaining awareness of group memberships (Brown & Hewstone, 2005). We need to retain knowledge and awareness of group memberships to make contact meaningful—intergroup contact where we simply forget that we are with an outgroup member isn't really intergroup contact. At the same time, unfortunately, awareness of group boundaries tends to lead to less positive interaction as a result of intergroup anxiety (Paolini, Harwood, & Rubin, 2010) and differing intergroup agendas (Bergsieker, Shelton, & Richeson, 2010). Music provides a setting in which group memberships can be displayed in a non-competitive and agenda-free manner, and where the benefits of diversity are explicitly on display (see also below).

The structure of music also enables a variety of *types* of musical contact. People from different social groups can *play* music together, thus experiencing peak synchronization activities. They can jointly experience music as *listeners*. And, of course, listeners can experience music played by outgroup members, and performers can experience the responses of outgroup members. One interesting context of musical contact is in *observing* people from different groups making music together (vicarious intergroup musical contact). This type of contact has the potential for strong effects, given that it *models* positive intergroup relations so strongly (Bandura, 1986), and in many contexts also models the uniquely beneficial outcomes that come from intergroup diversity (e.g., when the resulting music is an engaging blend or hybrid that couldn't occur without the combination). Such phenomena can occur around musical styles that cross-cultural groups (Ska, Norteño, Latin jazz) or specific musical projects that feature musicians from multiple groups (e.g., Paul Simon's "Graceland"; Yo-Yo Ma's "Silk Road Ensemble"). Harwood, Qadar and Chen (2016) provide data suggesting that exposure to such collaborations is more powerful in influencing positive intergroup relations than exposure to non-musical collaborations.

Music, of course, does not offer a panacea for social relations—as noted earlier, it can exacerbate intergroup tensions (Harwood, 2017). Technological developments since the invention of sound recording have also shifted the ways in which humans encounter music and engage with it socially. Recording has increased our ability to listen to music alone, and our ability to consume music without interacting with the performer (Harwood, 2018). It has also increased our ability to consume music privately (e.g., via headphones), even when in social environments, thus making music consumption a technique for actively blocking social interaction (e.g., when donning headphones in a crowded airplane). Schäfer et al., (2013) note that, particularly in the West, the use of music for personal fulfillment and mood management may be becoming more important than its use for social connection (Heye & Lamont, 2010; Roberts & Foehr, 2008). That said, the continuing popularity of live music, music festivals, and dancing in bars and club all suggest that music is not doomed to a solitary and private future. The growth of technologies such as music streaming have also made it increasingly easy for people to access diverse music. While most people may seek the familiar most of the time, streaming services offer the opportunity for the more adventurous to find music from different cultures—access that was considerably more difficult in the days of physical media, and extremely rare in the pre-recording era.

Incremental Sound Organizer of Music Therapy (ISO Principle)

The fifth theorem of imagined interaction conflict-linkage theory states: Thinking about conflict may be facilitated through exposure to contextual cues including music, chemical dependency, and media (Honeycutt, 2003; p. 81). Support for this theorem is reviewed, elsewhere (e.g., Honeycutt,

2004). The brain's neurotransmitters are affected by the rhythm of the music.

The ISO (Incremental Sound Organizer) principle of music therapy is designed to deal with changing a person's emotions as they listen to a medley of music. The mood of the person is measured using a series of scales reflecting a continuum of sadness to happiness and the music is designed to matches the mood of the patient to the music being played and/or listened to, which in turn fosters the achievement of an altered state of consciousness (Honeycutt, Keaton, Hatcher, & Hample, 2014). For example, if you are angry, start with music that is loud gradually switch to a more tranquil piece of music. "The vectoring power of music is that we change the mood or emotion of persons from one affective pole (joy) to its opposite (anger) through small incremental changes in the rhythm and intensity of the music" (Honeycutt, 2003; p. 82).

The theory of musical equilibration explains the emotional impact of music as a process in which the listener identifies with the content of the will encoded in the music (Willimek & Wilimek, 2014). For example, if a person is somber; music in the minor keys of F or G minor can reinforce melancholy feelings while music in the majors keys sounds more exhilarating (e.g., D and G majors; Also see http://www.wmich.edu/mus-theo/courses/keys.html).

Earlier research has found that "instrumental music may be conducive to conflict resolution because the harmonics, rhythm, and intensity involved are such that individuals can mimic these attributes verbally or nonverbally without having consciously or subconsciously to process language in the form of lyrics" (Honeycutt & Eidenmuller, 2001; p. 30). Indeed, instrumental music which is not as recognizable by the individuals, may be desirable in order to rule out effects of familiarity with the recording artist.

In order to change a person's mood, it is best to offer a medley of songs. For example, if a person reports being sad, you could songs in minor keys. Songs in major keys tend to sound cheerful (Bowling et al., 2010). The pattern of pitches in excited speech mimics music played in major keys, while those of dejected speech matched minor music. Hence, happy music tends to be faster while sad music is slower (Honeycutt, 2019). Alternatively, if a person is feeling irritable or angry, the musical therapist starts with music that is not too quiet so that the listener may transfer some of his or her anxiety over to the music. There is a parallel here in clinical psychology known as the transference effect, in which individuals in therapy may transfer feelings of anger about others to the psychotherapies. For example, many people listen to music while driving.

Music and Stress Reduction

There are numerous studies revealing how background music can alleviate stress (e.g., Belkhuis, 2009; Brown, Martinez, & Parsons, 2004; Hodges, 2010). For example, listening to relaxing music has been found to affect endocrine, cognitive, and emotional responses in healthy women. It has been found that people listening to relaxing music or sounds of rippling water in an acoustic control condition prior to a stress test had the highest cortisol concentrations if they were listening to relaxing music while the lowest concentrations were found in those who were listening to the sound of rippling water. Although there was no significant effect of music regarding autonomic responses, we observed a trend towards a faster recovery in salivary alpha-amylase activity and in respiratory sinus arrhythmia in the music group.

Depression, Music Therapy and IIs

An early dissertation examined the use of IIs to deal with depression. Kroll-Mensing (1992) found that anxiety and depression were positively associated with the frequent occurrence of IIs. Anxiety was associated with reporting that IIs that clarify thoughts (self-understanding function), relieve tension (catharsis), and rehearsal. The presence of an increased frequency of IIs for anxious and depressed individuals makes sense in terms of the view that suggests that the relationships of anxious and depressed individuals are characterized by conflict and dissatisfaction (e.g., review, Honeycutt, 2004). Their IIs may reflect the conflict that they are experiencing in their interpersonal relationships. Hence, IIs can be used constructively to manage conflict as well as destructively, depending on the motives and desires of the individual.

Studies included in the review compared music therapy with either standard care or with CBT or a combination of both. Hsu and Lai (2004) assessed the effectiveness of soft music compared to bed rest for treatment of major depression. They found significantly lesser depressive scores in the music group. A meta-analysis of the effects of music therapy on a variety of mental health conditions including depression and anxiety reveals that music therapy is an effective treatment and that slight improvements are observed with a few therapy sessions, while longer courses or more frequent sessions result in more substantial benefits (Gold, Solli, Krüger, & Lie, 2009).

Visual imagery is a mode of imagery when having IIs along with verbal and a combination (Honeycutt, 2003). Related the specificity attribute of IIs describes how there are individual differences as people report having either abstract or specific lines of dialogue and specific images of the scene of II. They can tell you what the interaction partners were wearing and where it took place (e.g., car, rooms in an office, home, etc.). A combination of IIs and visualization helps people high in communication apprehension to prepare for a speech (Choi, Honeycutt, & Bodie, 2015).

Research reveals that the visual cortex area of the brain plays an important role in mental health (Romer et al., 2018). The visual cortex helps us understand and recognize what we see. It affects the visual imagery of IIs and daydreaming. In fact, damage to the occipital lobe of the brain can result in decreased visual imagery (Klinger, 1991). The results show that a person's risk of mental illness broadly increases when the visual cortex has trouble communicating with brain networks responsible for focus and introspection. Participants were given a series of psychiatric tests that measure depression and anxiety. Magnetic Resonance Imaging (MRI) was used to scan their brains. The analysis revealed that people with higher anxiety scores had four regions of the visual cortex that didn't work together well.

Research reveals that the brain is focused when working on tasks. However, mind-wandering and daydreaming are the default mode of the brain. Indeed, there is voluminous research demonstrating how the brain's default-mode network provides the substrate for mind-wandering (e.g., Andrews-Hanna, Reidler, Huang, & Buckner, 2010; Christoff, Gordon, Smallwood, Smith, & Schooler, 2009; Klinger, 2013; Mason et al., 2007; Stawarczyk, Majerus, Maquet, & Argembeau, 2011). There is a network of several "hubs" and "subsystems" (Andrews-Hanna, 2012) that constitutes a majority of the brain's energy consumption (Raichle, 2009). More importantly, several important functions must be served which include a variety of mental processes, including retrieval of past experiences and imagining future scenarios (Buckner, Andrews-Hanna, & Schacter, 2008), which are essential for planning and are also stock components of mind-wandering sequences. Hence, Buckner and his associates are referring to the retroactivity and proactivity attributes of IIs including the rehearsal function. Music facilities mind wandering, allowing the use of IIs to deal with stress. It can be effective in chronic, non-malignant pain including burn pain (Siedliecki & Good, 2006; Tan, Yowler, Super, & Fratianne, 2010).

Popular Love Songs and Using IIs to Deal with Relationships

A mixed-method master's thesis conducted in the West Indies by Amanda Lewis analyzed correlations between SII features and measures of listening to popular love songs. Focus group interviews were used to analyze how they used IIs while listening to their songs and how they helped deal with relational issues, breakups, and maintenance. The quantitative data revealed that the self-understanding function of IIs was negatively correlated with music influencing your moods ($r = -.28$, $p =. 029$), maintain your relationship with a loved one ($r = .43$, $p = .001$), and relieving tension ($r = -.45$, $p = .000$). Hence, what this means is that the more you understand the reasons for your values, attitudes, and ideology; the less that popular love songs influence moods, relieve tension, and maintain relationships. For example, one respondent reported, "I prefer love-lamenting songs because it has emotionally advised me how to confront the disappointment in love. I can relate to these songs, especially as they relate to my past, failed relationships" (Lewis, 2014, p. 44).

Other listeners reported how listening to popular love songs made them feel as if they understand themselves better. For example, a person said, "It allows me to appreciate what I have now with my partner and also reminds me of what not to do, so she would not end up as another ex" (Lewis, 2014, p. 49). A recurring theme was how love-lamenting songs was associated with the II function of conflict linkage and learning from prior mistakes ("If I heard a love-lamenting song, I tend to dwell on our arguments and hiccups in the relationship," p. 46). Popular love songs helped some listeners to appreciate their present relationship with their partners and reminded them not repeat past mistakes, while relieving tension. Additionally, there was a significant correlation of $-.29$ ($p = .024$) between the beat of a song and having retroactive IIs while the frequency of having IIs was slightly associated with liking the content and language of the lyrics ($r = .25$, $p = .05$). Finally, the specificity of IIs was associated with liking the theme of popular love songs ($r =.26$, $p = .043$).

Hence, it can be argued that listening to certain types of music relives pleasant as well as painful memories (remembrances of exes) that can help people learn from their experiences to the extent that are motivated, resilient, and focused on self-improvement. IIs can facilitate in this process of cognitive learning, which reinforces the theme of this volume.

Summary

Music has been called the universal language due to tonality and rhythm. It can unite people through anthems. Music affects moods and emotion and can help people in dealing with stress. Music therapy has been shown to reduce pain and cope with depression as people deal with trauma. In fact, the ISO (Incremental Sound Organizer) principle of music therapy reveals how people's emotions can change while listening to a medley of music. Research is reviewed in which people have imagined interactions while listening to music as memories are recalled. Music is used to maintain relationships as couples often have their own song. Music fulfills the catharsis function of imagined interactions as people release anxiety or tension. Music serves numerous functions, which can be subsumed into (1) achieving self-awareness, (2) expressing social relatedness, and (3) regulating, arousal and mood. Respectively, these functions are similar to the II features of valence, self-understanding, and relational maintenance. Music could have emerged as a form of coalition signaling by using music in groups, we signal to others that our group is organized, resource-rich, synchronized, and "in tune" (both literally and metaphorically) with one another.

Discussion Questions

1. *What are three of your most memorable songs? Are they instrumental or lyrical? Do any of the songs remind you of someone important in your life? What do you typically say to them while listening to the song?*
2. *Have you been in a close relationship with someone, in which both of you considered a piece of music as "your song"? Why does the song serve the relational maintenance function of IIs in bonding you together?*
3. *Do you listen to music when you are feeling sad (e.g., "blues" music), happy, or both?*
4. *What do you think about the findings that music therapy can assist with pain alleviation? Do you listen to music when you are ill at home?*
5. *When driving, how often do you listen to music, audiobooks, drive in silence, or use Wi-Fi phone apps? Do you ever perform car karaoke to musical selections?*

References

Allport, G. W. (1954). *The nature of prejudice*. Cambridge, MA: Addison-Wesley.

Andrews-Hanna, J. (2012). The brain's default network and its adaptive role in internal mentation. *Neuroscientist*, *18*(3), 251–270. doi: 10.1177/1073858411403316

Andrews-Hanna, J., Reidler, J. S., Huang, C., & Buckner, R. L. (2010). Evidence for the default network's role in spontaneous cognition. *Journal of Neurophysiology*, *104*(1), 322–335. doi: 10.1152/jn.00830.2009

Arnett, J. J. (1995). Adolescents' uses of media for self-socialization. *Journal of Youth and Adolescence*, *24*(5), 519–533. doi: 10.1007/BF01537054

Bandura, A. (1986). *Social foundations of thought and action: A social cognitive theory*. Englewood Cliffs, NJ: Prentice Hall.

Belkhuis, T. (2009) Music therapy may reduce pain and anxiety in children undergoing medical and dental procedures. *Journal of Evidentiary Based Dental Practice*, 9(4), 213–214. doi:10.1016/j.jebdp.2009.03.00

Bergsieker, H. B., Shelton, J. N., & Richeson, J. A. (2010). To be liked versus respected: Divergent goals in interracial interactions. *Journal of Personality and Social Psychology*, 99(2), 248–264. doi: 10.1037/a0018474

Bicknell, J. (2007). Explaining strong emotional responses to music: Sociality and intimacy. *Journal of Conscious Studies*, *14*(12), 5–23. doi: 10.1057/97802302338365

Bodie, G. D., Honeycutt, J. M., & Vickery, A. J. (2013). An analysis of the correspondence between imagined interaction attributes and functions. *Human Communication Research*, 39(2), 157–183. doi: 10.1111/hcre.12003

Bowling, D. L., Gill, K., Choi, J. D., Prinz, J., & Purves, D. (2010). Major and minor music compared to excited and subdued speech. *Journal of the Acoustical Society of America*, *127(1)*, 491–503. doi: 10.1121/1.3268504.

Brown, R., & Hewstone, M. (2005). An integrative theory of intergroup contact. *Advances in Experimental Social Psychology*, *37*, 255–343. doi: https://doi.org/10.1016/S0065-2601(05)37005-5

Brown, S., Martinez, M. J., & Parsons, L. M. (2004). Passive music listening spontaneously engages limbic and paralimbic systems. *Neuroreport*, *15*(13), 2033–2037. doi: 10.1097/00001756-200409150-00008

Buckner, R. L., Andrews-Hanna, J. R., & Schacter, D. L. (2008). The brain's default network. *Annals of the New York Academy of Sciences*, *112*, 1–38. doi: 10.1196/annals.1440.011

Choi, C. E., Honeycutt, J. M., & Bodie, G. D. (2015). Effects of imagined interactions and rehearsal on speaking performance. *Communication Education*, 64, 25–44. doi:10.1080/03634523.2014.978795

Christoff, K., Gordon, A. M., Smallwood, J., Smith, R., & Schooler, J. W. (2009). Experience sampling during fMRI reveals default network and executive system contributions to mind wandering. *Proceedings of the National Academy of Sciences*, U.S.A. *106*(21), 8719–8724. doi: 10.1073/pnas.0900234106

Conard, N. J., Malina, M., & Münzel, S. C. (2009). New flutes document the earliest musical tradition in southwestern Germany. *Nature*, *460*(7256), 737–740. doi: 10.1038/nature0816

Cooke, D. (1959). *The language of music*. Oxford, England: Oxford University Press.

Cross, I., & Morley, I. (2009). The evolution of music: Theories, definitions and the nature of the evidence. In S. Malloch, & C. Trevarthen (Eds.), *Communicative musicality: Exploring the basis of human companionship* (pp. 61–81). Oxford, England: Oxford University Press.

Darwin, C. (1871). The Descent of Man, and Selection in Relation to Sex. In: E. O. Wilson (Ed.). *From so simple a beginning: The four great books of Charles Darwin*. New York: W. W. Norton (2006).

Dissanayake, E. (2009). Root, leaf, blossom, or bole: Concerning the origin and adaptive function of music. In S. Malloch, & C. Trevarthen (Eds.), *Communicative musicality* (pp. 17–29). New York, NY: Oxford University.

Falk, D. (2004a). Prelinguistic evolution in early hominins: Whence motherese. *Behavioral and Brain Science, 27*(4), 491–503. doi: 10.1017/S0140525X04000111

Falk, D. (2004b). The "putting the baby down" hypothesis: Bipedalism, babbling, and baby slings. *Behavioral and Brain Science, 27*(4), 526–534. doi: 10.1017/S0140525X0448011X

Garrido, S., & Schubert, E. (2013). Adaptive and maladaptive attraction to negative emotions in music. *Musicae Scientiae, 17*(2), 147–166. doi: https://doi.org/10.1177/1029864913478305

Gold, B. P., Frank, M. J., Bogert, B., & Brattico, E. (2013). Pleasurable music affects reinforcement learning according to the listener. *Frontiers in Psychology, 4*, 1–19. doi: 10.3389/fpsyg.2013.00541

Gold, C., Solli, H. P., Krüger, V., & Lie, S. A. (2009). Dose-response relationship in music therapy for people with serious mental disorders: Systematic review and meta-analysis. *Clinical Psychology Review, 29*(3), 193–207. doi: 10.1016/j.cpr.2009.01.001

Hagen, E. H., & Bryant, G. A. (2003). Music and dance as a coalition signaling system. *Human Nature, 14*(1), 21–51. doi: https://doi.org/10.1007/s12110-003-1015-z

Hall, M. L., & Magrath, R. D. (2007). Temporal coordination signals coalition quality. *Current Biology, 17*(11), 406–407. doi: https://doi.org/10.1016/j.cub.2007.04.022

Harwood, J. (2017). Music and intergroup relations: Exacerbating conflict and building harmony through music. *Review of Communication Research*, 5, 1–34. doi: 10.12840/issn.2255-4165.2017.05.01.012

Harwood, J. (2018). *Communication and music in social interaction*. San Diego, CA: Cognella.

Harwood, J., Qadar, F., & Chen, C-Y. (2016). Harmonious contact: Stories about intergroup musical collaboration improve intergroup attitudes. *Journal of Communication*, 66, 937–959. doi: https://doi.org/10.1111/jcom.12261

Heye, A., & Lamont, A. (2010). Mobile listening situations in everyday life: The use of MP3 players while travelling. *Musicae Scientiae, 14*(1), 95–120. doi: 10.1177/102986491001400104

Hodges, D. A. (2010). Psychophysiological responses to music. In J. A. Juslin, & J. A. Sloboda (Eds.), *Handbook of music and emotion: Theory, research, applications* (pp. 279–311). New York, NY: Oxford University Press.

Honeycutt, J. M. (2003). *Imagined interactions: Daydreaming about communication*. Cresskill, NJ: Hampton.

Honeycutt, J. M. (2004). Imagined interaction conflict-linkage theory: Explaining the persistence and resolution of interpersonal conflict in everyday life. *Imagination, Cognition, and Personality, 23*, 3–25. doi: 10.2190/240J-1VPK-K86D-1JL8

Honeycutt, J. M. (2019). Intrapersonal communication and imagined interactions: A musical application. In D. W. Stacks, & K. Eichhorn (Eds.), *An integrated approach to communication theory and research*. New York, NY: Routledge.

Honeycutt, J. M., & Eidenmuller, M. E. (2001). An exploration of the effects of music and mood on intimate couples' verbal and nonverbal conflict-resolution behaviors. In V. Manusov, & J. H. Harvey (Eds.), *Attribution, communication behavior, and close relationships* (pp. 37–60). London: Cambridge University Press.

Honeycutt, J. M., Keaton, S. A., Hatcher, L. C., & Hample, D. (2014). Effects of rumination and observing marital conflict on observers' heart rates as they advise and predict the use of conflict tactics. In J. M. Honeycutt, C. R. Sawyer, & S. A. Keaton (Eds.), *The Influence of Communication on Physiology and Health* (pp. 73–92). New York, NY: Peter Lang.

Honeycutt, J. M., & Sheldon, P. (2018). *Scripts and communication for relationships* (2nd ed.). New York, NY. Peter Lang.

Hsu, W. C., & Lai, H. L. (2004). Effects of music on major depression in psychiatric inpatients. *Archives of Psychiatric Nursing, 18*(5), 193–199. doi: http://dx.doi.org/10.1016/j.apnu.2004.07.007

Huron, D. (2001). Is music an evolutionary adaptation? In R. J. Zatorre, & I. Peretz (Eds.), *The biological foundations of music* (pp. 43–61). New York, NY: New York Academy of Sciences.

Juslin, P. N., & Timmers, R. (2010). Expression and communication of emotion in music performance. In P. N. Juslin, & J. Sloboda (Eds.), *Handbook of music and emotion: Theory, research, and applications* (pp. 453–437). Oxford, England: Oxford University Press.

Klinger, E. (1991). *Daydreaming: Using waking fantasy and imagery for self-knowledge and creativity*. Los Angeles, CA: Jeremy P. Tarcher.

Klinger, E. (2013). Goal commitments and the content of thoughts and dreams: Basic principles. *Frontiers in Psychology, 4*, 415. doi: http://doi.org/10.3389/fpsyg.2013.00415

Kroll-Mensing, D. (1992). Differentiating anxiety and depression: An experience sampling analysis. (Unpublished doctoral dissertation). Minneapolis, MN: University of Minnesota.

Laukka, P., Eerola, T., Thingujam, N. S., Yamasaki, T., & Beller, G. (2013). Universal and culture-specific factors in the recognition and performance of musical affect expressions. *Emotion, 13*(3), 434–449. doi: 10.1037/a0031388

Lewis, A. (2014). The link between popular love songs and imagined interactions of romantic relationships: A mixed method study. *Unpublished Master's thesis*, The University of the West Indies. doi: https://sta.uwi.edu/conferences/15/humancommunication/documents/Programme.pdf

Lumsden, J., Miles, L. K., & Macrae, C. N. (2014). Sync or sink? Interpersonal synchrony impacts self-esteem. *Frontiers in Psychology*, 5, 1064. doi: 10.3389/fpsyg.2014.01064

Mason, M. F., Norton, M. I., Van Horn, J. D., Wegner, D. M., Grafton S. T., & Macrae C. N. (2007). Wandering minds: The default network and stimulus-independent thought. *Science, 315(5810)*, 393–395. doi: 10.1126/science.1131295

Mehr, S. A., Kotler, J., Howard, R. M., Haig, D., & Krasnow, M. M. (2017). Genomic imprinting is implicated in the psychology of music. *Psychological Science*, 28(10), 1455–1467. doi: 10.1177/0956797617711456

Mithen, S. (2006). *The singing neanderthals: The origins of music, language, mind, and body*. Cambridge, MA: Harvard University Press.

Newberg, A., D'Aquili, E., & Rause, V. (2001). *Why God won't go away: Brain science and the biology of belief*. New York, NY: Ballantine.

Nizamie, S. H., & Tikka, S. K. (2014). Psychiatry and music. *Indian Journal of Psychiatry*, *56*(2), 128–140. doi: 10.4103/0019-5545.130482

Norris, J. (2012). *Marching to the drums: A history of military drums and drummers*. Stroud, UK: History Press.

Paolini, S., Harwood, J., & Rubin, M. (2010). Negative intergroup contact makes group memberships salient: Explaining why intergroup conflict endures. *Personality and Social Psychology Bulletin*, *36*(12), 1723–1738. doi: https://doi.org/10.1177/0146167210388667

Pettigrew, T. F., & Tropp, L. R. (2006). A meta-analytic test of intergroup contact theory. *Journal of Personality and Social Psychology*, *90*(5), 751–783. doi: 10.1037/0022-3514.90.5.751

Raichle, M. E. (2009). A paradigm shift in functional brain imaging. *Journal of Neuroscience*, *29*(41), 12729–12734. doi: 10.1523/JNEUROSCI.4366-09.2009

Roberts, D. F., & Foehr, U. G. (2008). Trends in media use. *Future of Children*, *18*, 11–37. doi: 10.1353/foc.0.0000

Romer, A. L., Knodt, A. R., Houts, R., Brigidi, B. D., Moffitt, T. E., Caspi, A., & Hariri, A. R. (2018). Structural alterations within cerebellar circuitry are associated with general liability for common mental disorders. *Molecular Psychiatry*, *23*, 1084–1090. doi:10.1038/mp.2017.57

Salimpoor, V. N., Benovoy, M., Larcher, K., Dagher, A., & Zatorre, R. J. (2011). Anatomically distinct dopamine release during anticipation and experience of peak emotion to music. *Nature Neuroscience*, *14*(2), 257–262. doi: http://dx.doi.org/10.1038/nn.2726

Schäfer, T., & Sedlmeier, P. (2009). From the functions of music to music preference. *Psychology of Music*, *37*(3), 279–300. doi: 10.1177/0305735608097247.

Schäfer, T., Sedlmeier, P., Städtler, C., & Huron, D. (2013). The psychological functions of music listening. *Frontiers in Psychology*, *4*, 511. doi: http://doi.org/10.3389/fpsyg.2013.00511

Siedliecki, S. L., & Good, M. (2006). Effect of music on power, pain, depression and disability. *Journal of Advanced Nursing*, *54*(5), 553–562. doi: 10.1111/j.1365-2648.2006.03860.x

Smeijsters, H. (1995). The functions of music in music therapy. In T. Wigram, B. Saperton, & R. West (Eds.), *The art and science of music therapy: A handbook* (pp. 385–394). Chur, Switzerland: Harwood Academic.

Stawarczyk, D., Majerus, S., Maquet, P. D., & Argembeau, A. (2011). Neural correlates of ongoing conscious experience: Both task-unrelatedness and stimulus-independence are related to default network activity. *PLoS ONE* 6(2), e16997. doi: 10.1371/journal.pone.0016997

Tan, X., Yowler, C. J., Super, D. M., & Fratianne, R. B. (2010). The efficacy of music therapy protocols for decreasing pain, anxiety, and muscle tension levels during burn dressing changes: A prospective randomized crossover trial. *Journal of Burn Care and Research*, *31*(4), 590–597. doi: 10.1097/BCR.0b013e3181e4d71b

Trappe, H. J. (2010). The effects of music on the cardiovascular system and cardiovascular health. *Heart*, 96, 1868–1871.

Trappe, H. J. (2014). Johann Sebastian Bach: Life, works, and his significance for the cardiology. *DMW, German Medical Weekly Journal*. *139*, *(51–52)*, 2619–2625.

Trappe, H. J., & Voit, G. (2016). The cardiovascular effect of musical genres—a randomized controlled study on the effect of compositions by W. A. Mozart, J. Strauss, and ABBA. *Dtsch Arztebl Int.*,*513(20)*, 347–352. doi: 10.3238/arztebl.2016.0347.

Wallace, S. D., & Harwood, J. (2018). Associations between shared musical engagement and parent-child relational quality: The mediating roles of interpersonal coordination and empathy. *Journal of Family Communication*, *18*(3), 202–216. doi: 10.1080/15267431.2018.1466783

Weiner, J. (2013). Scenes from the life of a legend who can't stand still. *Rolling Stone*,1195, 40–46. Rollingstone.com

Willimek, D., & Willimek, B. (2014). Why do minor chords sound sad? The theory of musical equilibration and the emotions of chords. *Journal of Psychology and Psychotherapy*, *4*, *139*. doi: 10.4172/2161-0487.100013

Zane, W. (2015). *Petty: The biography*. New York, NY: Henry Holt.

· 6 ·

THE ROLE OF IMAGINED INTERACTIONS IN BODY IMAGE AND EATING DISORDERS

Pavica Sheldon

In the United States, an estimated 20 million women and 10 million men suffer from an eating disorder at some point in their life, including Anorexia Nervosa, Bulimia Nervosa, Binge Eating Disorder, and Other Specified Feeding or Eating Disorder (National Eating Disorders Association [NEDA], 2018).

A majority of experts believe that eating disorders such as anorexia are caused by a combination of biological, environmental, and psychological factors. Eating disorders often run in families, especially those with a conformist communication style and those that encourage perfectionism (Sheldon, 2010; 2013; Wade, Bulik, Neale, & Kendler, 2000). There is an evolutionary explanation for anorexia nervosa as well. Anorexics try to control food and being in self-control has always been an indication of a higher social status (Kardum, Gračanin, & Hudek-Knežević, 2008).

In order to manage stigma and to find social support, many individuals with an eating disorder turn to pro-anorexic (also known as Pro-Ana) or pro-bulimic (also known as Pro-Mia) websites (Yeshua-Katz & Martins, 2013). Sheldon, Grey, Vickery, and Honeycutt (2015) examined what types of messages individuals communicate to one of the most popular pro-Ana blog sites in terms of imagined interactions. Their content analysis of 587 blogs entries revealed that they journal about food, weight, and mental illness the most. About 15% of all the entries coded featured imagined interactions (IIs);

defined as a social cognitive process in which persons imagine themselves communicating with others (Honeycutt, 2003–2004; 2010). In this chapter we explain the role of imagined interactions in managing eating disorders and body image. We first explain what eating disorders are, their causes, and relief IIs can provide in individuals with an eating disorder.

Eating Disorders Explained

Of all the eating disorders, three are the most common ones: Anorexia Nervosa, Bulimia Nervosa, and Binge Eating Disorder. *Anorexia nervosa* has the highest mortality rate of any mental illness (Sullivan, 1995), and is characterized by a relentless pursuit of thinness, a distortion of body image and intense fear of gaining weight (National Association of Anorexia Nervosa and Associated Disorders [ANAD], 2014). People suffering from anorexia are called anorexics. Their persistent energy intake restriction can be a way to control areas of life that feel out of their control. It can also be a way of expressing emotions that might feel too complex (ANRED, 2018).

Bulimia nervosa is another serious and potentially life-threatening eating disorder characterized by a cycle of bingeing and self-induced vomiting designed to undo or compensate for the effects of binge eating (NEDA, 2018). Research suggests that comfort foods—high in sugar, fat, and calories—seem to calm the body's response to chronic stress (ANRED, 2018). A study has also suggested a link between fast-paced modern life and increasing rates of overeating (Dallman et al., 2003).

Binge eating disorder is one of the newest eating disorders formally recognized by the Diagnostic and Statistical Manual of Mental Disorders (DSM–5). It is a severe, but treatable eating disorder characterized by recurrent episodes of eating large quantities of food (often very quickly and to the point of discomfort). It is the most common eating disorder in the United States (NEDA, 2018). The lifetime prevalence of binge eating disorder among US adolescents is more than five times greater than that of anorexia and twice that of bulimia (Swanson, Crow, Le Grange, Swendsen, & Merikangas, 2011).

What Causes Eating Disorders

Various explanations have been given about causes of eating disorders. Most research focuses on anorexia nervosa, the most serious and life-threatening eating disorder. Anorexia nervosa has the highest mortality rate of any mental illness, and a 12 times higher rate than that associated with all other causes of death for females 15–24 years old (Sullivan, 1995). In fact, one out of 10 anorexics die within 10 years after contracting the disease (South Carolina Department of Mental Health, 2014). Majority of experts believe that anorexia nervosa is caused by a combination of biological, environmental, and psychological factors.

Anorexia nervosa runs in families. It is estimated to have a heritability of 58% (Wade et al., 2000). In addition, environmental factors such as exposure to thin models in mass and social media, strained family relationships, as well as stressful life events, are associated with anorexia (Sheldon, 2010; 2013). Kinzl, Traweger, Guenther, and Biebl (1994) found that having an adverse family background (including fighting between parents, lack of warm parent-child interactions, and parental neglect) was associated with higher scores on a measure of eating disorder pathology in general. Families of patients with eating disorders are less supportive of personal growth (Latzer, Hochdorf, Bachar, & Canetti, 2002), and have conformist communication style (Sheldon, 2010; 2013). Another group of researchers (Kent & Waller, 2000; Wonderlich et al., 2007) found that emotional abuse is associated with eating disorder pathology. Psychological factors such as being perfectionistic, and having a negative self-image were found to be associated with anorexia as well (Sheldon, 2010). Perfectionism can cause an individual to become obsessed with their weight, diet, and body image, as well as exercise, all in order to portray the perfect image to the world.

Some scholars (e.g., Gatward, 2007; Raphael & Lacey, 1994) also argue that there might be an evolutionary explanation for anorexia. When starving, anorexics try to self-regulate. Those who occupy a high, dominant position within the group feel more in control compared to those in a more submissive position (Kardum et al., 2008). It is likely that they will be more prone to developing eating disorders as they see dietary restrictions as a sign of high status and self-control. Think about the recent gluten-free craze. Poor people do not choose which food they eat. This explains why anorexia is so frequent in western developed nations (Kardum et al., 2008; Södersten, Bergh, & Zandian, 2006). Button and Warren (2002) offered another explanation for anorexia. Anorexic people try to avoid anxiety derived from repeated invalidating experiences in the relational field by focusing on issues such as eating and weight, with the aim of making their life more manageable. Some scholars (e.g., Button, 1993; Winter & Button, 2010) even argued that it is the fear of maturity and a fear of change that cause the control.

Unlike anorexia, bulimia can be more difficult to diagnose due to more normal physical appearance and a body mass index within the normal range (Wilson, 1998). Bulimia nervosa predominantly affects adolescent girls, occurring in approximately 1–2% of the female population (Fairburn & Harrison, 2003). Low self-esteem and confidence are risk factors for bulimic pathology. Mond, Hay, Rodgers, and Owen (2008) found that low self-esteem is the most likely cause of bulimia nervosa among a community sample of women.

Although binge eating is the most prevalent eating disorder, not much research has been done to learn about the underlying triggers of binge eating. Schulte (2016) examined key predictors of binge eating among youths in the United Arab Emirates (UAE). She found two key emotions—boredom and loneliness— to be significant predictors of binge eating. Unlike for other eating disorders, depressive symptoms were not a significant predictor of binge eating. Other research has found that binge eating correlates to body mass, negative affect, stress, emotional eating, body dissatisfaction, and boredom (Freeman & Gil, 2004; Mason & Lewis, 2014; Stein et al., 2007).

Eating Disorders Blogs

Overcoming an eating disorder can be difficult. For many people, one way to cope with anorexia or bulimia is to look for support online. A classic symptom of someone with eating disorder is the desire to hide their behavior from the world. They either try to avoid the stigma associated with a mental illness, or they are not accepting that they suffer from an eating disorder. However, some individuals might turn to social media and blogs to avoid social stigma upon sharing their stories in face-to-face interactions (Whitney, Haigh, Weinman, & Treasure, 2007).

Several studies have analyzed the content of pro-ana blogs. Research (e.g., Mantella, 2007; Yeshua-Katz & Martins, 2013) has shown that the top reason that pro-ana bloggers reported joining these blogs was to obtain social and emotional support and to express themselves. Unlike other websites, blogs are unique as they allow sharing personal feelings, thoughts, and issues that individuals might not feel comfortable communicating in offline situations (Tierney, 2006; Tong, Heinemann-LaFave, Jeon, Kolodziej-Smith, & Warshay, 2013).

Tong et al. (2013) analysis of 48 blogs revealed that the average pro-ana blogger reveals information regarding her sex, height, weight, and physical location. It was also common that these bloggers revealed their "goal weight" or the weight they hoped to obtain in the future. Their analysis also indicated that emotional support was most frequently communicated form of social support among pro-ana bloggers. Blogs also encouraged sharing of one's personal situations. Bloggers disclosed personal stories on a variety of topics, including specific (anti-recovery stories), relational (friends, family, and romantic partners) and mundane (school and exams) stories.

Another content analysis of pro-ana blogs was conducted by Sheldon et al. (2015). The authors content analyzed Pro-Ana LiveJournal blogs to find out what individuals blog about. The study results revealed that the main topics anorexics blog about include food, weight, and mental illness (see Table 6.1). Fifteen to 20% of blogs discussed purging and binging, both characteristics of bulimia nervosa. Many bloggers choose to relieve their struggles by journaling about their prior conversations with family, friends, and medical professionals. Some of those conversations including imagined interactions (IIs).

Table 6.1. Topics Communicated on Pro-Ana Blog (%).

Topics	%
Food	57.6
Weight	39.4
Mental illness	33.9
Advice	23.7
Family talk	21.8
Body image	21.5
Purging	19.6
Binging	14.5
Exercise	13.6
Peer talk	11.8
Expert talk	8.0
Trigger	6.8
Suicide talk	6.5
Partner talk	6.0

(Source: Sheldon, P., Grey, S. H., Vickery, A. J., & Honeycutt, J. M. (2015). An analysis of imagined interactions with Pro Ana (Anorexia): Implications for mental and physical health. *Imagination, Cognition, and Personality*, 35, 166–190. doi:10.1177/0276236615587493)

Imagined Interactions in Pro-Ana Blogs

Imagined Interactions (IIs) are a form of social cognition in which actors imagine conversations with others using visual and verbal imagery (Honeycutt, 2003). IIs fulfill various functions, and have been studied in conjunction with individual differences, such as communication apprehension (Honeycutt, Choi, & DeBerry, 2009), sex differences (Edwards, Honeycutt, & Zagacki, 1989), relational quality (Honeycutt, 2008–2009), personality (Honeycutt & Keaton, 2012), as well as body image disturbances (Sheldon et al., 2015).

Honeycutt (2010) proposed six functions of IIs that explain motivations for their usage: (1) catharsis, or using IIs to relieve tension; (2) compensation, or substituting IIs for real interactions; (3) conflict-linkage, or using IIs between arguments, thereby creating an ongoing conflict; (4) rehearsal, or mentally preparing for interactions prior to engaging in them; (5) relational maintenance, or using IIs psychologically to maintain a relationship by thinking about a partner; and (6) self-understanding, or using IIs to gain a deeper understanding of the individual's attitudes, values, and beliefs. When it comes to the relation to actual conversations, IIs can be proactive and retroactive (Honeycutt, Vickery, & Hatcher, 2015). Proactive IIs occur before an anticipated encounter, whereas retroactive IIs occur after the encounter. In Sheldon et al.' (2015) study analyzing 587 anorexics' blogs, the majority of IIs were retroactive and served the cathartic function (83% of entries). This means that individuals with an eating disorder use IIs to relieve tension and anxiety and to release emotions. They ruminate about past conversations and those ruminations help them to relieve the stress that they experience in dealing with their mental illness.

In terms of catharsis, individuals with eating disorders may subliminally release emotions directed at family members, friends, doctors, peers, and others of significance as a way of envisioning frustrations with their disapproval (Honeycutt, 2003). Research on rumination reveals that it is difficult to either forgive or forget despite the cultural maxim to the contrary (McCullough, Bellah, Kilpatrick, & Johnson, 2001). People often dwell on arguments and may be obsessed with the topic (e.g., eating disorder) or another person's (e.g., "My father doesn't understand my eating disorder" (also see Honeycutt, 2003; 2010). Rosenblatt and Meyer (1986) proposed IIs as means of emotional catharsis in counseling sessions which have found that IIs serve as an outlet for their patients to release unresolved tension. Individuals are using IIs as a means of "getting things off their chest."

For individuals suffering from anorexia nervosa, IIs might also serve as a mechanism for dealing with suppressed conflict that is not being discussed openly (see Honeycutt, 1995).Honeycutt and Ford (2001) proposed imagined interactions as a means of problem solving by allowing an individual to think through a problem. Individuals with an eating disorder suffer from multiple problems related to the mental illness. Journaling about those problems aids them not just in releasing emotions, but also in self and other understanding. For example, Sheldon et al. (2015) found that self and other understanding, and conflict-linkage, were the second most important functions of having IIs during blogging on a Pro-Ana site. Individuals replaying arguments with family members are doing it to understand themselves and their parents. Zagacki, Edwards, & Honeycutt, (1992) studied the role of mental imagery and emotion in IIs and found that IIs that involved more conflict were related to an increase in self-understanding. IIs accompanied by a more negative affect are also more memorable than more pleasant IIs. Perhaps this explains why anorexics recall negative information more readily (Sheldon et al., 2015).

Family is the predominant partner in IIs of individuals suffering from an eating disorder (Sheldon et al., 2015). Families who restrict an open conversation with their children negatively influence their body satisfaction. This is especially true for an opposite-sex parent (Sheldon, 2013). Conformist fathers ten to have daughters who are unhappy with their weight. Parents who become exceedingly conscious of their own weight may consequently be similarly concerned with keeping their daughters in "perfect" shape (Byely, Archibald, Graber, & Brooks-Gunn, 2000; Vincent & McCabe, 2000). Striegel-Moore and Kearney-Cooke (1994) found that parents were more likely to rate their daughters as overweight than their sons, although boys are proportionately heavier than girls (Fritz & Carnett, 2007). Regarding parenting styles, anorexia nervosa is associated with rejective/neglectful style, while bulimia nervosa with overprotective style (Horesh, Sommerfeld, Wolf, Zubery, & Zalsman, 2015). Think about a daughter who is looking for more affection from her parents. Rosenblatt and Meyer (1986) indicated that an individual may choose to use IIs in place of actually confronting a loved one in fear that the loved one would be hurt by the message.

After the family, the second most reported II partners were peers (Sheldon et al., 2015). Individuals with an eating disorder ruminate and complain to the Pro-Ana community about what their friends say about their looks. Most of the blogs discussing peers tend to be negative. Previous research (Graziano, Jensen-Campbell, Shebilske, & Lundgren 1993) found that young women and men are sensitive to same-sex peers' comments about their physical looks, as they are socialized from a very young age to be oriented to others to receive validation of their self-worth (Cash & Henry, 1995; Sheldon, 2010). Thus, research has shown that a sorority member's binge eating could be predicted from the binge-eating level of her friends (Crundall, 1988). From an evolutionary standpoint, achieving a slender figure is a sign of winning amongst other women (Austin, 2007). Women have always been competing for mating resources (Geary, 2010) and therefore place a higher importance on physical attractiveness (Rhodes, Simmons, & Peters, 2005). Researchers (Hill & Buss, 2006; Nolen-Hoeksema & Jackson, 2001) argue that the process of female competition often leads to invidious comparison and excessive rumination. For example, women often make negative comments about another girl's looks if she is with a partner to whom they are attracted. Recently, there has been an increase of body dissatisfaction among men as well (Sheldon, 2010). For American men, the ideal is a lean, muscular body shape (Ricciardelli, McCabe, & Ridge, 2006). According to the same researchers, the appearance of the ideal, almost unachievable V-shaped male physique has increased in men's magazines over the past 30 years. This has caused an increased rate of eating disorders.

Food is also associated with imagined interactions (Sheldon et al., 2015). The capacity for self-regulation, including control over appetites, is much more extensive in humans than what is found in other animals (Baumeister, Gailliot, DeWall, & Oaten, 2006). Research (Baumeister & Leary, 1995; Gatward, 2007; Gilbert, 2004) suggests that humans have had to cope with periods of famine for thousands of years. This would pressure them to starve, but also to compete for status within the group. From an evolutionary perspective, this can explain how anorexics tolerate starvation. Fear of weight gain is explained as a fear of entering the competition for food (Gatward, 2007). Another evidence supporting an evolutionary standpoint is that anorexia nervosa has existed for a long time (Bemporad, 1996) and is hereditary (Wade et al., 2000). In addition, food-related activities, such as shopping, cooking and eating are conventionally presented as female-centered. Women tend to purchase, prepare and provide food and may therefore be more obsessed about it (Astani & Mandia, 2017).

In line with the internal structure of imagined interaction, various studies have revealed that conflict linkage and catharsis have more negative emotions than those used for compensation and relational maintenance functions (Bodie, Honeycutt, & Vickery, 2013; Honeycutt, Vickery, & Hatcher, 2014).

In Sheldon et al., (2015) study about IIs and body image, most of the blog entries featuring IIs reflected negative affect (63%). This is not surprising as a major function of IIs is compensating for the lack of real communication.

Table 6.2 presents the results of a technique called logistic regression analysis in which persons either used IIs to deal with eating disorders or they did not. Significant predictors were discussing food as expected, mental illness, talk about family, binging, and talking with peers as well as experts.

Table 6.2. Logistic Regression Analysis Predicting IIs on Pro-Ana Blog.

Predictor	B	S.E.	*Wald*	*df*	*Sig.*	*Exp (B)*
Food	.92	.33	7.91	1	.005	2.500
Weight	.20	.30	.46	1	.497	1.225
Mental illness	–.70	.33	4.38	1	.036	.498
Advice	–.04	.33	.01	1	.906	.961
Family talk	2.53	.30	69.83	1	.000	12.493
Body image	.41	.36	1.33	1	.249	1.507
Purging	.45	.36	1.53	1	.217	1.565
Binging	–1.41	.49	8.19	1	.004	.243
Exercise	–.44	.42	1.13	1	.287	.643
Peer talk	1.53	.38	15.94	1	.000	4.621
Expert talk	1.47	.43	11.59	1	.001	4.366
Trigger	.61	.52	1.37	1	.241	1.848
Suicide talk	.56	.56	1.01	1	.315	1.757
Partner talk	.85	.46	3.42	1	.064	2.332
Model χ^2 =	343.41	$p<.000$				
Pseudo R^2 =	.20					
N =	587					

Note: The dependent variable in this analysis is an entry featuring IIs so that 0 = not an II and 1 = qualifies as an II. Overall, 82 entries featured II, and 505 entries did not feature II.
(Sheldon et al., 2015)

Summary

Eating disorders such as anorexia and bulimia nervosa, as well as binge eating, have serious health consequences. Individuals with eating disorders use Internet websites to express emotions directed at family members, peers, medical professionals, and other significant others who often disapprove of their actions. Dysfunctional family life is the main reason young adults develop eating disorders. Food is often the only thing they can control in their lives.

Overall, therapists should study imagined interactions of individuals with an eating disorder. One way is to study blogs (online diaries) to better understand the kinds of issues with which they struggle, and the identities of the people they are talking to. Future studies should focus on the negative emotions present in pro-ana blogs, including fear (of gaining weight), disgust (for eating food), and anger (parents' talk). They should examine the language used to describe those feelings.

Imagined interactions cannot explain all the factors that cause eating disorders such as anorexia and bulimia nervosa, however, they are another facet to take into account when trying to understand the interplay between psychological and evolutionary motives for wanting to lose weight.

Discussion Questions

1. *Have you, or anyone you know, had an eating disorder? If yes, have they ever talked to you about their struggle? If you had it, have you shared your struggles with others? Have you engaged in imagined interactions?*
2. *What are some of the* major *risks for developing* eating disorders*?*
3. *How can imagined interactions (IIs) help with coping with a mental illness, such as eating disorder pathologies?*

References

ANRED (Anorexia Nervosa and Related Eating Disorders). (2018). Retrieved from https://www.anred.com/

Astani, A., & Mandia, A. (2017). Risk factors involved in the development and maintenance of dysfunctional eating behaviors: A theoretical review. *Journal of Experiential Psychotherapy / Revista De Psihoterapie Experientiala, 20*(3), 44–56.

Austin, L. (2007). Possible cause of eating disorders among women: Theory of competition for mates and status. *Psi Chi Journal of Undergraduate Research, 12*(4), 146–153.

Baumeister, R. F., Gailliot, M., DeWall, C., & Oaten, M. (2006). Self-regulation and personality: How interventions increase regulatory success, and how depletion moderates the effects of traits on behavior. *Journal of Personality, 74*(6), 1773–1802. doi: 10.1111/j.1467-6494.2006.00428.x

Baumeister, R. F., & Leary, M. R. (1995). The need to belong: Desire for interpersonal attachments as a fundamental human motivation. *Psychological Bulletin, 117*(3), 497–529. doi: 10.1037/0033-2909.117.3.497

Bemporad, J. R. (1996). Self-starvation through the ages: Reflections on the pre-history of anorexia nervosa. *International Journal of Eating Disorders*, *19*(3), 217–237. doi: 10.1002/(SICI)1098-108X(199604)19:3<217::AID-EAT1>3.0.CO;2-P

Bodie, G. D., Honeycutt, J. M., & Vickery, A. J. (2013). An analysis of the correspondence between imagined interaction attributes and functions. *Human Communication Research*, 39(2), 157–183. doi: 10.1111/hcre.12003

Button, E. J. (1993). *Eating disorders: Personal construct therapy and change*. Chichester, UK: John Wiley & Sons.

Button, E. J., & Warren, R. L. (2002). Selfimage in anorexia nervosa 7.5 years after initial presentation to a specialized eating disorders service. *European Eating Disorders Review, 10*(6), 399–412. doi:10.1002/erv.484

Byely, L., & Archibald, A. B., Graber, J., & Brooks-Gunn, J. (2000). A prospective study of familial and social influences on girls' body image and dieting. *International Journal of Eating Disorders*, *28*(2), 155–164.

Cash, T. F., & Henry, P. E. (1995). Women's body images: The results of a national survey in the USA. *Sex Role*, *33*(1–2), 19–28. doi: 10.1007/BF01547933

Crundall, I. (1988). *Survey of drug use among young people in Victorian Youth Training and Reception Centres*. Melbourne, Australia: Health Department, Alcohol and Drug Services Unit.

Dallman, M. F., Pecoraro, N., Akana, S. F., la Fleur, S. F., Gomez, F., Houshyar, H., & . Manalo, S. (2003). Chronic stress and obesity: A new view of 'comfort food'. *Proceedings of The National Academy of Sciences of The United States of America*, *100*(20), 11696–11701.

Edwards, R., Honeycutt, J. M., & Zagacki, K. S. (1989). Gender differences in imagined interactions. *Sex Roles*, *21*(3), 259–268. doi:10.1007/BF00289906

Fairburn, C. G., & Harrison, P. J. (2003). Eating disorders. *Lancet, 361(9355)*, 407–416.

Freeman, L. M. Y., & Gil, K. M. (2004). Daily stress, coping, and dietary restraint in binge eating. *International Journal of Eating Disorders*, 36(2), 204–212. http://dx.doi.org/10.1002/eat.20012

Fritz, S., & Carnett, S. (2007, May). *"Mom, dad, am I fat?": The effects of physique, parental body image, and parental communication on satisfaction with one's body*. Presented at the International Communication Association Annual Meeting, San Francisco.

Gatward, N. (2007). Anorexia nervosa: An evolutionary puzzle. *European Eating Disorders Review*, *15*(1), 1–12. doi:10.1002/erv.718

Geary, D. C. (2010). *Male/female: The evolution of human sex differences* (2nd ed.). Washington, D. C.: American Psychological Association.

Gilbert, P. (2004). Evolutionary approaches to psycho-pathology and cognitive therapy. In P. Gilbert (Ed.), *Evolutionary theory and cognitive therapy* (pp. 3–44). New York, NY: Springer.

Graziano, W. G., Jensen-Campbell, L. A., Shebilske, L. J., & Lundgren, S. R. (1993). Social influence, sex differences, and judgments of beauty: Putting the interpersonal back in interpersonal attraction. *Journal of Personality and Social Psychology*, *65*(3), 522–531.

Hill, S. E., & Buss, D. M. (2006). Envy and positional bias in the evolutionary psychology of management. *Managerial and Decision Economics*, *27*(2–3), 131–143. doi: 10.1002/mde.1288

Honeycutt, J. M. (1995). The oral history interview and reports of imagined interactions as marital therapy. *Journal of Family Psychotherapy*, 6, 63–69. doi: 10.1300/j085V06N04_06

Honeycutt, J. M. (2003). *Imagined interactions: Daydreaming about communication*. Cresskill, NJ: Hampton.

Honeycutt, J. M. (2003–2004). Imagined interaction conflict-linkage theory: Explaining the persistence and resolution of interpersonal conflict in everyday life. *Imagination, Cognition, and Personality*, *23*, 3–25. doi: 10.2190/240J-1VPK-K86D-1JL8

Honeycutt, J. M. (2008–2009). Symbolic interdependence, imagined interaction, and relationship quality. *Imagination, Cognition, and Personality*, *28*(4), 303–320. doi:10.2190/IC.28.4.b

Honeycutt, J. M. (2010). Forgive but don't forget: Correlates of rumination about conflict. In J. M. Honeycutt (Ed.), *Imagine that: Studies in imagined interaction* (pp. 17–29). Cresskill, NJ: Hampton.

Honeycutt, J. M., Choi, C. W., & DeBerry, J. R. (2009). Communication apprehension and imagined interactions. *Communication Research Reports*, *26*(3), 228–236. doi:10.1080/08824090903074423

Honeycutt, J. M., & Ford, S. G. (2001). Mental imagery and intrapersonal communication: A review of research on imagined interactions (IIs) and current developments. *Communication Yearbook 25* (pp. 315–345). Mahwah, NJ: Lawrence Erlbaum Associates. doi: http://dx.doi.org/10.1207/s15567419cy2501_9

Honeycutt, J. M., & Keaton, S. A. (2012). Imagined interactions and personality preferences as predictors of relationship quality. *Imagination, Cognition, and Personality*, *32*(1), 3–21. doi:10.2190/IC.32.1.b

Honeycutt, J. M., Vickery, A. J., & Hatcher, L. C. (2015). The daily use of imagined interaction features. *Communication Monographs*, *82*(2), 201–223. doi: 10.1080/03637751.2014.953965

Horesh, N., Sommerfeld, E., Wolf, M., Zubery, E., & Zalsman, G. (2015). Father-daughter relationship and the severity of eating disorders. *European Psychiatry: The Journal of the Association of European Psychiatrists*, *30*, 114–120. doi: 10.1016/j.eurpsy.2014.04.004

Kardum, I., Gračanin, A., & Hudek-Knežević, J. (2008). Evolutionary explanations of eating disorders. *Psychological Topics*, *17*(2), 247–263.

Kent, A., & Waller, G. (2000). Childhood emotional abuse and eating psychopathology. *Clinical Psychological Review*, *20*(7), 887–903.

Kinzl, J. F., Traweger, C., Guenther, V., & Biebl, W. (1994). Family background and sexual abuse associated with eating disorders. *American Journal of Psychiatry*, *151*(8), 1127–1131.

Latzer, Y., Hochdorf, Z., Bachar, E., & Canetti, L. (2002). Attachment style and family functioning as discriminating factors in eating disorders. *Contemporary Family Therapy*, *24*(4), 581–599.

Mantella, D. G. (2007). *"Pro-Ana" web-log uses and gratifications: Towards understanding the pro-anorexia paradox.* (Masters thesis). Georgia State University, Atlanta, GA.

Mason, T. B., & Lewis, R. J. (2014). Profiles of binge eating: The interaction of depressive symptoms, eating styles, and body mass index. *Eating Disorders, 22*(5), 450–460. http://dx.doi.org/10.1080/10640266.2014.931766

McCullough, M. E., Bellah, C. G., Kilpatrick, S. D., & Johnson, J. L. (2001). Vengefulness: Relationships with forgiveness, rumination, well-being, and the big five. *Personality and Social Psychology Bulletin, 27*(5), 601–610. doi: 10.1177/0146167201275008

Mond, J. M., Hay, P., Rodgers, B., & Owen, C. (2008). Mental health literacy and eating disorders: What do women with bulimic eating disorders think and know about bulimia nervosa and its treatment? *Journal of Mental Health, 17*(6), 565–575.

National Association of Anorexia Nervosa and Associated Disorders, ANAD (2014). *About eating disorders.* Retrieved from http://www.anad.org/get-information/about-eating-disorders

National Eating Disorders Association, NEDA (2018). *What are eating disorders?* Retrieved from https://www.nationaleatingdisorders.org/learn/by-eating-disorder/anorexia

Nolen-Hoeksema, S., & Jackson, B. (2001). Mediators of the gender difference in rumination. *Psychology of Women Quarterly, 25*, 37–47. doi: 10.1111/1471-6402.00005

Raphael, F. J., & Lacey, J. H. (1994). The etiology of eating disorders: A hypothesis of the interplay between social, cultural, and biological factors. *European Eating Disorders Review, 2*(3), 143–154.

Rhodes, G., Simmons, L. W., & Peters, M. (2005). Attractiveness and sexual behavior: Does attractiveness enhance mating success? *Evolution and Human Behavior, 26*(2), 186–201. doi: https://doi.org/10.1016/j.evolhumbehav.2004.08.014

Ricciardelli, L. A., McCabe, M. P., & Ridge, D. (2006). The construction of the adolescent male body through sport. *Journal of Health Psychology, 11*(4), 577–587.

Rosenblatt, P. C., & Meyer, C. (1986). Imagined interactions and the family. *Family Relations, 35*(2), 319–324. doi: 10.2307/583641

Schulte, S. J. (2016). Predictors of binge eating in male and female youths in the United Arab Emirates. *Appetite, 105*, 312–319. doi:10.1016/j.appet.2016.06.004

Sheldon, P. (2010). Pressure to be perfect: Influences on college students' body esteem. *SouthernCommunication Journal, 75*(3), 277–298. doi: 10.1080/10417940903026543

Sheldon, P. (2013). Testing parental and peer communication orientation influence on young adults' body satisfaction. *Southern Communication Journal, 78*(3), 215–232. doi: 10.1080/1041794X.2013.776097

Sheldon, P., Grey, S. H., Vickery, A. J., & Honeycutt, J. M. (2015). An analysis of imagined interactions with Pro Ana (Anorexia): Implications for mental and physical health. *Imagination, Cognition, and Personality, 35*(2), 166–190. doi: 10.1177/0276236615587493

Södersten, P., Bergh, C., & Zandian, M. (2006). Understanding eating disorders. *Hormones and Behavior, 50*(4), 572–578. doi: https://doi.org/10.1016/j.yhbeh.2006.06.030

South Carolina Department of Mental Health. (2014). *Eating disorder statistics.* Retrieved from http://www.state.sc.us/dmh/anorexia/statistics.htm

Stein, R. I., Kenardy, J., Wiseman, C. V., Dounchis, J. Z., Arnow, B. A., & Wilfley, D. E. (2007). What's driving the binge in binge eating disorder? A prospective examination of precursors and consequences. *International Journal of Eating Disorders*, *40*(3), 195–203. doi:10.1002/eat.20352

Striegel-Moore, R. H., & Bulik, C. M. (2007). Risk factors for eating disorders. *American Psychologist*, *62*(3), 181–198. doi: 10.1037/0003-066X.62.3.181

Striegel-Moore, R. H., & Kearney-Cooke, A. (1994). Exploring parents' attitudes and behaviors about their children's physical appearance. *International Journal of Eating Disorders*, *15*(4), 377–385. doi: http://dx.doi.org/10.1002/eat.2260150408

Sullivan, P. F. (1995). Mortality in anorexia nervosa. *American Journal of Psychiatry*, *152*(7), 1073–1074. doi: https://doi.org/10.1176/ajp.152.7.1073

Swanson, S. A., Crow, S. J., Le Grange, D., Swendsen, J., & Merikangas, K. R. (2011). Prevalence and correlates of eating disorders in adolescents: Results from the national co-morbidity survey replication adolescent supplement. *Archives of General Psychiatry*, *68*(7), 714–723. doi:10.1001/archgenpsychiatry.2011.22

Tierney, S. (2006). The dangers and draw of online communication: Pro-anorexia websites and their implications for users, practitioners, and researchers. *Eating Disorders*, *14*(3), 181–190. doi:10.1080/10640260600638865

Tong, S., Heinemann-LaFave, D., Jeon, J., Kolodziej-Smith, R., & Warshay, N. (2013). The use of pro-ana blogs for online social support. *Eating Disoders*, *21*(5), 408–422. doi: 10.1080/10640266.2013.827538

Vincent, M. A., & McCabe, M. P. (2000). Gender differences among adolescents in family and peer influences on body dissatisfaction, weight loss, and binge eating behaviors. *Journal of Youth and Adolescence*, *29*(2), 205–221. doi: 10.1023/A:1005156616173

Wade, T. D., Bulik, C. M., Neale, M., & Kendler, K. S. (2000). Anorexia nervosa and major depression: Shared genetic and environmental risk factors. *American Journal of Psychiatry*, *157*(3), 469–71. doi: 10.1176/appi.ajp.157.3.469

Whitney, J., Haigh, R., Weinman, J., & Treasure, J. (2007). Caring for people with eating disorders: Factors associated with psychological distress and negative caregiving appraisals in carers of people with eating disorders. *British Journal of Clinical Psychology*, *46*(4), 413–428. doi: 10.1348/014466507X173781

Wilson, G. T. (1998). The clinical utility of randomized controlled trials. *International Journal of Eating Disorders*, *24*, 13–29. doi: https://doi.org/10.1002/(SICI)1098-108X(199807)24:1<13::AID-EAT2>3.0.CO;2-3

Winter, D. A., & Button, E. J. (2010). A personal construct perspective on control in eating disorders. In S. Sassaroli, & G. M. Ruggiero (Eds.), *Cognitive therapy of eating disorders on control and worry* (pp. 28–50). New York, NY: NOVA.

Wonderlich, S. A., Rosenfeldt, S., Crosby, R. D., Mitchell, J. E., Engel, S. G., Smyth, J., & Miltenberger, R. (2007). The effect of childhood trauma on daily mood lability and comorbid psychopathology in bulimia nervosa. *Journal of Trauma Stress*, *20*, 77–87. doi: 10.1002/jts.20184

Yeshua-Katz, D., & Martins, N. (2013). Communicating stigma: The pro-ana paradox. *Health Communication*, *28*(5), 499–508. doi: 10.1080/10410236.2012.699889

Zagacki, K. S., Edwards, R., & Honeycutt, J. M. (1992). The role of mental imagery and emotion in imagined interaction. *Communication Quarterly*, *40*, 56–68. doi: 10.1080/01463379209369820

SECTION 3

ATTACKS ON PUBLIC POLICY CONCERNS

· 7 ·

FRACKING OUT!

Using Imagined Interactions to Manage the Trauma of Environmental Degradation

Andrea J. Vickery, Michael F. Rold,
Kayla J. Hastrup, and Stephanie Houston Grey

On September 20, 2016, the *Times-Picayune* newspaper published an article entitled, "After 2 ½ years, St. Tammany Parish fracking saga abruptly ends." Starting at the presumed end may at first appear an unlikely place to open this chapter, but it serves to illustrate the trauma and stress felt in this Louisiana community. In 2014 Helis Oil & Gas announced their plans to conduct exploratory drilling to determine the potential value in fracking the local land. Fracking is the abbreviation of hydraulic fracturing: Sand, water, and chemicals are injected into small cracks, or fissures, in shale rock formations to trigger the release of gas and oil. This process contaminates groundwater and initiates seismic activity (Owen, 2014), both indicators of environmental degradation. Local activists began conversations, developed social media campaigns, and held information sessions informing citizens about fracking and its effects. One group, Concerned Citizens of St. Tammany Parish (CCSPT), was created to unify and amplify individual efforts. CCSTP joined the parish government in filing a lawsuit against Helis based on permitting, but local courts and subsequent appeals to the state courts ruled against CCSTP and St. Tammany Parish (Roberts, 2016). The *Times-Picayune* article reported that Helis would be abandoning their fracking plans as the endeavor would not be profitable enough for the New Orleans based company (Rhoden, 2016).

This abrupt ending reflects the unfinished story of fracking and environmental degradation in St. Tammany Parish. Helis could decide to reopen their fracking campaign tomorrow, next week, or next year and there are no court orders in place to stop them. Activists would then have to start their educational and legal efforts all over again. As trauma is shaped by individual, societal, and institutional reactions to events (Grey, 2007), the unresolved and unfinished nature of fracking is undoubtedly present in the self-talk, mental imagery, and experiences of the community. The activists of St. Tammany Parish represent how a group of people might come together to protect the environment. Given the inevitable changes in our environment, we owe it to ourselves to seriously consider how people might manage trauma in relation to environmental destruction.

This chapter explores narratives and imagined interactions (IIs) in the sense-making activities of local environmental activists. After a brief background, we present a thematic analysis from three semi-structured interviews as a case study to understand how self-talk and IIs in narrative discourses keep the efforts to stop fracking alive in the minds of local environmental activists. We then discuss how these narratives embody the trauma and stress still felt by environmental activists, providing some insight and applications for all citizens concerned with the environment.

Background Studies

A national survey of over 1,000 Americans in 2012 revealed that 52% of respondents reported knowing very little or nothing at all about fracking (Boudet et al., 2014), but that number may change as more communities face fracking proposals. LSU Public Policy survey data from 2013 suggests over 40% of Louisiana-based respondents had read some or a lot about fracking (Climek, Brou, Means, & Goidel, 2013). Community characteristics shape the identity of people who view themselves as environmentalists (Owen, Videras, & Wu, 2010); personality traits like openness and altruism also correlate with pro-environmental behaviors (Markowitz, Goldberg, Ashton, & Lee, 2012). II features like frequency are also associated with openness (Honeycutt, Pence, & Gearhart, 2013). II theory assumes that intrapersonal communication or internal talk is the "foundation on which other types of communication rest" (Honeycutt, 2008, p. 79), complementing environmental activism studies which primarily focus on public or rhetorical communication like Grey and Broussard's (2017) essay on the CCSTP community.

While there is not yet a quantitative investigation linking II features, personality traits, pro-environmentalism identity, and activism, such an investigation might not be sensitive to ongoing stress and trauma and unresolved nature in local communities facing fracking. Instead, an exploratory and qualitative study giving activists the space to share their narratives may be more appropriate for understanding IIs while also activating the power and health benefits of stories (Pennebaker & Seagal, 1999). Prior explorations of narratives and IIs are situated in marital relationships and utilize quantitative methodologies (Honeycutt, 1999), suggesting the need to extend the theoretical and contextual boundaries of II research (Honeycutt, 2008) and provide an alternative to the primarily quantitative extensions of II theory (Bodie, Honeycutt, & Vickery, 2013).

Imagined interactions provide an important catharsis function that effectively enables an individual to release and measure emotions in the aftermath of trauma and tragedies (Honeycutt, 2003). Honeycutt, Nasser, Banner, Mapp, and DuPont (2008) found students with high levels of trauma anxiety after Hurricanes Rita and Katrina used the catharsis function of imagined interactions as a way to release tension. They also found that the basic emotions that predicted trauma anxiety were fear, anger, sadness, and guilt. Therefore, we can better understand how a person might attempt to deal with traumatization from environmental concerns by identifying when these emotions surface and which II features appear in the narratives of environmental activists. These features, including II functions and attributes, are detailed in other sources (see Introduction, this volume; Honeycutt, 2003; 2008).

Environmental activism encompasses multiple simultaneous activities, not unlike the II where II functions and attributes co-occur together (Bodie et al., 2013; Honeycutt, Vickery, & Hatcher, 2015). Example activities shared by our interviewees included: researching fracking, learning about the effects on groundwater and nature, creating social media pages to share information, going to the state Capitol to speak with legislators, protesting at the state Capitol, attending court hearings, presenting information at community meetings, asking petroleum industry representatives questions, among other individual and community actions. This list is not exhaustive as it focuses on specific behaviors reported in our interviews in response to fracking. We provide this glimpse into our interviews now because their personal experiences shared in the interviews mirror a psychological model by Matsuba and Pratt (2013) where an individual's pro-environmental identity begins with experiences with nature, environmental education, and concern for the next generation (i.e., generativity).

Specifically, the activities described can be as a response to the actions of Helis starting in 2014. Of course, interviewees also reported on general pro-environmental behaviors like recycling, selecting zero-waste food packaging, participating in beach cleanups, advocating for hybrid vehicles, or supporting other causes. The importance of framing activism as a response to local corporate activities is integral to our investigation for two reasons. First, this framing theoretically intersects with a conceptualization of trauma in communication studies as the impact of events on individuals and communities (Grey, 2007). Second, this framing unites differences in our interviewees' backgrounds as not all interviewees may have identified themselves as environmental activists prior to 2014. Perhaps one of our interviewees said it best when asked why fracking was his top environmental cause: He replied, "*It's not the most important environmental cause, but it's the most immediate for me. You know, I think like we don't even know what the most important environmental cause is*." While these interviews will be discussed in more detail shortly, this insight from one of our interviewees reinforces the theoretical and methodological framing of our study. There is no singular cause or activity associated with environmentalism. Nor can one singular narrative represent the experiences of environmental activists in St. Tammany Parish, resulting in our general research direction and question guiding our forthcoming analysis:

> RQ: What II features are present in the narrative accounts of environmental activists involved in the anti-fracking efforts in St. Tammany Parish?

Current Study

Interviewees

A total of three interviewees participated in our qualitative case study. All three interviewees were residents of St. Tammany Parish and had participated in environmental activism using various combinations of the activities described in the previous section. Interviewee #1 (Female) is an educator who serves on local community committees dedicated to environmental issues. Interviewee #2 (Male) is an educator with research knowledge and expertise in a STEM field. Interviewee #3 (Female) currently works for an environmental non-profit but has previously worked in the Oil and Gas industry.

Procedures

After receiving IRB approval from the Louisiana State University office, two authors were responsible for conducting the semi-structured interviews (for similar procedures, see Honeycutt, 1996). Interviewees completed the informed consent document, verbally affirmed consent to be recorded, and then were given a reference document describing II functions and attributes. Interviews began with a general question asking interviewees to describe their involvement in and with local environmental causes. Follow up questions were asked about IIs and environmental activism. Within the interviews, participants were directly asked questions about the use of II features to solicit "yes" or "no" responses, as well as follow-up questions about II features. These interviews ranged from 1.5 to 2 hours in length. Both transcripts (created by one of the interviewing authors) and audio recordings were consulted during the thematic analysis.

Analysis

Two authors were responsible for analyzing the interviews for II features. Independently, these authors listened to the audio recordings and consulted the transcripts to identify II features. These notes were then compared with the notes of II features generated by one of the interviewing authors. Due to the exploratory nature of the project, no intercoder reliability estimates were generated. Results present features agreed upon by all three authors, or features where two of the three authors agreed; final decisions were based on expertise and knowledge of the two authors in agreement. Only examples relevant to activist efforts of 2014–2016 are reported.

Results

In response to our guiding research question, many of the identified features of II functions and attributes were present in our interviews. All three of our interviewees reported using IIs as a form of rehearsal, reinforcing the frequency and importance of the rehearsal function (Honeycutt et al., 2015). Interviewee #1 shared, "*At every single public meeting [...], I was rehearsing in my head what I was going to say when I got up. As soon as I started rehearsing, my heart would pound and I would get cold sweats and I couldn't do it.*" From this II, we can infer the rehearsal function was used as a way to practice what will be said, but did not help the interviewee to feel more confident and relaxed before the actual talk. However, with more frequency, the rehearsal function of the IIs did work to relieve some sense of apprehension and also illustrates the function of catharsis. The same interviewee noted: "*I did have talking points inside my heart. They just weren't getting to my head and far enough for me to get them out of my mouth. So I rehearsed inside of my head frequently and every time there was an opportunity to speak I was ready to say it.*" Rehearsal, then, may have helped Interviewee #1 distinguish between the emotional and factual content of her planned presentations.

The other interviewees also revealed the use of the rehearsal function. When asked by the interviewer if he used rehearsal IIs before presentations, Interviewee #2 stated, "*I've never been one for rehearsing even in the classroom. I just have a rough idea of what I'm going to do.*" Applying II attributes to this statement, the "rough idea" noted here may encapsulate the attribute of *specificity* in rehearsal IIs. The same interviewee later explains what he does rehearse prior to his presentation: "*Okay, right, yes, there's one thing I imagine. Like you know when I saw '780 million gallons'*[1] *I said okay, how could this relate to something? So I looked up on the internet and found out the size of Lake Pontchartrain, the average depth [...] I did some calculations and came up with the same rough size, so now you have something an ordinary person can understand [...] So those are the sort of things I might have been thinking.*" When Interviewee #2 does use rehearsal IIs, we can infer there is a high degree of specificity on preparing and imagining how audience members will react and understand the numerical facts of fracking.

Interviewee #3 affirmed her use of IIs to rehearse when directly questioned about it by the lead interviewer. She replies, "*I do that like a schooling to try and figure out how to do it better next time [...] especially if it didn't go right, I try and figure out how I could have done or said something to make it go better [...] or whether or not I feel like it's something I can reuse again.*" While she does not report any specific examples of rehearsal IIs, her revelation suggests past conversations are potentially replayed to develop scripts and schemas for future conversations, acknowledging the attributes of proactivity and retroactivity may occur in her IIs. Additionally, these examples suggest self-understanding is of particular importance to this interviewee. She notes at other points in the interview that she consistently focuses on gaining self-understanding from all her experiences, explaining that "*my ability to handle the spontaneity of it is because of my background, assimilating so much information from different sources [...] I hadn't done that exactly before but I think learning and going through so many different types of scenarios helps me to be more able to react.*" For the third interviewee, replaying conversations helps her understand her own conversational strengths, gaining self-understanding. Self-understanding and other functions are prevalent in only one or two interviews, unlike rehearsal which was present in all three interviews.

In contrast with the previous infrequency of compensatory IIs (Honeycutt et al., 2015), Interviewees #2 and #3 described compensatory IIs which make up for, or compensate for, actual interactions in their activism. Interviewee #3 stated, "*In the environmental world, we need children from little on up to young adults screaming and saying, 'you cannot keep polluting our air and water,' you know, 'you can't keep doing this,' 'This is ridiculous, you can't just because it makes money for you now, you greedy bastards, you can't keep doing this.*" This experience is framed as a potential compensatory encounter because of the interviewee's desire to see these interactions happen in actual activism. As a follow-up question, the lead interviewer asked Interviewee #3 who the "you" was in this scenario, only to receive the answer of "*the Koch Brothers.*" Often, interviewees are unable to directly converse with all stakeholders in their environmental activist efforts, which may explain Interviewee #3's IIs with the Koch Brothers.

Third-party IIs involve the same features of IIs but represent the times where an individual imagines a conversation for which he or she was not present (Porter, 2010); third party IIs may explain the use of compensatory IIs. Interviewee #3 spent time providing a historical, compensatory, third-party near-II detailing how industries research and share information with the public "*A few of the second-tier scientists basically just totally sold out to the Tobacco industry. They became this group of scientists that had fairly good credentials and so forth but would, you know, go around saying there is no evidence of causation and so forth. This same group of scientists after the tobacco thing they migrated over to the situation with the fluorocarbons up in the ozone layer saying all that's bunk.*" We have no way of knowing how discrepant this II is from the actual conversations, but this excerpt illustrates another class of stakeholders – in this case, scientists – with whom the activists are unable to converse with directly.

General impressions of the interviews from those authors present and those who listened only to recordings revealed how talking about activism and environmentalism were highly charged emotional experiences and thus connected to catharsis as a general concept (Honeycutt, 2003). Interviewee #3's visual imagery reveals, "*I do feel sort of alone … sometimes in my head — that—I would just run away if it gets too deep, I will run away. Take my children and run back to [state]. I'll sell the house and I'll get out of dodge.*" While other examples from narratives may touch on catharsis more generally, this quote contains cathartic mental imagery visualizing an escape from the environmental landscape of Louisiana.

Imagined interaction conflict-linkage theory explains how conflict can persist in interpersonal communication through mental imagery and rumination whereby conflict is relived through the replaying of arguments and preparation for potential future arguments (Honeycutt, 2010). Conflict is central to our interviewees' experiences as environmental activists; after all, their experiences are represented in legal conflict with Helis. General reports during the narratives invoke the II attributes of negative valence and other-dominated. For instance, Interviewee #2 spoke about a meeting he attended with members of the DEQ (Department of Environmental Quality) and receiving a less-than-enthusiastic response from the board concerning his arguments. When asked if he had imagined the negative response he received from the DEQ members, the interviewee responded, "*... because of my experience with the state and with Baton Rouge I kind of was just not surprised; clearly their minds are made up.*" Interviewee #3 talked about how the majority of her IIs are with those who oppose her environmental views and concerns and how those IIs might assist her in future conflicts by allowing her to alter her argument and "*trying to get it better ... [to determine] what [points] seemed to have an effect and which things didn't.*" Finally, Interviewee #2 responds in the affirmative when asked if he is imagining future conflicts with oil and gas executives, "*I've been watching the price of oil regularly so I've been imagining at some point [a conflict is] possible.*"[2] Not only is this person imagining future conflicts with representatives from the oil and gas industry, he is also seeking data in the form of oil prices to better equip himself for future disagreements, or proactively readying himself for future conflict. In addition to its proactive nature this situation could also exemplify both the rehearsal and conflict management functions of imagined interactions. While ruminating on these previous conversations, the interview subjects were utilizing their IIs as a form of conflict management. Since the nature of the real interaction was in a moment of conflict, it is reasonable to assume they were thinking about the interaction as a way to manage what was said (Honeycutt, 2003).

The third interviewee discusses past conversations she has had with her daughter concerning the television shows and movies of famed French oceanographer Jacques Cousteau as a way of introducing her daughter to environmental concerns. But one could imply that these discussions also served to develop and strengthen the bond between mother and child through conversations about environmentalism and the films of Cousteau, representing potential relational maintenance IIs. While individuals certainly use IIs to foster close personal relationships with family members, there are examples of our interviewees using IIs to maintain relationships in a professional environment. Interviewee #3 discusses a time she worked for a company that was in favor of fracking. Upon receiving a book from the head of her department that attempted to debunk much of the scientific evidence for climate change, Interviewee #3 spent time fact-checking the book in preparation for any future climate discussions with her manager: "*When I read it I was making notes [...] and then I had the figure back then which was something like 90% of the [climate] scientists at that time believed in global warming caused by humans.*" The interviewee wrote that 90% figure down in the margins of the book in order to prepare herself for a future discussion with her manager about climate change, a conversation that the interviewee tried her best to avoid. While clearly this situation is an example of conflict management function of IIs, the interviewee could also be using IIs as a means to maintain relationships at work by avoiding disagreements with coworkers, thereby creating a more harmonious work environment. This inference is supported by Interviewee #3's admission of her challenges managing tensions as she balanced her identity as an environmentalist in her work environment.

We frame the invocation of media imagery as representative of discrepancy because we infer that our interviewees hope the visual imagery in media will not accurately represent the real world of environmental degradation. Indirect and direct references to the films *Elysium* (2013), *Hunger Games* (2012), and *Waterworld* (1995), suggest a desire for discrepancy between visual media depictions of the future and the more positive and clean futures likely envisioned by our interviewees. Discrepant IIs often catastrophize future outcomes (Honeycutt, 2003), but these catastrophized images of the future are of real concern for environmentalists. A final example occurs when Interviewee #3 shares her desire to have executives that make the ethical and environmental decisions even if profit suffers, referencing a scene in the 1978 film, *Heaven Can Wait*. While we can never know all actions of boardroom executives, discrepant conversations are likely imagined where environmental needs could take first billing compared to profits, even if the inverse may better represent reality. In exploring the features of IIs from our research question, we find catastrophizing, rumination, and third-party IIs—in addition to common functions and attributes—in the narratives and interviews of our three environmental activists.

Applications to Mental Health Status in View of Stress and Trauma

The use of positive visual imagery may help combat appraisals involving catastrophizing and feelings of helplessness and frustration: One could take a moment to visualize the decrease in plastic waste every time he or she uses a glass container or reusable bag, or one could take pictures before and after he or she picks up litter on a local trail or beach. Sharing emotions verbally and nonverbally in conversations and social media posts should activate supportive responses from friends and family like advice and comfort messages valuing and acknowledging actions, emotions, and cognitions (Barbee & Cunningham, 1995). Through cognitive reappraisal (Lazarus & Folkman, 1984), individuals may then reappraise their actions as helpful and valuable in managing individual stress levels and preventing further environmental degradation. Self-understanding IIs may play a role here as well.

Managing the stress and trauma associated with environmental issues and activism involve not only individual efforts, but the integration of the individual in the community. Collective efficacy efforts indeed help determine individual coping and pro-environmental behaviors (Homburg & Stolberg, 2006). Individuals may help manage stress by engaging in collective efforts to enact positive changes to the local environment. Reducing the frequency of compensatory third-party IIs with community stakeholders in favor of seeking actual conversation with stakeholders may reduce uncertainty. With many behaviors to enact, possibilities include protesting in spaces visible to legislators and executives, performing the future envisioned by our third interviewee.

Popular press articles advocate to lay audiences that being in nature helps individuals reduce stress and depressive symptoms (Khazan, 2015). Similarly, managing hydration levels to manage physiological symptoms of stress is recommended (Shaw, n.d.). If readers reach for a glass of water or go for a nature hike to manage stress, we unfortunately acknowledge that people may still be exposed to the deleterious effects of economic degradation. A recently announced expansion of a chemical plant producing PVC plastic in Louisiana (Associated Press, 2018) will undoubtedly expose citizens to phthalates and dioxins in the air and water (National Library of Medicine). If it is happening in Louisiana, it is happening in other communities. The individual and collective cycle of environmental activism thus continues involving education, positive (re)appraisals, individual behaviors, and community engagement.

Limitations and Future Research

The semi-structured narrative interview format has benefits for interviewees and trauma survivors, but these benefits reveal the major limitations of our study. Some II features were not present in the interviews. And we can only infer the trauma-related outcomes for our interviewees. Because these interviews focused on a specific context where individuals have IIs, variety is artificially constrained to environmental issues and partners. Our interviewees were all opposed to fracking and desired to see a stop to environmental degradation. The decision by Helis to suspend fracking may result in different traumas for employees and supporters of fracking who are more concerned with economic versus environmental issues.

For future research on environmental activism, we recommend both narrative and quantitative approaches, depending on which communities and activists are the subjects and audience. Quantitative analyses may be more appropriate for general trait-like use of IIs and pro-environmental behaviors, but caution should be exercised and qualitative methods considered for acute, recurring, and immediate events shaping perceptions of trauma. Qualitative investigations in II research should continue, with samples inclusive of individuals both in support and against issues which change the environment. We recommend specific II features like compensation receive focused attention, particularly if these efforts focus on parasocial relationships with entities like the Koch Brothers with whom activists cannot directly engage to enact environmental change (Madison, Porter, & Greule, 2016).

Summary

Our study recognizes the power of Fisher's (1984) paradigm framing humans as "homo narrans" or storytelling persons. Reports of IIs were woven in narrative accounts of environmental involvement, reinforcing the symbolic nature of IIs in storytelling and sense-making. The narrative interviews may have made it challenging to apply traditional coding to II features as interviewees often described experiences rather than specific IIs, but this narrative approach may have been more appropriate for the interviewees, given their proximity to the issue and the unresolved nature of fracking within St. Tammany Parish.

Interviewees frequently used rehearsal IIs to consider speaking points and consider their audience when educating others about fracking, intuitively advocating for education and knowledge about fracking and other environmental issues in our communities. Compensatory IIs, third-party IIs, and (hopefully) discrepant IIs between real-life and movie-life suggest a use of IIs to cope with the unresolved tension where industries prioritize profits over the environment. We acknowledge the importance of these features for coping with trauma, but we hope readers and activists consider the role of positive mental imagery and self-talk in managing stress.

We hope this call to action inspires you to use IIs to enact positive environmental change in your community and continue pro-environmental behaviors, even if being an activist is not part of your current identity. We end with a connection to media and trauma, inspired by our interviewees' own thoughts. Film and television may sell trauma to their audiences (Rothe, 2011), but we also acknowledge how environmental events depicted on screens big and small provide a visualization of potential future trauma. We do not have to wait until our planet looks like real-life versions *Elysium* or *Waterworld*. Activists can use this imagery to help others envision the effects of fracking and hopefully persuade others to become involved, enact pro-environmental behaviors, and enact a pro-environmental identity through individual and communal symbolic and behavioral actions.

Discussion Questions

1. *Have a few IIs on your own about an environmental issue relevant to your community and imagine who you might talk to about these issues. Focusing on the attribute of variety, identify the conversational partners and subtopics related to the main topic. Then, share and discuss these IIs. Identify similarities and differences in what environmental issues are named and which conversational partners are shared across your IIs.*
2. *Think of a recent conversation you had concerning an environmental issue that went poorly. Perhaps you tried to encourage a friend or roommate to recycle, but they were not very receptive to your suggestion. As you retroactively replay this conversation in your mind, think of what you might say differently if you have another opportunity to converse with this person about the same environmental issue. Write down aspects of the original conversation that were not effective and replace those with new ideas you think have a better chance of succeeding.*
3. *Why might visual imagery be more powerful compared to verbal imagery in IIs in the realm of environmental degradation?*

Notes

1. The "780 million gallons" referenced here refers to a 2011 Hydraulic Fracking Report which reported an estimated780 million gallons of chemical waste were generated by fracking companies http://www.conservation.ca.gov/dog/general_information/Documents/Hydraulic%20 Fracturing%20Report%204%2018%2011.pdf
2. The prices referenced here can be found at: https://www.eia.gov/dnav/pet/pet_pri_ spt_s1_m.htm. Lower prices on crude oil may be one reason Helis halted operations in 2016.

References

Associated Press. (2018, July 24). Chemical Plant Shintech announces $1.5B Louisiana Expansion. *US News*. Retrieved from https://www.usnews.com/news/best-states/louisiana/articles/2018-07-24/chemical-plant-shintech-announces-15b-louisiana-expansion.

Barbee, A. P., & Cunningham, M. R. (1995). An experimental approach to social support communications: Interactive coping in close relationships. In B. R. Burleson (Ed.), *Communication Yearbook 18* (pp. 318–413). Mahwah, NJ: Erlbaum.

Bodie, G. D., Honeycutt, J. M., & Vickery, A. J. (2013). An analysis of the correspondence between the functions and attributes of imagined interactions. *Human Communication Research*, *39*(2), 157–183. doi: 10.1111/hcre.12003

Boudet, H., Clarke, C., Bugden, D., Maibach, E., Roser-Renouf, C., & Leiserowitz, A. (2014). "Fracking" controversy and communication: Using national survey data to understand public perceptions of hydraulic fracturing. *Energy Policy*, *65*, 57–67. doi: 10.1016/j.enpol.2013.10.017

Climek, M., Brou, L., Means, M., & Goidel, K. (2013, July 24). *Fracking and polarization of public opinion*. Report published by the Louisiana State University Public Policy Research Lab. Retrieved from http://pprllsu.com/wp-content/uploads/2015/12/Fracking-and-Polarization-of-Public-Opinion.pdf

Grey, S. (2007). Wounds not easily healed: Exploring trauma in communication studies. In C. S. Beck (Ed.), *Communication Yearbook 31* (pp. 174–222). Mahwah, NJ: Erlbaum.

Grey, S., & Broussard, J. M. (2017). Dominance and danger in South Louisiana: Social media and the construction of risk and authority in the fight over fracking. *The Electronic Journal of Communication*, *27*(1), 1–14. doi: 10.1016/j.jenvp.2006.03.003

Homburg, A., & Stolberg, A. (2006). Explaining pro-environmental behaviour with a cognitive theory of stress. *Journal of Environmental Psychology*, *26(1)*, 1–14. doi: 10.1016/j.jenvp.2006.03.003

Honeycutt, J. M. (1996). The oral history interview and report of imagined interactions. *Journal of Family Psychotherapy*, 6(4), 63–69. doi: 10.1300/j085V06N04_06

Honeycutt, J. M. (1999). Typological differences in predicting marital happiness from oral history behaviors and imagined interactions (IIs). *Communication Monographs*, 66(3), 276–291. doi: 10.1080/03637759909376478

Honeycutt, J. M. (2003). *Imagined Interactions*. Cresskill, NJ: Hampton.

Honeycutt, J. M. (2008). Imagined Interaction theory: Mental representations of interpersonal communication. In L. A. Baxter & D. O. Braithwaite (Eds.), *Engaging Theories in Interpersonal Communication: Multiple Perspectives* (pp. 77–87). Thousand Oaks, CA: Sage.

Honeycutt, J. M. (2010). Forgive but don't forget: Correlates of rumination about conflict. In J. M. Honeycutt (Ed.), *Imagine That: Studies in Imagined Interactions* (pp. 17–30). Cresskill, NJ: Hampton.

Honeycutt, J. M., Nasser, K. A., Banner, J. M., Mapp, C. M., & DuPont, B. W. (2008). Individual differences in catharsis, emotional valence, trait anxiety, and social networks among Hurricane Katrina and Rita victims. *Southern Communication Journal, 73*(3), 229–242. doi: 10.1080/10417940802219728

Honeycutt, J. M., Pence, M. E., & Gearhart, C. C. (2013). Using imagined interactions to predict covert narcissism. *Communication Reports*, *26*, 26–38. doi: 10.1080/08934215.2013.773051

Honeycutt, J. M., Vickery, A. J., & Hatcher, L. C. (2015). The daily use of imagined interaction features. *Communication Monographs*, *82*(2), 201–223. doi: 10.1080/03637751.2014.953965

Khazan, O. (2015, June 30). "How walking in nature prevents depression." *The Atlantic*. Retrieved from https://www.theatlantic.com/health/archive/2015/06/how-walking-in-nature-prevents-depression/397172/

Lazarus, R., & Folkman, S. (1984). *Stress, appraisal and coping*. New York, NY: Springer.

Matsuba, M. K., & Pratt, M. W. (2013). The making of an environmental activist: A developmental psychological perspective. *New Directions in Child and Adolescent Development*, *2013* (142), 59–74. doi: https://doi.org/10.1002/cad.20049

Madison, P., Porter, L. V., & Greule, A. (2016). Parasocial compensation hypothesis: Predictors of using parasocial relationships to compensate for real-life interaction. *Imagination, Cognition, and Personality*, 35(3), 258–279. doi: 10.1177/0276236615595232

Markowitz, E. M., Goldberg, L. R., Ashton, M. C., & Lee, K. (2012). Profiling the 'pro-environmental individual': A personality perspective. *Journal of Personality*, 80, 81–111. doi: 10.1111/j.1467-6494.2011.00721.x

National Library of Medicine. (n.d.). "Polyvinyl Chloride." Retrieved from https://toxtown.nlm.nih.gov/chemicals-and-contaminants/polyvinyl-chloride-pvc

Owen, A., Videras, J., & Wu, S. (2010). Identity and environmentalism: The influence of community characteristics. *Review of Social Economy*, 68(4), 465–486. doi: 10.1080/00346760903480533

Owen, G. (2014). Fracking. In J. A. Matthews (Ed.), *Encyclopedia of Environmental Change* (p. 428). Thousand Oaks, CA: Sage. doi: 10.4135/9781446247501.n1551

Pennebaker, J. W., & Seagal, J. D. (1999). Forming a story: The health benefits of narrative. *Journal of Clinical Psychology*, 55(10), 1243–1254. doi: 10.1002/(SICI)1097-4679(199910)55:10<1243::AID-JCLP6>3.0.CO;2-N

Porter, M. (2010). *Third party imagined interactions: Expanding imagined interactions as false memories in understanding interactions* (Doctoral dissertation). Louisiana State University, Baton Rouge, Louisiana. Retrieved from http://www.lsu.edu/etd

Rhoden, R. (2016, September 20). After 2 ½ years, St. Tammany Parish fracking saga abruptly ends. *The Times-Picayune*. Retrieved from https://www.nola.com/environment/index.ssf/2016/09/st_tammany_fracking_saga_comes.html

Roberts, F. A. (2016, June 18). Louisiana Supreme Court refuses to hear St. Tammany fracking appeal, likely ending 2-year challenge vs. Helis. *The New Orelans Advocates*. Retrieved from https://www.theadvocate.com/new_orleans/news/communities/st_tammany/article_4964ee99-10e1-5d7f-a6b2-2e76566be1cb.html

Rothe, A. (2011). *Popular trauma cultures*. New Brunswick, NJ: Rutgers.

Shaw, G. (n.d.). Water and stress reduction: Sipping stress away. *WebMD*. Retrieved from https://www.webmd.com/diet/features/water-stress-reduction#1

· 8 ·

USING IMAGINED INTERACTIONS TO DEAL WITH HURRICANE EVACUATIONS

Michael Navarro

In the summer of 1900, a fierce race was developing between two Texas cities on the Gulf coast. Both Houston and Galveston sought to become the primary port city for the state, a title with which would come vast financial benefits, as well as the massive growth in population that would accompany growth in business. At the time, Galveston was quickly pushing ahead in the race, due not only to its ideal coastal location, but also because of the efforts of the wealthy elite of the city, who saw the success of Galveston in this race to be a matter of personal civic pride (Larsen, 1999). The chief meteorologist in Galveston was a well-respected man in the community named Issac Kline. Kline had built a reputation by creating accurate flood-prediction and freeze models, and he was highly thought of by the upper members of the U.S. Weather Bureau. After a hurricane hit the Texas coastal town of Indianola in 1891, Kline wrote an editorial for the newspaper insisting that it was virtually impossible for a massive hurricane to strike Galveston. This article helped sway the city against building a sea wall along the coast, which would have cost thousands of dollars and created an unsightly shoreline (Larsen, 1999).

In the early days of September, 1900, reports began to arrive from Cuba that a massive hurricane was in the Gulf of Mexico. The Cuban meteorologists informed the U.S. Weather Bureau that their models had the storm heading straight towards the Texas coast. The bureau, in what was described by author Erik Larsen (1999) as a moment of extreme hubris, disregarded the Cuban warnings, instead believing that the storm would head towards Florida. In Galveston, Isaac Kline received both models as well. He reported the U.S. Weather Bureau's forecast, and as a result the residents of Galveston remained in the city. On September 9th, 1900, a Category 4 hurricane struck the city of Galveston. A twelve foot storm surge swept across the entire island, causing catastrophic damage to every building in the city. Reports indicated between 6,000 and 12,000 casualties, as well as nearly 30,000 people left homeless. To this day it is still the deadliest natural disaster in American history (Larsen, 1999).

The story of Galveston has long served as an example of the terrible wrath that hurricanes are capable of inflicting upon coastal cities. However, it can also be seen as an example of how inaccurate perceptions of risk can result in devastating consequences. How the risk surrounding a given threat is perceived individually is influenced by a number of factors, from personal experience to individual understanding of that risk as a social construct. It is in this understanding of the social construction of risk that imagined interactions become so important. The purpose of this chapter is to examine the ways in which we perceive risk surrounding hurricanes, and the impact that imagine interactions can have on individual intent to engage in preventative actions.

Literature Review and Background Studies

Several different theories address the topic of how individuals process information to form their perception of risk. Perhaps the oldest and most influential theoretical foundation in the study of risk perception is the psychometric paradigm (Slovic, 1987) which operates on the assumption that individuals base their evaluations of risk on two distinct factors: dread risk and unknown risk (Fischhoff, Slovic, Lichtenstein, Read, & Combs, 1978). High dread risk equates to greater feelings of a loss of control, dread, and a high perceived probability of catastrophic potential and fatal consequences (Bodemer & Gaissmaier, 2015). High unknown risk means that "the hazard is unobservable, unknown, new, and delayed" (Bodemer & Gaissmaier, 2015, p. 12). For laypeople, dread risk was found to be a better predictor of risk perception and desire for risk regulations than unknown risk (Slovic, 1987). It should be noted, however, that the psychometric paradigm model predicts risk perception on an aggregate level across all participants and hazard types. When separated by individual hazards, the amount of variance explained by the model is reduced by 60% (Bodemer & Gaissmaier, 2015).

Another predictor of individual risk perception is forwarded by the Risk-As-Feelings hypothesis (Dickert, Vastfjall, Mauro, & Slovic, 2015). This hypothesis outlines a dual-process model of risk perception by which individuals process information about risk either intuitively and through instinctual reactions (risk-as-feelings) or more logically, deliberatively, and through scientifically reasoned action (risk-as-analysis). This framework follows the tenants of the affect heuristic, which holds that people refer to their feelings in judgements and decisions, so much so that feelings of the severity of outcomes may outweigh the consideration of an event's likelihood of actually occurring (Dickert et al., 2015, p. 44; Slovic, Finucane, Peters, & MacGregor, 2002). As a result, individuals may be more likely to perceive a catastrophic event as being more likely to occur than it actually is (Dickert et al., 2015). For example, if the risk of nuclear power is communicated as low, then an individual may perceive the benefits to be high, and vice versa. Likewise, if the benefits are communicated to be high, then risk is perceived to be low (Slovic et al., 2002). Affective processing is also likely to be more influenced by narratives rather than data, and it is also important to acknowledge that individuals differ in their ability to create the vivid mental imagery associated with producing a heavily affective response (Dickert et al., 2015). Research also has shown that "[r]isk communication that arouses affective responses is likely to motivate action, but if unguided, this does not guarantee effective risk management or proper risk-reducing measures." (Dickert et al., 2015, p. 51).

One theory that attempts to address both analytical and emotional processing of risk information is fuzzy-trace theory (Reyna, 2008). Fuzzy-trace offers another dual-process model of information processing by proposing that individuals mentally represent risks through either verbatim or gist representations (Bodemer & Gaissmaier, 2015). Verbatim representations are objective and analytical, but also rote, involving little interpretation of the data presented (Brust-Renck, Reyna, Corbin, Royer, & Weldon, 2015). On the other hand, gist representations are more subjective interpretations of data, and are subject to outside influences such as culture, emotion, education, and experience (Brust-Renck et al., 2015). Findings generally suggest that gist representations are more stable and less prone to interference, while verbatim representations may be more prone to error (Bodemer & Gaissmaier, 2015). Furthermore, gist processing relies on the ability of the individual to not only read the relevant data, but also interpret that data in such a way as to inform their perception of risk (Brust-Renck et al., 2015). Given the effectiveness of gist processing, "risk communication should convey absolute (categorical) or relative (ordinal) comparisons rather than only exact, detailed information," and "[m]essages should express accurate meaning based on expert validations" (Brust-Renck et al., 2015, p.139).

Another aspect of risk that is important to consider is that individual perceptions of risk are not made within a vacuum. Culture and society play an important role in determining what risks should be taken into consideration, and, equally important, what risk should be disregarded. Arnoldi (2009) advocates for a constructionist approach to risk, meaning "first, recognition that understanding of any object is influenced by its surrounding culture and meaning, not only it's given qualities, and second, a "strong focus on power and the discursive processes in which reality is constructed ranging from the idea that the culture and meaning influence the perception of reality to the argument that culture and meaning determine our conception of reality" (p. 16)" (Burgess, 2015, p. 57). In essence, the constructionist approach shifts the focus from an objective definition of a particular risk to the process by which the definition is made. As Burgess (2015) states, "[i]mportantly, it is an approach that understands that perception need not have any direct relation to the problem that it reflects," and that "[t]he general pattern of human problem creation and resolution indicates that a problem only becomes defined as such when the possibility of a solution becomes real. Otherwise, conditions are absorbed in a fatalistic fashion" (p. 59).

In order to understand how a particular problem becomes seen as such in a society, Spector and Kitsuse (1987) set forth a four-stage typographical model of problem creation. First, an outside group asserts the existence of a problem, creating a public or political issue over the matter. Second, the legitimacy of the outside group is acknowledged by the powers that be, leading to an official investigation into the outside group's claims. Third, there is a reemergence of the claims by the outside group, accompanied by expressions of dissatisfaction with the established procedures for dealing with issue at hand. Fourth, the outside group rejects the institutional response, opting instead for counter institutions as a response to the established procedures (Burgess, 2015). An example of this model in action can be seen in the public outcry over the health dangers of electromagnetic fields (EMF). Journalist Paul Brodeur first stimulated the controversy, which lead to further scientific investigation over the effects of EMF. The concerns were reignited with the introduction of new technologies such as microwaves and computers, along with claims that existing guidelines were no longer appropriate for these new technologies. The final stage resulted in a countermovement claiming collusion in the current government, followed by the creation of a dedicated network to spread awareness of the perceived ill-effects of EMF (Burgess, 2015).

Douglas and Wildavsky's Risk and Culture (1983) offers a further exploration into why particular societies—in this case, Americans—chose to focus on certain risks and ignore others. The authors were particularly interested in the rise of public concern over the risks of pollution in the 1960's. Douglas and Wildavsky (1983) state that overall populations become segmented over certain issues, either toward the center or the borders: central positions assess risk in terms of either the market or in a hierarchical manner, while those on the border are defined as sectarian. Those that fall near the center are more likely to stay the course, viewing and acting toward risk as they have always done, and change comes about very slowly. Sectarian groups on the border "expect life in the future to undergo a radical change for the worse," and that the cause for this change rest solely at the feet of the central: "corrupt worldliness, social distinctions, division of labor, materialistic values, and unfeelingness for human suffering" (Douglas & Wildavsky, 1983, p. 127). Douglas and Wildavsky also claim "that the success of the ecology movement in this country represents a shift of the more vocal parts of American life towards the border" (p. 151). The authors conclude by stating "[s]ectarianism, we contend, has always had some strength in America. Its potential has increased because of widespread changes in education, industry, and political mobilization that manifested themselves in the mid-century; and its recent successes were gained because of its ability to make use of new political technology in the midst of other contemporaneous challenges to trust in American institutions" (Douglas & Wildavsky, 1983, p. 152).

Each of these processes affects how every individual creates their own perceptions of risk. The most important fact to remember is that the actual level of harm attached to a given threat is not necessarily as important, as in most cases it is an unknown commodity. Instead, what matters most, at least in terms of making decisions on how to properly counter the threat, is the amount of risk individuals *perceive* to be assigned to the threat. As previously discussed, there are numerous processes involved in creating this perception. In the terms of a hurricane, we can look to the psychometric paradigm to examine the amount of dread risk an individual may feel about the approaching storm, or the potential for catastrophic consequences. The affect heuristic focuses on how the feelings an individual has about an approaching hurricane, for example fear of flooding or irritation at the inconvenience of an evacuation.

As noted throughout this volume, imagined interactions can act as a type of self therapy in dealing with trauma. Recall, that imagined interactions (II) are defined as "a type of social cognition and mental imagery theoretically grounded in symbolic interactionism, in which individuals imagine conversations with significant others for a variety of purposes" (Honeycutt 2003, p. 2). IIs serve six separate cognitive functions: relationship maintenance, rehearsing, self-understanding, catharsis, compensation, and conflict management. In addition, there are nine distinct attributes of IIs: frequency, emotional valence, discrepancy, self-dominance, proactivity, retroactivity, specificity, and variety (Honeycutt, 2003). All IIs can be thought of as intrapersonal communication that has the potential to inform how an individual will communicate interpersonally. Given that IIs are explicitly an intrapersonal phenomenon, it is reasonable to assume that IIs are a method by which individuals can negotiate their personal attitudes and beliefs with their understanding or interpretation of particular social constructs, such as severe weather warnings.

If we examine the existing research in the realm of risk perception through the lens of IIs, it is not difficult to quickly see the applicability. In particular, individual affective responses and gist representations are heavily influenced by external sources. Studies have also shown that the stronger an individual's social network is, the more likely they are to respond to warning messages (Aguirre, Anderson, Balandran, Peters, & White, 1991; Anderson, Keaton, Saarinen, & Wells, 1984). One potential cause for this effect could be that the more people are in a person's social network, the more defined the individual's social construction of risk becomes. However, in an evacuation situation, an individual is placed in the position of evaluating several potential threats at once: the threat of the storm, the threat of an unnecessary evacuation, the financial threat, the threat to property, et cetera. Engaging in IIs with members of the individual's social network—for example, a parent or spouse—could allow the individual to focus their attention on the threat of the storm specifically. Fuzzy-trace examines the verbatim representations of the storm such as wind data and probability charts, as well as gist representations which rely more on the subjective interpretation of that data from not only the individual, but society at large. The cultural construction of the risk surrounding hurricanes plays an equally important role in how individual's perceptions take shape. This social construction is based not only on past events, but also influencers such as the mass media, political affiliations, and other power structures (an example of the politicization of a hurricane could be seen in late 2016, when Matt Drudge of the *Drudge Report* suggested that the government may have lied about the intensity of Hurricane Matthew to send a message about climate change [Samenow, 2016]).

Regarding hurricane evacuation messages, there are three functions of IIs which stand out. First, the catharsis function, which serves to relieve tension and uncertainty. The actual threat surrounding hurricanes is almost always unknown and uncertain. This makes it difficult to get an accurate perception of the risk surrounding a given storm. For many individuals, this uncertainty can cause a great deal of anxiety and unease. By having an II about the storm, individuals may experience some level of catharsis about this anxiety. The second function of interest is that of compensation. Should an individual live alone in an area receiving a hurricane evacuation message, they may wish to talk about their decision-making process with someone who may not physically be there, for example, a parent. IIs allow the individual to compensate for the lack of the physical presence of that trusted conversational partner. Third, the self-understanding function of IIs may help the individual negotiate their own personal perceptions of risk with those of society at large.

Current Study

The goal of the current study is to examine individual risk perception in regards to hurricanes—specifically, an individual's likeliness to comply with an evacuation order. The basic thought process behind the study is as follows: it is understood that every individual percieves the risk attributed to the threat of a hurricane in a different way. For some individuals, the risk of flooding and damage to property may be the most relevant, while for others, the risk of leaving their home unattended for an undetermined amount of time may be more salient. Personal experiences with hurricanes and storm evacuations vary, and individual understanding of the hard meteorological data describing the hurricane will also differ. However, prior research has shown that the societal construction of risk is an important influencing factor on personal risk perceptions. As such, the goal of the current study is to uncover whether individuals who are prompted to have an imagined interaction with a respected other about their personal intentions to comply with an evacuation order are more likely to evacuate than those that do not have an II.

Study participants were drawn from a sample of 123 students enrolled in a general education courses in the communication studies department of Louisiana State University using the research protocol system that lists a variety of studies that they can participate in for course credit. The sample consisted of 60% male and 40% female participants, 73% of which identified as white. 22% and 39% identified as freshman and sophomores, while 20% and 18% identified as juniors and seniors. In this case, class rank is notable, as there was a notable severe flooding event which occurred on the participants' campus during the summer of 2016, a time at which many freshmen may not have been living in the area. Participants were then asked to report their personal experiences with storm evacuations and storm damage, as well as the experiences of those close to them. Over 57% reported having prior personal experience with storm evacuations, and 80% reported having family or friends with experience. Additionally, 65% reported having personal experience with storm damage, with the average amount of damage reported as $\mu = 5.42$ (1 = *very light damage*, 10 = *total loss*) while 88% reported having close friends or family that have suffered storm damage, with the average amount of damage reported as $\mu = 7.86$.

Participants were randomly assigned to one of six conditions. In condition 1, participants read a hypothetical mandatory evacuation notice from the Mayor of the city in which the university is located. After reading the notice, the participants were prompted to imagine having a conversation with a respected other about their intentions to evacuate, and provide a script for how they imagine that conversation going. This particular methodology is adapted from the Survey of Imagined Interactions to fit the context of the current study (Honeycutt, 2010, p. 205). Condition 2 had participants read the mandatory evacuation script, but did not include the prompt for an II. Conditions 3 and 4 followed the same pattern, the exception being that the evacuation order in these conditions was voluntary. Finally, conditions 5 and 6 followed the same pattern, but provided limited information ("An evacuation notice has been issued for your area due to an approaching storm."). After each condition, participants were asked the simple question: "Based on the information you were given in the previous text, would you comply with the evacuation order?" After answering, participants were given an open text area in which to answer why they chose their decision.

A series of six binomial tests were run in which the decision to evacuate or not evacuate is counted beyond chance accuracy. Table 8.1 presents the binomial results.

Table 8.1. Binomial Tests.

Condition		N	Observed Prop.*	Exact Sig. (2-tailed)
1. Mandatory Evacuation With II	Will evacuate	18	.90	.000
	Will not evacuate	2	.10	
	Total	20	1.00	
2. Mandatory Evacuation With No II	Will evacuate	18	.86	.001
	Will not evacuate	3	.14	
	Total	21	1.00	
3. Voluntary Evacuation With II	Will evacuate	20	.95	.000
	Will not evacuate	1	.05	
	Total	21	1.00	
4. Voluntary Evacuation With No II	Will evacuate	17	.81	.007
	Will not evacuate	4	.19	
	Total	21	1.00	
5. Limited Information for Evacuation With II	Will evacuate	17	.89	.001
	Will not evacuate	2	.11	
	Total	19	1.00	
6. Limited Evacuation With No II	Will evacuate	15	.71	.078
	Will not evacuate	6	.29	
	Total	21	1.00	

Note: Test probability = .50.

In the groups in which imagined interaction scripts were prompted after receiving an evacuation notice (mandatory, voluntary, and no information), the percentage of participants who said they would evacuate (category 1) were 90%, 95%, and 89% respectively. The fact that the percentage was so high in the 'no information' category is of particular interest, as previous research has shown that individuals are **less** likely to comply with evacuation orders when they perceive there to be not enough information to make an informed decision (Balluz, Schieve, Holmes, Kiezak, & Malilay, 2000; Bateman & Edwards, 2002; Mileti & Darlington, 1997). In the categories where IIs were not prompted, the intent to comply with evacuation orders went down to 86% in the mandatory condition, 81% in the voluntary condition, and 71% in the no information condition. Each of these binomial tests were significant at the 0.50 test proportion level, with the exception of the no information, no II condition ($p = 0.078$). The tests do however support the hypothesis that prompting an II will make individuals more likely to comply with an evacuation order across all conditions.

The intent of the current study was to determine if prompting imagined interactions would have an effect on individuals' intentions to comply with hurricane evacuation orders. Based on the results of the binomial tests, those individuals who imagine a dialogue with a respected other concerning their decision are, in all conditions, more likely to comply. It should be noted that there are several limitations to this study. First, the number of participants in each condition is somewhat small, averaging around twenty. Future studies should seek to increase this number. Second, although participants in the non-II conditions were not prompted to have an II, it is unknown whether they may have still had one. Some of the responses participants entered to justify their evacuation decisions would appear on the surface to indicate that this may have been the case:

- *Yes because if my family is leaving then that is a sign to me that this storm is serious and I should leave as well.*
- *My family has lost a lot, both in property in life, because of storms and so we don't take evacuation orders lightly.*
- *I usually have gone along with the decisions the elders in my family make about evacuation proceedings in the past.*

Each of these responses was given in the non-II condition, yet indicates that the participants may have engaged in an II with a family member when making their decision.

Another item that is interesting to note is the somewhat shockingly large percentage of participants who reported either personal experience with storm damage (57%) or knowing a close friend or relative with experience (88%). Furthermore, the reported mean damage experienced in both cases (personal = 5.42, know someone = 7.86) is also very high. Upon reading some of the participant responses as to why they chose to evacuate or not, the impact of this experience becomes even clearer:

- *"Yes because I am from New Orleans and I saw firsthand the devastation that Katrina caused to my hometown in 2005. Although it may be tough for me to leave behind all of my belongings, my health comes first."*
- *"Although I would want to stay in town and protect my property from looters, it would be safer to leave town and avoid worrying my friends and family."*

- *"I've seen what major storms can do. If the evacuation is mandatory, the threat must be real and serious enough for me to leave."*
- *"My family has lost a lot, both in property in life, because of storms and so we don't take evacuation orders lightly."*

The current study set out to examine the impacts that IIs might have on evacuation intentions. However, the memory of the devastation wrought by storms of the past appears to still be fresh in the minds of the majority of participants in the sample. Certainly a limitation of the current study is the small sample size of n = 123, but it should also be noted that a major limitation of this study is that the sample population lies within an area of the country with a relatively recent history of massive destruction from hurricanes and flooding, and that as a result it makes sense that many of the study participants would have some level of direct or indirect experience with storms such as the one described in the hypothetical evacuation orders. However, these results do call into question recent research findings on certain biases that individuals may fall in to when responding to a potential disaster.

Applications to Mental or Physical Health Status in View of Stress and Trauma

The findings of the current study indicate that when individuals are determining whether or not they will comply with an evacuation order, whether voluntary or mandatory, they are more likely to comply after having an II with a respected other. The most obvious application of these findings is in terms of hurricane evacuation messaging, where IIs could be utilized to achieve a higher rate of compliance with evacuation orders in the future. The actual, real threat surrounding a hurricane is extremely difficult to predict. For example, a twenty mile per hour wind gust may result in no damage, while a twenty one mile an hour gust could result in a tree falling down onto a house. While flooding in the past may not have impacted a particular neighborhood, construction or flood plain erosion in the time since may now result in flooding. When creating their perceptions of the risk surrounding an incoming hurricane, individuals may draw heavily on past experience when that experience may not be at all applicable to the current threat.

By invoking imagined interactions, individuals may think beyond their own personal experiences and perceptions and engage more fully with the social construction of risk. This becomes even more important when the individual is making evacuation decisions for a group of people, like a family. Evacuation messaging can utilize IIs to ensure that individuals think not only about their own abilities to withstand a hurricane, but also others. For example, a young woman may have a high self-efficacy about her abilities to not only make it through a hurricane, but also live in a city post-disaster, when electricity, food, and water may be scarcer. However, if she is stimulated to have an II with a respected other about her decision, she may be reminded of all the variable that she may not have control over, and be more likely to comply. In addition to hurricane messaging, it is not unreasonable to think that IIs could be utilized for other health related messaging relating to risk. For example, when individuals need to make decisions about preventative medical procedures, stimulating an II may have a similar effect as was experienced in the current study.

Summary and Future Research

The study discussed previously has many limitations which should be addressed through future research. As previously stated, the sample size was small, but more perhaps importantly was composed entirely of individuals who reside along the Gulf coast region that was heavily effected by Hurricane Katrina in 2005. As such, a majority of the study participants had personal experience with severe storm damage and hurricane evacuations. Future research should examine whether the impact of Iis would be the same for a natural disaster evacuation for an event that the sample population may have more limited experience with (for example, a wild fire). The current study also raises an interesting question about age and experience with disaster.

In the 2017 book *The Ostrich Paradox: Why We Underprepare for Disasters*, authors Dr. Robert Meyer and Dr. Howard Kunreuther of the Wharton Risk Management and Decision Process Center enumerate six biases that impact individuals' abilities to make reliable decisions in regards to high-impact, low-probability events, such as hurricanes. One of these biases is historical amnesia, defined as a general tendency to quickly forget lessons learned from past disasters (Meyer & Kunreuther, 2017, p. 21). If this is the case, then respondents in the current study would not be impacted as much by the memories of a hurricane which happened over 12 years ago. However, as the results and subsequent open responses have shown, memories from this storm are indeed still fresh, and built into the social construction of risk surrounding hurricane evacuations. Further research should be done to examine this historical amnesia bias to learn exactly how long it takes before people start to forget lessons learned from the past. Additionally, it would be interesting to learn whether trauma from natural disasters that individuals experience when they are younger is more likely to influence risk perceptions of hurricanes later in life.

Further research should also examine the specific functions of IIs, and which ones impact risk perception the most. For the current study, the functions of catharsis, compensation, and self-understanding were primary focus. However, the functions of conflict management, relational maintenance, and rehearsal could also be present when making decisions based on risk perception. While the focus of the current study, and this entire chapter, is specifically on IIs and hurricane evacuation intentions, the lessons learned could be applicable in any number of areas where individual decision processes based on risk perceptions are made. For example, the same decisions are made in the area of preventative medical procedures. Any number of other similar situations in which decisions are made based on individual risk perceptions could all benefit from the inclusion of imagined interactions in the messaging process. For decisions such as preventative medical procedures, it is not difficult to see how these other functions of IIs could be applicable. An individual may elect to participate in the preventative action so as to avoid an argument with a significant other, or could use IIs to rehearse the process of telling their friends and family about the procedure.

Hurricanes are extremely complex events which are often unpredictable in nature. Despite their sheer destructive power, there is a high level of uncertainty assigned to when and where the storm may reach land. Individuals living in at-risk areas perceive a certain level of risk for hurricanes in general, and for those which they may come into direct contact with. This perceived risk is based not only on the individual's personal experience with hurricanes and evacuation processes, but also on the socially constructed risk of the event. This social construction is what society at large believes the risk of hurricanes to be, but also what the neighborhood, the local area, and family and friends believe the risk to be. Based on all of this input, an individual will perceive a level of risk to assign to a hurricane, and make judgements about whether or not they should evacuate based on that perception.

However, that perception of risk is not always in-line with the actual threat of the hurricane. When there is a reasonable probability that a hurricane may strike a certain area, government officials may issue voluntary or mandatory evacuation warnings. In many cases, some individuals may choose not to comply, believing that their perception of risk is more accurate. In order to ensure that the most highest amount of residents in an at-risk area comply with evacuation orders, it may be useful to incorporate imagined interactions into the risk messaging process.

According to the current study, individuals who are prompted to have an II with a respected other about their decision of whether they should evacuate or not are more likely to report that they would choose to evacuate in both voluntary and mandatory conditions. Having an imagined interaction forces an individual to think not only of their own personal perceptions of risk assigned to a storm, but also of the perceptions of the respected other, and of the socially constructed risk as well. By incorporating IIs into evacuation messaging, it may be possible to increase evacuation participation among those residents in at risk areas. Future research should examine the effectiveness of IIs in other disaster-related messaging, as well as other situations involving decision-making based on risk perceptions, such as preventative medical procedures.

Discussion Questions

1. *What is your personal perception of the risks surrounding a hurricane? In your opinion, what are the societal views of the risks of a hurricane? In what ways do you believe this social construct is influenced by media, politics, and other influencers?*
2. *Imagine that you are in an area under threat of a hurricane strike, and you have been given a voluntary evacuation order. Describe an imagined interaction that you might have with a respected other about your intentions to comply with this order. Would you comply? Why or why not?*
3. *What are some other decision-making processes based on risk perception that could also benefit from the use of imagined interactions? What functions of IIs would be most useful for this situation?*

References

Aguirre, B. E., Anderson, W. A., Balandran, S., Peters, B. E., & White, H. M. (1991). *Saragosa, texas, tornado, May 22, 1987: An evaluation of the warning system*. Washington, D. C.: National Academy Press. doi: 10.17226/1766

Anderson, L., Keaton, J., Saarinen, T., & Wells, W. (1984). *The Utah landslides, debris flows and floods of May and June 1983*. Washington D. C.: National Academy Press. doi: 10.1177/030913338901300201

Arnoldi, J. (2009). *Risk: An introduction*. Cambridge, UK/Malden, MA: Polity Press.

Balluz, L., Schieve, L., Holmes, T., Kiezak, S., Malilay, J. (2000). Predictors for people's response to a tornado warning: Arkansas, 1 March 1997. *Disasters, 24*, 71–77. doi: 10.1111/1467-7717.00132

Bateman, J. M., & Edwards, B. (2002). Gender and evacuation: A closer look at why women are more likely to evacuate for hurricanes. *Natural Hazards Review, 3*(3), 107–117. doi: 10.1061/(ASCE)1527-6988(2002)3:3(107)

Bodemer, N., & Gaissmaier, W. (2015). Risk perception. In H. Cho, T. Reimer, & K. A. McComas (Eds.), *The SAGE handbook of risk communication* (pp. 10–23). Thousand Oaks, CA: SAGE. doi: 10.4135/9781483387918

Burgess, A. (2015). Social construction of risk. In H. Cho, T. Reimer, & K. A. McComas (Eds.), *The SAGE handbook of risk communication* (pp. 56–68). Thousand Oaks, CA: SAGE. doi: 10.4135/9781483387918

Brust-Renck, P. G., Reyna, V. F., Corbin, J. C., Royer, C. E., & Weldon, R. B. (2015). The role of numeracy in risk communication. In H. Cho, T. Reimer, & K. A. (Eds.), *The SAGE handbook of risk communication* (pp. 134–145). Thousand Oaks, CA: SAGE. doi: 10.4135/9781483387918

Dickert, S., Vastfjall, D., Mauro, R., & Slovic, P. (2015). The feeling of risk: Implications for risk perception and communication. In H. Cho, T. Reimer, & K. A. (Eds.), *The SAGE handbook of risk communication* (pp. 41–53). Thousand Oaks, CA: SAGE. doi: 10.4135/9781483387918

Douglas, M., & Wildavsky, A. (1983). *Risk and culture: An essay on the selection of technological and environmental dangers*. Berkeley and Los Angeles, CA: University of California Press.

Fischhoff, B., Slovic, P., Lichtenstein, S., Read, S., & Combs, B. (1978). How safe is safe enough? A psychometric study of attitudes toward technological risks and benefits. *Policy Sciences*, 9(2), 127–152. doi: 10.1111/j.0272-4332.2004.00433.xHoneycutt, J. M. (2003). *Imagined interactions: Daydreaming about communication*. Cresskill, NJ: Hampton Press. doi: 10.1002/9781405186407

Honeycutt, J. M. (2010). Imagined interactions. *American Psychologist*, 65(2), 129–130. doi: 10.1037/a0018052

Larsen, E. (1999). *Isaac's storm: A man, a time, and the deadliest hurricane in history*. New York, NY: Crown.

Meyer, R., & Kunreuther, H. (2017). *The ostrich paradox: Why we underprepare for disasters*. Philadelphia, PA: Wharton Digital Press.

Mileti, D. S., & Darlington, J. D. (1997). The role of searching in shaping reactions to earthquake risk information. *Social Problems*, 44, 89–103. doi: 10.2307/3096875

Reyna, V. F. (2008). A theory of medical decision making and health: Fuzzy-trace theory. *Medical Decision Making*, 28(6), 829–833. doi: 10.1177/0272989X08327066

Samenow, J. (2016, October 6). Drudge Report's playing down and politicizing of Hurricane Matthew was 'deplorable.' *The Washington Post*. Retrieved from https://www.washingtonpost.com/news/capital-weather-gang/wp/2016/10/06/drudge-report-posts-infuriating-and-flawed-comments-on-hurricane-matthew/?noredirect=on&utm_term=.92bb715c08b3

Slovic, P., 1987. Perception of risk. *Science*, *236*(4799), 280–285. doi: 10.1126/science.3563507

Slovic, P., Finucane, M., Peters, E., & MacGregor, D. G. (2002). Rational actors or rational fools? Implications of the affect heuristic for behavioral economics. *Journal of Socio-Economics*, *31*(4), 329–342. doi: 10.1016/S1053-5357(02)00174-9

Spector, M., & Kitsuse, J. I. (1987). *Constructing social problems*. New York, NY: de Gruyter.

· 9 ·

THE ROLE OF IMAGINED INTERACTIONS IN ACTUAL AND VICARIOUS EXPERIENCE WITH POLICE OFFICERS

Laura B. Carper

Recent events of reported racial bias and mistreatment have generated much heated and negative press toward law enforcement, especially from African-Americans (Noble, 2014). However, while researchers have found that a person's race does affect perceptions of law enforcement (Gabbidon, Higgins, & Potter, 2011; Wu, Smith, & Sun, 2013), few studies have analyzed the impact of actual and vicarious experiences (experiences described by people other than the direct individual) with police officers. Researchers analyzing actual experiences have found that the race of the individual affects the person's perceptions of police officers (Callanan & Rosenberger, 2011; Noble, 2014), but few, if any, studies have analyzed how these experiences affect imagined interactions. Although most research on experiences with police officers has analyzed actual interactions, fewer studies have analyzed how vicarious experiences impact perceptions of police officers. Research on vicarious experiences suggests the importance of social ties and the dissemination of messages about police officers; particularly, African Americans have more negative stories about police officers in their social groups (Browning, Bourguignon, Chiappori, & Lechene, 1994; Rosenbaum, Shuck, Costello, Hawkins, & Ring, 2005; Weitzer & Tuch, 2005). While, the findings about race and actual and vicarious experiences with police are important, the researcher will analyze how actual and vicarious experiences differ in the use of imagined interactions and dealing with possible trauma.

Research by Buhmann, Nordentoft, Ekstroem, Carlsson, and Mortenson (2018) found that trauma-affected refugees who used cognitive behavioral therapy had improvement after treatment. Cognitive behavior therapy encourages patients to change destructive patterns of behavior through reflection over time. Additionally, research has found that children who have experienced trauma can also benefit from the use of cognitive behavior therapy (Wamser-Nanney & Steinzor, 2016). One way in which trauma from vicarious and actual experiences with police officers could be analyzed is through the use of imagined interactions. To understand the differences between vicarious and actual experiences and a person's imagined interactions, the following study was conducted.

Experiences with Law Enforcement

Much research has been performed to understand the connection between race and the perceptions of law enforcement. Consistently, results have found that African-Americans and other minorities report lower levels of satisfaction, distrust, racial bias, discrimination, unfair treatment, and less favorable attitudes toward police (Brown & Benedict, 2002; Davis, 2000; Gabbidon et al., 2011; Hagan & Albonetti, 1982; Redner-Vera & Galeste, 2015; Warren, 2010; Wu, 2014; Wu et al., 2013; Weitzer & Tuch, 2005), while Caucasian Americans are more likely to trust the police, remain neutral, and see law enforcement as color blind (Brunson, 2007; Henderson, Cullen, Cao, Browning, & Kopache, 1997; Hurwitz & Peffley, 2005; Wu, 2014).

Actual Experiences

Personal experiences with law enforcement consist of one-on-one contact with police. Much research has analyzed how actual experiences and race influence perceptions of police officers. Specifically, many findings suggest that African-Americans report strong negative perceptions of law enforcement for receiving rough and unfair treatment, excessive force, unequal treatment, and disrespect (Noble, 2014). In areas where crime rates are normally high, prior interactions with police can influence negative attitudes. Taylor, Wyant, & Lockwood (2013) state, "Aggressive policing in low income, minority urban neighborhoods can lead to direct and retold negative experiences (or highly publicized events) with police and especially among young black males" (p. 235). Furthermore, African-Americans are more likely to report negative perceptions of law enforcement based on the experience that occurred, the severity of the experience, behavior of the police, and the number of experiences. Caucasians, however, are more likely to report more positive experiences (Callanan & Rosenberger, 2011; Mbuba, 2010; Rome, Son, & Davis, 1995; Russell-Brown, 2009; Williams & Close, 2008). The personal and vicarious experiences with police are fundamental in shaping the negative perceptions of law enforcement (Mbuba, 2010; Warren, 2010). While much research shows the importance that actual experiences play when shaping personal perceptions of law enforcement, few studies have analyzed the significance that vicarious experiences play in shaping perceptions, especially in the context of imagined interactions (IIs).

Vicarious Experiences

Vicarious experiences are the indirect contacts with police that people hear from their family, friends, people they know, and the media. The primary difference between actual and vicarious experiences is whether the observer appraises an event that has occurred to the individual person or someone else (Wondra & Ellsworth, 2015); in other words, how one interprets his or her own situation or a third-party's interaction and whether or not one understands it in the same way as the other (Wondra & Ellsworth, 2015). This suggests that vicarious experiences can be interpreted differently from those of the person who experienced first-hand.

Research in vicarious experiences has increased in recent years, particularly in regards to how vicarious experiences differ across racial groups (Browning et al., 1994; Rosenbaum et al., 2005; Weitzer & Tuch, 2006; Wortley & Owusu-Bempah, 2011). Researchers have generally found that African-Americans have more negative stories about police circulating within their own social networks. In fact, Browning et al. (1994) found that 66% of African-Americans compared to only 13% Caucasians reported knowing someone who had been mistreated by police. This is essential information when performing any study that analyzes how people's perceptions are shaped by experiences, specifically in regards to a person's race. While this research is becoming increasingly important in today's current climate in regards to police brutality, the researcher seeks to understand how these negative perceptions are not only influenced by vicarious experiences, but how these vicarious experiences affect a person's emotional cognition in the form of IIs. To further understand vicarious experiences and emotions, the researcher will suggest the appraisal theory of emotions as a way to interpret IIs and experiences.

Research performed by Joshua Wondra and Phoebe Ellsworth (2015) on how the appraisal theory of empathy is affected by actual experiences and vicarious experiences is an important consideration into the dynamics of experiences and possibly imagined interactions. The researchers define appraisal theory of empathy as how an observer's appraisal or assessment of another's situation or experience is essential to understanding how the observer's emotions, particularly empathy, are influenced by the other person (Wondra & Ellsworth, 2015). The appraisal theory of emotion could be applied to vicarious experiences with police officers. If a person views family members' or friends' experiences with police officers as important, whether positive or negative, the individual could then be influenced by the same emotions that friends or family were. Finally, Waller and Boschen (2015) asked female students to imagine a non-consensual kiss as a teenager to determine if the imagination created a feeling of dirtiness, and they found that just the imagination of the event created a feeling of unease, and none of the methods tried reduced that impact. The past research suggests that vicarious experiences can be powerful for individuals, even if they have not actually experienced anything. While some research has analyzed how race impacts actual and vicarious experiences, no study has analyzed how individuals deal with the trauma from the events using IIs.

Imagined Interactions (IIs)

As noted in this volume, imagined Interaction (IIs) is a process by which individuals imagine conversation with a variety of people and relationships for a range of purposes. IIs are formed from the work of symbolic interactionism and cognitive scripts (Mead, 1934). Symbolic interactionism suggests that individuals create and maintain society through repeated, meaningful interactions (Carter & Fuller, 2015) and cognitive scripts. Cognitive scripts are created by experiences or past scripts and are used in the creation of new scripts in new encounters (Honeycutt, 1989; Honeycutt, 2015; Zagacki, Edwards, & Honeycutt, 1992). IIs have eight attributes and serve six functions. The eight attributes include frequency (how often does one have IIs), proactivity (II engaged in prior to conversation), retroactivity (reviewing the interaction after it occurs), variety (diversity of topics), discrepancy (IIs rate of how similar or dissimilar to actual event), self-dominance (who is more prominent in the II), valence (how negative or possible the II is), and specificity (level of detail) (Honeycutt, 1989). The current study will analyze how frequency, retroactivity, discrepancy, valence, and specificity apply to IIs with police officers after actual or vicarious encounters, as well as three functions of IIs: conflict management, rehearsal, and catharsis.

Obviously, if a person has an actual encounter with a police officer, whether positive or negative, that interaction will influence the IIs with a police officer in the future. What about vicarious experiences? Studies in psychology have shown that experiences that we do not have any actual memory of can impact decision making as well as social interactions (Cramer, 2000). Researchers have analyzed the idea of third party imagined interactions (TPIIs). TPIIs are imagined interactions that occur during conversation between two other individuals, where the person observing is not a conversational partner (Porter, 2010–2011). Porter (2010–2011) also found that TPIIs and IIs attributes and functions are more similar than different. This means that a person's imagined TPII will still serve the same functions and attributes as IIs. Furthermore, Berkos and Denham (2016) found that having TPIIs negatively impacted relational intimacy. This research could be applied to how a person is influenced by experiences that a family member or friend has with police officer because it is likely that the observer was not present at the incident which the family or friends describe. Importantly, as described by Wondra and 'Ellsworth, as people listen to others about their vicarious experiences, they, in turn, feel the emotion of those situations, further influencing the person's IIs.

Current Study

Frequency

Frequency is an important attribute to analyze in regards to how people deal with the trauma of interaction with police officers either from actual or vicarious experiences. Kroll-Mensing (1992) found that as IIs became more frequent about a topic, the more anxious and depressed people became, impacting their overall level of satisfaction in their relationships. Furthermore, research by Allen, Edwards, Hayhoe, and Leach (2005) found that as students had more frequent IIs about financial issues, they reported less pleasant IIs. Results from Allen et al. were supported by Zagacki et al. (1992) who found that more frequent IIs were associated with more mixed emotions than positive, as well as imagery. Considering actual encounters with police officers have a face-to-face encounter with more visual imagery, I suggest the following hypothesis:

> *H1: Frequency will be used more in actual encounters than in vicarious experiences.*

Retroactivity and Proactivity

Retroactivity refers to how people review the interaction once the interaction has taken place. Retroactive IIs help to understand what has happened, what to do in the future, and how to reduce stress and tensions (Honeycutt, 2003). Through retroactivity, people are able to replay conversations after they happen. However, by replaying these conversations, the conflict remains intact and can lead to rumination and mulling, which will be discussed further in the conflict management function (Honeycutt, 2003). Zagacki et al. (2002) discovered that retroactive conflict tends to be more verbal instead of visual, leading to higher amounts of discrepancy. The research suggests that retroactivity in IIs could play a role in vicarious experiences, where there may be a lack of visual imagery. Thus, retroactivity could be used when reviewing experiences with police officers and dealing with the trauma from the event.

> *H2: There will not be a significant difference in the use of retroactive IIs between vicarious and actual experiences.*

Similar to retroactivity, proactivity refers to IIs that occur before an interaction occurs. Proactivity can help individuals plan future interactions as well as reduce stress and tensions (Honeycutt, 2003). Proactive IIs have been found to correlate with imagined success in competition, but not with actual success (Gotcher & Honeycutt, 1989). Retroactive IIs work in tandem with proactive IIs; after the event has occurred, individuals review proactive IIs and compare. Honeycutt (1989) found that retroactivity and proactivity were correlated. Based on the link between retroactivity and proactivity I suggest the following hypothesis:

> *H3. There will not be a significant difference in the use of proactive IIs between vicarious and actual experiences.*

Discrepancy

In addition to the conflict management function of IIs, another important function one should consider when framing perceptions of law enforcement is discrepancy. Discrepancy relates to how different the actual encounter is from the II. Studies have demonstrated that relationship satisfaction was predicted by being engaged and having pleasant IIs with one's partner, rather than highly discrepant IIs (Honeycutt & Wiemann, 1999). Additionally, higher discrepancy leads to less communication competency and comes from the participant's lack of skill with expecting outcomes from the other person the participant is interacting with (Honeycutt, 2003). Lastly, relating to retroactivity and proactivity, highly discrepant IIs tend to be more verbal based instead of visual (Zagacki et al., 1992).

> *H4: Higher amounts of discrepancy will be present in vicarious experiences more than in actual experiences.*

Valence

As discussed previously, valence is how negative or positive one views IIs (Honeycutt, 1989). Research by Honeycutt (2003) found that more pleasant IIs have a more positive effect on a person; conversely, more negative IIs have a more negative effect on a person. In fact, the more negative impact an event has on an individual, the more likely the memory and II will be recalled (Honeycutt, 1992). People who have more positive feelings report fewer IIs as well as fewer retroactivity IIs (Honeycutt, 2003). Obviously, valence is essential to understanding how people deal with actual and vicarious experiences with police officers. If the experience has a more negative impact, people will be more likely to remember the event. I postulate the following hypothesis:

> *H5: IIs from actual encounters with police officers will have more negative valence than in vicarious encounters.*

Specificity

In regard to IIs about police, specificity in IIs is essential. The level of detail in the IIs can shed light on how people remember and build IIs from experiences with police officers. In fact, Honeycutt, Zagacki, and Edwards (1992–1993) found that more specific IIs suggest a better understanding of the meanings in other messages, as well as a strong memory of the event. Importantly, Honeycutt (1999) found that couples reporting a secure attachment style experience higher levels of detailed visual and verbal imagery. These findings imply that higher levels of visual and verbal imagery suggest greater specificity in IIs. Furthermore, research on experiences with police officers indicates the race of the police officers impacts the interaction (Cochran & Warren, 2012). Through these findings, the following hypotheses are suggested:

> *H6: Higher specificity in IIs will be present for actual experiences compared to vicarious experiences.*

> *H7: The race of the police officer will positively impact specificity in encounters.*

While the attributes describe the specific details about IIs and how we make sense of them, IIs serve six functions of communication.

Functions of IIs

While all of the attributes of IIs are incorporated into the different II functions in a variety of ways, different functions and attributes are used in different situations. IIs serve six functions: maintaining relationships, conflict management and resolution, rehearsal, self-understanding, catharsis, and compensation (Honeycutt, 2003). Depending on the situation, IIs' functions are used differently in congruence with the attributes. The current study will analyze how conflict management and resolution, rehearsal, and catharsis functions of IIs are used when people have IIs about actual or vicarious experiences with police officers.

Conflict Linkage Function

Without realizing it, people create and experience IIs every day for a variety of reasons, whether it is to reduce anxiety or depression or to improve relationships. For example, II research has found that when a person's norm is violated, he or she seeks rehearsal, self-understanding, and catharsis functions (Berkos, Allen, Kearney, & Plax, 2001). The conflict-linkage theory describes how conflict can be kept alive and maintained by having retroactive and proactive IIs in relationships (Honeycutt, 2003). Conflict-linkage theory suggests that conflict is continuously recreated when people imagine future negative interactions, and these IIs lead to negative actual encounters as a form of self-fulfilling prophecy. Cloven and Roloff (1991) found that dwelling on and ruminating about the problem increased the belief that the problem is serious. The effect was even stronger when couples reported having more volatile arguments. The conflict management function can also be seen in research in actual interactions with police officers.

In areas where crime rates are normally high, prior interactions with police can influence negative attitudes. Taylor et al. (2015) state, "Aggressive policing in low income, minority urban neighborhoods can lead to direct and retold negative experiences (or highly publicized events) with police and especially among young black males" (p. 235). The past research suggests the following hypothesis:

H8: The conflict management function of IIs will be used more in actual experiences than in vicarious experiences.

H9: Higher retroactivity IIs will negatively impact the conflict management function of IIs when dealing with police officers for people with actual encounters with police officers versus vicarious experiences.

Rehearsal Function

The rehearsal function can be used to plan and anticipate encounters and help relieve stress (Honeycutt, 2003). Rehearsal can also be used to enhance confidence in future interactions (Honeycutt, 1989). The rehearsal function could be used by people who have had traumatic encounters with police officers as a way to prepare for future interactions. Because of the lack of contact with police officers, I hypothesize that individuals who have had an actual experience with police officers will use the rehearsal function more than those who have vicarious experiences.

H10: The rehearsal function will be used in actual experiences more than in vicarious experiences.

Catharsis Function

Catharsis is a way of releasing strong emotions and therefore providing relief from the stress. Gotcher and Edwards (1990) found that cancer patients used cathartic IIs to improve communication practices with providers as well as to reduce fear. Furthermore, Honeycutt (1996) found that when unhappy couples used cathartic IIs, the couples experienced a therapeutic effect. Furthermore, Treat (2010) suggested that the cathartic function of IIs could be used as a form of therapy for traumatic encounters. Because an actual encounter with police officers can be a traumatic event for a person, I hypothesize that people who have had an actual experience with police officers will use catharsis more than individuals with vicarious experiences.

H11: The catharsis function of IIs will be used in actual more than in vicarious experiences.

Current Study

Participants were recruited from Amazon's Mechanical Turk. After completing a shortened II (SII) survey by Honeycutt (2003), participants received $0.40. The SII with 38 statements was developed by Honeycutt (2003) and altered to refer to interactions with police officers which measured the six attributes (frequency, retroactivity, proactivity, discrepancy, valence, specificity) and three functions of IIs (conflict management, rehearsal, and catharsis), for a total of 42 questions. Two open-ended questions were presented to participants to describe both an Imagined Interaction with a police officer and an actual experience with police officers; 74 had usable responses. To analyze the relationship between experience and imagined interactions, a dichotomous variable were created, actual experience only (1= had an experience, 0 = did not). Furthermore, OLS regression was used. Regression analysis is a statistical technique that estimates the strength and direction of a relationship between two or more variables (Anderson, 2013; also see chapter 10). Two different regression models were generated for each attribute and function. The first model includes a simple bivariate regression (the function/attribute and actual experience yes or no). A simple bivariate regression analyzes a single independent variable (the actual experience) and a dependent variable (the function or attribute of IIs) (Anderson, 2013). The second model, uses multiple regression, which controlling for gender, age, race, race of cop in experience, and the feelings from the interaction (more independent variables).

Findings from the regressions indicated support for hypotheses 1–3, and 7–9; all others were not supported. Table 9.1 indicates the support of the hypotheses. Furthermore, means and standard deviations are reported. A mean is an average of the data in a sample, whereas a standard deviation is the distance or spread of the numbers in a data set, or how varied the sample size is (Anderson, 2013).

Before discussing the intricacies between vicarious and actual experiences with police officers, regardless of race, it is important to note that individuals with vicarious experiences reported mixed feelings with a slight indication toward negativity from the II ($M = 3.07$, $SD = .99$) on a scale of 1 = extremely negative to 5 = extremely positive, whereas individuals with an actual experience had an average score of 2.57 ($SD = 1.21$, negative leaning), suggesting that regardless of II function, people are reporting generally more negative leaning reactions from experiences with police officers. Furthermore,

Table 9.1. Support for Hypotheses.

Hypothesis	*Supported or Not Supported*
H1: Frequency will be used more in IIs from actual encounters than in vicarious encounters.	Supported
H2: There will not be a significant difference in the use of retroactive IIs between vicarious and actual experiences.	Supported
H3. There will not be a significant difference in the use of proactive IIs between vicarious and actual experiences.	Supported
H4: Higher amounts of discrepancy will be present in vicarious experiences more than in actual experiences.	Not supported
H5: IIs from actual encounters with police officers will have more negative valence than in vicarious encounters.	Not Supported
H6: Higher specificity in IIs will be present when one has an II from actual experience compared to vicarious experiences.	Not Supported
H7: The race of the police officer will positively impact specificity in encounters.	Supported
H8: The conflict management function of IIs will be used more in actual experiences than in vicarious experiences.	Supported
H9: Higher retroactivity IIs will positively impact the conflict management function of IIs when dealing with police officers, regardless of experience.	Supported
H10: The rehearsal function will be used in actual more than in vicarious experiences.	Not Supported
H11: The catharsis function of IIs will be used in actual more than in vicarious experiences.	Not Supported

hypotheses 1 and 8 will be discussed first because of support for the differences between vicarious and actual experiences.

Interestingly, frequency (ß = .17) and the conflict linkage function of IIs (ß = .16) was found to be statistically significant at predicting a relationship between the type of experience and the use in IIs. As noted in chapters 3 and 11, Beta values range from -1 to 1 indicating a negative or positive relationship with what is predicted. In other words, people who had actual experiences used frequency and the conflict management function of IIs differently from participants who had vicarious experiences. Participants who had an actual experience with police officers more frequently (M = 2.23, *SD* = .98) had IIs about their experiences than those with vicarious experiences (M = 1.67,

SD =1.10), regardless of their feelings from the interactions, suggesting that regardless of valence, individuals with actual encounters had IIs about these encounters more. The conflict management function on the other hand, was used more for those who had an actual experience (M = 2.76, SD = 0.67) than those with a vicarious experience (M = 2.33, SD = 1.13). Individuals who had an actual experience with police officers managed and coped with their interaction slightly higher than those who had vicarious experiences, suggesting that because they actually experienced a confrontation with a police officer, they have the ability to deal with the matter at hand more than those who have heard about the experience but were not the primary target. However, the lower conflict management score for vicarious experiences suggests a growing problem as more and more incidents between police officers and innocent civilians occur: How do people who did not have the interaction cope with the trauma? For example, comments from the open-ended questions suggest the importance of vicarious interactions. One participant described an encounter he had witnessed riding in the car with his friend, "I should mention that my friend is black. It felt like a great injustice that the officer would stop him of all people," as well as a white participant who reported his family telling him of a negative experience they had in which his response was,

There are times where I'm walking down the street and get nervous when a police officer drives by. I have a high level of anxiety and can rarely bring myself to complete these imagined interactions. I stop them quickly and remove myself from any situation where there's even a chance I have to interact with someone of authority. I just want to walk free of distraction and bother, but that anxiety always haunts me and prevents me from doing what I want.

Results indicated there were distinct differences in how the type of experiences influenced participants' IIs; however, other than frequency and conflict management function, no other differences were found, suggesting that overall, people with vicarious experiences use IIs in a similar fashion as those with actual experiences. Additionally, retroactivity was also found to impact the conflict management function of IIs (hypothesis 9) when interacting with police officers.

Results indicated as individuals had more retroactive IIs about the encounter, the higher the individual managed the conflict regardless of experience. Research by Johnson and Roloff (1998) found that mentally reliving an encounter repeatedly through the use of retroactive IIs can lead to mulling over a conflict. Furthermore, similar to mulling is rumination, where an individual continuously dwells on the conflict leading to depression and stress (Sukhodky, Golub, & Cromwell, 2001). The results of this study relate to results by Honeycutt (2003) that found that retroactivity was associated to rumination over conflict. Thus, IIs could be used as a form of cognitive behavioral therapy, discussed in the literature review, to refer to the past interaction to cope with the trauma, instead of ruminating and mulling over the incident and creating stress and anxiety, as in this example:

The officer, male, white, 40s, was immediately aggressive, threatening to give me a ticket for speeding. I was afraid because he repeatedly yelled at my passenger (who yelled back). I imagined him arresting my passenger based on his behavior. I imagined being arrested right then for some imagined offense; the event occurred 9 years ago.

Additionally, retroactivity and proactivity were found to not be impacted by the type of experiences (hypotheses 2 and 3). In other words, retroactivity and proactivity in IIs play an important role in both vicarious and actual experiences, suggesting individuals, after hearing about a police interaction from friends and family, do retroactively have IIs about the encounter to deal with the interaction and plan for the future. Interestingly, age was found to be a significant influence to proactivity in IIs (ß = −.24). The mean for proactivity in IIs for the youngest participant, age 18, was 4.16 (*SD* = 1.18) and the oldest participant, age 85, (M = 2.33), signifying that as age increases in the sample, the less proactive IIs they have about police officers. The results imply that as people get older and have more experience with police officers, they are less likely to plan these interactions before they take place, whereas younger people may not have many past experiences to rely on to influence how they react as experiences occur. Research by Croghan and Croghan (2010) proposes that managers who have fewer experiences are less likely to have ability to plan interaction. Furthermore, feelings during the interaction as well as the type of experience were close to significance at impacting proactivity in IIs; further research is need to analyze how proactivity is impacted during police interactions. Additionally, support for hypotheses 7–9 was found.

In addition, to frequency, proactivity, and retroactivity, the race of the police officer was found to impact specificity in IIs. The means for specificity in II by the race of the police officer in the encounter were for a White police officer (M = 3.00, *SD* = .82), Black (M = 2.18, *SD* = 1.03), and Hispanic (M = 2.55, *SD* = .90), indicating that when white police officers were a part of an II, the more specific they were. Furthermore, the race of the police officer had a Beta score of −.24, suggesting a weak inverse relationship. This is not surprising considering several respondents reported the race of the police officer in experiences, regardless of vicarious or actual. Participants described a wide variety of races including, "The policeman was a Cuban," "The officer, male, white, 40s was immediately aggressive," "Both white male cops, both unnecessarily aggressive," "I was pulled over by a male Caucasian police officer," "The main cop interrogating me was an African-American and male," and many others responded with specific details about the race of the police officers in their IIs. These responses along with the data suggest that race of the police officer is highly memorable in people's IIs about police officers. While the above-mentioned hypotheses were supported and the following were not, it does not remove the importance of the null results.

Null results for valence and the type of experience with police officer implies the similarity between how IIs are used in both interactions (hypothesis 5). However, it is important to remind that individuals with a vicarious experience had a valence in IIs score of 3.40 (more neutral leaning), whereas participants with an actual experience had a 2.89 (more negative leaning); thus, both groups reported neutral to negative valence in IIs, supporting prior findings by Honeycutt, Zagacki, and Edwards (1992) which found that more pleasant events are not remembered as much as negative encounters. After controlling for several factors, the type of experience did not influence valence in IIs, but a participant's feelings during the encounter significantly impacted the person's valence in II. Results indicated the more positive the feelings during the interaction, the more positive the overall valence in IIs (= .30), and conversely, the more negative the feelings from the encounter the more negative the IIs. More research is needed to understand how valence in vicarious interactions is lower than expected, what types of encounters are influencing IIs, how negative are these interactions, does media coverage about negative events impact these encounters, etc. In addition, to null results for valence in IIs, rehearsal and catharsis were as well.

While conflict management was an essential difference between vicarious and actual experiences, rehearsal and catharsis were not significant. As discussed in the literature review, rehearsal and catharsis work together to release stress and anxiety, but in the sample, participants with actual encounters reported a slightly higher rehearsal score of 3.23, while those with vicarious encounters had a 2.88 score. Regardless, both were low suggesting that participants need more training in IIs to deal with rehearsing prior to a conflict to have a potentially better experience. Similar results were found with the catharsis function of IIs. Both types of encounters had a mean score (actual = 3.04, vicarious = 3.02), suggesting their IIs are not being used appropriately to relieve stress from the situation.

Summary

The current study has analyzed the differences between vicarious and actual experiences and the attributes and functions of IIs present. While both frequency and conflict management in IIs were found to be different based on experiences, the other functions and attributes were not different across groups suggesting the importance of more vicarious experience research. These results gives credence to work by Crisp and Turner (2009) which found that IIs about interactions with police officers could be just as influential as actual experiences. The current research also adds to prior research in TPII's to suggest that IIs vary slightly across the type of interaction. Furthermore, Berkos and Denham (2016) found that TPII's, or IIs from a third party, similar to vicarious experiences, were negatively associated with intimacy and relational quality as well as higher levels of stress. In other words, people who have vicarious experiences with police officers may create more stress and anxiety about interacting in an actual experience with police officers by having retroactive IIs about an event and ruminating about an event that they were not a part of but are envisioning in their head how the event occurred. More research is needed to understand how rumination from the experiences with police officers impacts their current IIs, especially during vicarious encounters.

Finally, the current study highlights the necessity that IIs can be used to help overcome the trauma from encounters with police officers. Since vicarious and actual experiences with police officers were found to be similar in their use of the attributes and functions of IIs, IIs could be a useful tool to deal with the trauma from encounters regardless of the type of experience. Proper training and therapy could be used to help individuals who have had interaction with police officers to properly deal with their trauma. Importantly, this study has shown that those with vicarious experiences deal with the trauma in similar ways as those who have had an actual experience, indicating the importance of social ties and media influence. Clearly, more research is needed to understand the impact of social ties and media influence on a person's IIs from vicarious experiences.

Discussion Questions

1. *Think of an interaction you have had with a police officer versus an encounter that you have heard of from family or media. How were your IIs different in each situation? How were they similar?*
2. *When you overhear encounters with police officers from your family and friends, do these interactions impact how you view police officers? Does your negative/positive view impact IIs of future encounters with police officers?*
3. *How might the different levels of trauma (witnessing a shooting vs. getting pulled over) from an interaction with police officers impact one's IIs regardless of actual vs. vicarious interaction?*

References

Allen, M. W., Edwards, R. Hayhoe, C., & Leach, L. J. (2010). College students' imagined interactions with parents about spending and credit: The influence of attitudes toward money and family communication patterns. In J. M. Honeycutt (Ed.), *Imagine that: Studies in imagined interaction (pps. 127- 146)*. Cresskill, NJ: Hampton.

Anderson, A. (2013). *Business statistics for dummies*. Hoboken, NJ: Wiley.

Berkos, K. M., Allen, T. H., Kearney, P., & Plax, T. G. (2001). When norms are violated: Imagined interactions as processing and coping mechanisms. *Communication Monographs*, 68(3), 289–300. doi: https://doi.org/10.1080/03637750128066

Berkos, K. M., & Denham, J. A. (2016). Intimacy, marital satisfaction, and third party imagined interactions. *Imagination, Cognition, and Personality*, 36(3), 312–330. doi: 10.1177/0276236616683897

Brown, B., & Benedict, W. (2002). Perceptions of the police: Past findings, methodological issues, conceptual issues and policy implications. *Policing*, 25(3), 543–580. doi: https://doi.org/10.1108/13639510210437032

Browning, M., Bourguignon, F., Chiappori, P. A., & Lechene, V. (1994). Incomes and outcomes: A structural model of intrahousehold allocation. *Journal of Political Economy*, *102*(2), 1067–1096. doi: 10.1086/261964

Brunson, R. (2007). Police don't like black people: African-American young men's accumulated police experience. *Criminology & Public Policy*, 6, 71–102. doi: https://doi.org/10.1111/j.1745-9133.2007.00423

Buhmann, C., Nordentoft, M., Ekstroem, M., Carlsson, J., & Mortensen, E. (2018). The effect of flexible cognitive–behavioural therapy and medical treatment, including antidepressants on post-traumatic stress disorder and depression in traumatised refugees: Pragmatic randomised controlled clinical trial. *British Journal of Psychiatry*, 208(3), 252–259. doi:10.1192/bjp.bp.114.150961

Callanan, V. J., & Rosenberger, J. S. (2011). Media and public perceptions of the police: Examining the impact of race and personal experience. *Policing & Society, 21*(2), 167–189. doi: 10.1080/10439463.2010.540655

Carter, M. J., & Fuller, C. (2015). Symbolic interactionism. *Sociopediaisa.* doi: 10.1177/205684601561. Retrieved from http://www.sagepub.net/isa/resources/pdf/Symbolic%20interactionism.pdf

Cloven, D. H., & Roloff, M. E. (1991). Sense-making activities and interpersonal conflict: Communicative cures for the mulling blues. *Western Journal of Speech Communication,* 55(2), 134–158. doi: 10.1080/10570319109374376

Cochran, J. C., & Warren, P. Y. (2012). Racial, ethnic, and gender differences in perceptions of the police: The salience of officer race within the context of racial profiling. *Journal of Contemporary Criminal Justice, 28*(2), 206–227. doi: 10.1177/1043986211425726

Cramer, P. (2000). Defense mechanisms in psychology today: Further processes for adaptation. *American Psychologist, 55*(6), 637–646. doi: 10.1037/0003-066X.55.6.637

Crisp, R. J., & Turner, R. N. (2009). Can imagined interactions produce positive perceptions? *American Psychologist, 64*(4), 231–240. doi:10.1037/a0014718

Croghan, T., & Croghan, J. (2010). Visualizing success: Imagined interactions in organizational contexts. In J. M. Honeycutt (Ed.), *Imagine That: Studies in Imagined Interactions* (pp. 99–114). Cresskill, NJ: Hampton Press.

Davis, R. (2000). *Perceptions of the police among members of six ethnic communities in Central Queens, NY.* New York, NY: Safe Horizon.

Gabbidon, S. L., Higgins, G. E., & Potter, H. (2011). Race, gender, and the perception of recently experiencing unfair treatment by the police: Exploratory results from an all-black sample. *Criminal Justice Review, 36,* 5–21. doi:10.1177/0734016810379904

Gotcher, J. M., & Edwards, R. (1990). Coping strategies of cancer patients: Actual communication and imagined interactions. *Health Communication, 2*(4), 255–266. doi: http://dx.doi.org/10.1207/s15327027hc0204_4

Gotcher, J. M., & Honeycutt, J. M. (1989). An analysis of imagined interactions of forensic participants. *National Forensic Journal, 7,* 1–20.

Hagan, J., & Albonetti, C. (1982). Race, class, and the perception of criminal injustice in America. *American Journal of Sociology,* 88(2), 329–355. doi: https://doi.org/10.1086/227674

Hayhoe, C. R., Leach, L., Allen, M. W., & Edwards, R. (2005). Credit cards held by college students. *Financial Counseling and Planning, 16,* 1–10. doi:2006-11385-001

Henderson, M., Cullen, F. T., Cao, L., Browning, S. L., & Kopache, R. (1997). The impact of race on perceptions of criminal injustice. *Journal of Criminal Justice, 25*(6), 1–16. doi: https://doi.org/10.1016/S0047-2352(97)00032-9

Honeycutt, J. M. (1989). A functional analysis of imagined interaction activity in everyday life. In J. E. Shorr, P. Robin, J. A. Connelia, & M. Wolpin (Eds.), *Imagery: Current Perspectives.* New York, NY: Plenum Press.

Honeycutt, J. M. (1996). The oral history interview and reports of imagined interactions. *Journal of Family Psychotherapy,* 6(4), 63–69. doi:https://doi.org/10.1300/j085V06N04_06

Honeycutt, J. M. (2003). *Imagined interactions: Daydreaming about communication.* Cresskill, NJ: Hampton.

Honeycutt, J. M. (2015). Imagined interaction theory: Mental representations of interpersonal communication. In D. O. Braithwaite, & P. Schrodt (Eds.), *Engaging Theories in Interpersonal Communication*, (2nd ed., pp. 75–87). Thousand Oaks, CA: Sage.

Honeycutt, J. M. (Ed.). (2010). *Imagine that: Studies in imagined interaction*. Cresskill, NJ: Hampton Press.

Honeycutt, J. M., & Wiemann, J. M. (1999). Analysis of functions of talk and reports of imagined interactions (IIs) during engagement and marriage. *Human Communication Research*, *25*, 399–419. doi: 10.1111/j.1468-2958.1999.tb00451.x

Honeycutt, J. M., Zagacki, K. S., & Edwards, R. (1992–1993). Imagined interaction, conversational sensitivity and communication competence. *Imagination, Cognition, and Personality*, *12*, 139–157. http://dx.doi.org/10.2190/B9PC-51RJ-1D7N-4M94

Hurwitz, J., & Peffley, M. (2005). Explaining the great racial divide: Perceptions of fairness in the U.S. criminal justice system. *Journal of Politics*, *67*(3), 762–783. doi: https://doi.org/10.1111/j.1468-2508.2005.00338.x

Johnson, K., & Roloff, M. (1998). Serial arguing and relational quality: Determinants and consequences of perceived resolvability. *Communication Research*, 25(3), 327–343. doi. 10.1177/009365098025003004

Kroll-Mensing, D. (1992). *Differentiating anxiety and depression: An experience sampling analysis* (Unpublished doctoral dissertation). University of Minnesota, Minneapolis.

Mbuba, J. M. (2010). Attitudes toward the police: The significance of race and other factors among college students. *Journal of Ethnicity in Criminal Justice*, 8(3), 201–215. doi:10.1080/15377938.2010.502846

Mead, G. H. (1934). *Mind, self, and society*. Chicago, IL: University of Chicago Press.

Noble, S. U. (2014). Teaching trayvon: Race, media, and the politics of spectacle. *Black Scholar*, *44*, 12–29. doi:https://doi.org/10.1080/00064246.2014.11641209

Porter, M. A. (2010–2011). Third-party imagined interactions: Expanding mental imagery to the experience of others' communication. *Imagination, Cognition, and Personality*, 30, 147–169. doi: 0.2190/IC.30.2d

Redner-Vera, E., & Galeste, M. (2015). Attitudes and marginalization: Examining American Indian perceptions of law enforcement among adolescents. *Journal of Ethnicity in Criminal Justice*, *13*(4), 283–308. doi:10.1080/15377938.2014.984043

Rome, D. M., Son, I. S., & Davis, M. S. (1995). Police use of excessive force: Does the race of the suspect influence citizens' perceptions? *Social Justice Research*, 8, 41–56. doi: 10.1007/BF02334825

Rosenbaum, D. P., Shuck, A., Costello, S. K., Hawkins, D. F., & Ring, M. K. (2005). Attitudes towards the police: The effects of direct and vicarious experience. *Police Quarterly*, 8(3), 343–365. doi:10.1177/1098611104271085

Russell-Brown, K. (2009). *The color of crime* (2nd ed.). New York, NY: New York University Press.

Sukhodky, D., Golub, A., & Cromwell, E. (2001). Development and validation of the anger rumination scale. *Personality and Individual Differences*, *31*(5), 689–700. doi: https://doi.org/10.1016/S0191-8869(00)00171-9

Taylor, R. B., Wyant, B., & Lockwood, B. (2015). Variable links within perceived police legitimacy? Fairness and effectiveness across races and places. *Social Science Research*, *49*, 234–248. doi:10.1016/j.ssresearch.2014.08.004

Treat, S. R. (2010). Imagined interactions with Phantasy: Shared horizons for imagined interactions and fantasy theme analysis. In J. M. Honeycutt (Ed.), *Imagine that: Studies in imagined interaction (pps. 171- 192)*. Cresskill, NJ: Hampton.

Waller, K., & Boschen, M. (2015). Evoking and reducing mental contamination in female perpetrators of an imagined non-consensual kiss. *Journal of Behavior Therapy Experimental Psychiatry*, *49*, 195–202. doi: 10.1016/j.jbtep.2014.07.009

Wamser-Nanney, R., & Steinzor, C. (2016). Characteristics of attrition among children receiving trauma-focused treatment. *Psychological Trauma*, 8(6), 745–754. doi: 10.1037/tra0000143

Warren, P. Y. (2010). The continuing significance of race: An analysis across two levels of policing. *Social Science Quarterly*, *91*(4), 1025–1042. doi:10.1111/j.1540-6237.2010.00747.x

Weitzer, R., & Tuch, S. (2005). Racially biased policing: Determinants of citizen perceptions. *Social Forces*, *83*(3), 1009–1030. doi: https://doi.org/10.1353/sof.2005.0050

Williams, B. N., & Close, B. R. (2008). Perceptions of bias-based policing: Implications for police policy and practice. In M. J. Lynch, E. B. Patterson, & K. K. Childs (Eds.), *Racial divide: Racial and ethnic bias in the criminal justice system* (pp. 191–212). Monsey, NY: Criminal Justice Press.

Wondra, J., & Ellsworth, P. (2015). An appraisal theory of empathy and other vicarious emotional experiences. *Psychological Review*, *122*(3), 411–428. doi: 10.1037/a0039252

Wortley, S., & Owusu-Bempah, A. (2011). The usual suspects: Police stop and search practices in Canada. *Policing & Society*, *21*(4), 395–407. doi: http://dx.doi.org/10.1080/10439463.2011.610198

Wu, Y. (2014). Race/ethnicity and perceptions of the police: A comparison of white, black, Asian, and Hispanic Americans. *Policing & Society*, *24*(2), 135–157. doi: https://doi.org/10.1080/10439463.2013.784288

Wu, Y., Smith, B. W., & Sun, I. Y. (2013). Race/ethnicity and perceptions of police bias: The case of Chinese immigrants. *Journal of Ethnicity in Criminal Justice*, *11*(1–2), 71–92. doi:10.1080/15377938.2012.735989

Zagacki, K. S., Edwards, R., & Honeycutt, J. M. (1992). The role of mental imagery and emotion in imagined interaction. *Communication Quarterly*, *40*, 56–68. doi: https://doi.org/10.1080/0146337920936982

· 10 ·

WINNERS AND LOSERS

Depression, Learned Helplessness, and the Trauma of Losing Political Elections

T. Phillip Madison, James M. Honeycutt, Emily N. Covington, and Philip J. Auter

> *Donald Trump will not be the 45th president of the United States. Nor the 46th, nor any other number you might name. The chance of his winning nomination and election is exactly zero.*
>
> —James Fallows, *The Atlantic*

The Princeton Election Consortium predicted a 99-percent chance of Hillary Clinton winning the 2016 election—with a 95-percent confidence interval. In October of 2016 America visualized a Clinton win and seemed cocksure of itself, with that cocksureness heavily reinforced by polling agency results favoring Clinton and disseminated through both mainstream and social media. For many Americans the crippling blow came the night of Tuesday, November 8, and left a path of emotional devastation and confusion in its wake.

More than a year later the damage to the psyche of large segments of Americans persists and the wounds remain open due in-part to the proliferation of social media. In 2018, a common internet trope is to list the 2016 naysayers' predictions that Hillary Clinton would crush Donald Trump in the election. For some, such lists provide sources of humor while for others they remain sources of horror—and powerful reminders that we live in uncertain and constantly changing times.

This chapter explores the role of imagined interactions (IIs) with Donald Trump among those experiencing depression and learned helplessness as results of electoral defeat, as well as the winners—those who like Trump's policies. We identify the functions and attributes of IIs that predict affective discomfort and offer suggestions for how people may use visualization and imagination to overcome the trauma of unprecedented election results. Although the times may be terrifying for some, human imagination remains a powerful tool for coping with the past, the present, and the future.

Literature Review

Prior to the 2016 presidential election, over half of Americans (52%) reported that the election was either a very or somewhat significant source of stress (American Psychological Association, 2016). The APA (2016) found that pre-election stress was a bipartisan phenomenon with 55% of Democrats and 59% of Republicans reporting election-related stress. In 2017, 73% of Democrats felt stressed about the future of the United States while only 56% of Republicans and 59% of Independents felt the same (American Psychological Association, 2017).

While some discount election-related stress as trivial or refer to those who experience it as "snowflakes," such lasting and significant stress can have harmful effects. According to *Psychology Today* (n.d.), "prolonged or repeated arousal of the stress response...can have harmful physical and psychological effects, including heart disease and depression" (para. 2). The breadth of election-related stress in the post-2016 election era has led some mental health professionals to develop new classifications for the phenomena. Sweeton (2016), a clinical psychologist specializing in post-traumatic stress disorder, explains that while "Post-Election Stress Disorder" (PESD) is not an official mental illness, it certainly is a sensation that people are feeling. In response to the 2016 presidential election, many Americans reported "feeling triggered, traumatized, on edge, anxious, sleepless, angry, hopeless, avoidant of connection, alone, and suddenly haunted by past traumas they believed they had buried" (Sweeton, 2016, para. 1). For many women in particular, the election—and more specifically, allegations of Donald Trump's sexual misconduct and his crude Access Hollywood tapes—brought back memories of past sexual assault and abuse (Sweeton, 2016). The fight-or-flight response to post-election stress reflects, for many people, an intense fear of what may happen in the future (Sweeton, 2016).

Other psychologists are uneasy with the term PESD. In an interview between Goldberg (2017) and Dr. Philip Levendusky, the director of psychology at a Harvard-affiliated psychiatric hospital, Levendusky uses the term "post-traumatic stress *reaction*" to describe these intense levels of election-related stress. Levendusky breaks down the term as follows: "It's post, it's after the event. It was experienced as a trauma, so traumatic. And reaction is how you felt about it. And I'm not going to carry 'disorder' after it. That's where we would be treading in the land of diagnosis" (Goldberg, 2017, para. 15). With post-traumatic stress reactions, one certainly carries and is affected by the trauma but they will not necessarily develop a diagnosable disorder (Goldberg, 2017).

Levandusky attributes much of the election-related stress to a matter of perceived sense of control (Goldberg, 2017). Prior to the election, many were completely certain that Hillary Clinton would win the presidency, so they perceived high levels of control of the situation. When Clinton lost and Trump won though, these individuals' perceived senses of control plummeted and were "replaced with a lot of agitation, depression, upset" (Goldberg, 2017, para. 10). The grassroot activities that people have engaged in since the election, such as marches and protests, are a way for these individuals to regain some sense of control of the political situation, making them feel less helpless and, thus, decreasing anxiety; even engaging in conversations with friends about today's political climate can be helpful (Goldberg, 2017). When asked if those who feel triggered by Trump should either try to avoid him on television or expose themselves to him in an immersion therapy-like fashion, Levendusky stresses the importance of avoiding constant exposure to him (Goldberg, 2017).

Perception of control is linked to another psychological occurrence: learned helplessness. Seligman, Maier, and Geer (1968) spent many years electrocuting animals to explore the effects of such experiments on animal cognition in order to apply the findings to humans. One phenomenon revealed in these experiments was learned helplessness; the authors describe the process and results in dogs:

> When an experimentally naive dog receives escape-avoidance training in a shuttle box, the following behavior typically occurs: at the onset of the first traumatic electric shock, the dog runs frantically about, defecating, urinating and howling, until it accidentally scrambles over the barrier and so escapes the shock. On the next trial, the dog, running and howling, crosses the barrier more quickly than on the preceding trial. This pattern continues until the dog learns to avoid shock altogether …

> In dramatic contrast to a naive dog, however, a typical dog which has experienced uncontrollable shocks before avoidance training soon stops running and howling and sits or lies, quietly whining, until shock terminates. The dog does not cross the barrier and escape from shock. Rather, it seems to give up and passively accepts the shock. On succeeding trials, the dog continues to fail to make escape movements and takes as much shock as the experimenter chooses to give. (Seligman, 1972, p. 407)

While learned helplessness was first studied in animals like the dog mentioned above, it is now, more commonly, used to describe "the failure of human beings to pursue, utilize, or acquire adaptive instrumental responses" (Nuvvula, 2016). Individuals who suffer from learned helplessness, essentially, accept that bad things are or will happen to them and that they have little or no control over it (Nuvvula, 2016). According to Teodorescu and Erev (2014), "Exposure to uncontrollable outcomes has been found to trigger learned helplessness, a state in which the agent, because of lack of exploration, fails to take advantage of regained control" (p. 1). The empirical explanation of learned helplessness describes that when an organism perceives a lack of control it discerns that actions and outcomes are independent, turns helpless, and stops exploring its environment (Teodorescu & Erev, 2014). For example of a person who thought that Trump would lose the election might develop a lack of perceived control after election night, leading them to feel helpless and stop engaging in political happenings.

Teodorescu and Erev (2014) explain that understanding learned helplessness "can shed light on many important behavioral and social problems, including depression" (p. 1). Depression, according to Clark and Beck (1999), "is the second most common psychological disorder" (p. 1). The American Psychiatric Association (2017) cites the following depression symptoms: sadness, depressed mood, loss of interest in activities previously enjoyed, appetite change, sleep trouble or excessive sleeping, increased fatigue and energy loss, increased purposeless activity, feelings of worthlessness or guilt, trouble thinking, concentrating and making decisions, and suicidal thoughts. In order for depression to be diagnosed, symptoms must persist for at least two weeks (American Psychiatric Association, 2017). The main risk factors for depression include biochemistry, genetics, personality, and environmental factors (American Psychiatric Association, 2017).

Sub-clinical forms of depressive disorder that are milder and do not include enough symptoms to be classified as depression are even more common than major depressive disorder (Clark & Beck, 1999). Clark and Beck explain that the "presence of a depressive disorder or even a few depressive symptoms has been associated with significant reductions in physical and social functioning" (p. 1). Under that logic then, those who experience post-election stress disorder or election-related post-traumatic stress reactions may not have diagnosable, full-scale depression, but they do experience symptoms of depression, and therefore may experience a similar decline in physical and social functioning.

All of the mental health dilemmas outlined above are clearly connected. High levels of election-related stress lead people to experience what mental health professionals are calling "post-election stress disorder" or a post-traumatic stress reaction. Election-related stress is also linked to a perceived loss of control which may, in turn, but connected to learned helplessness. Learned helplessness is also related to depressive disorder and sub-clinical forms of depression, both of which are quite serious.

How can people get past the trauma of having their candidate lose an election? Imagined interactions are a form of daydreaming whose attributes, functions, and other aspects are covered thoroughly elsewhere in this book. In this chapter we look at their relationship with learned helplessness and depression within a political context. Emerging from the extant literature, we ask the following research questions that address liking Trump's policies, depression, and learned helplessness.

RQ1: Which functions and attributes of IIs with Donald Trump predict liking Trump policies?
RQ2: Which functions and attributes of IIs with Donald Trump predict depression?
RQ3: Which functions and attributes of IIs with Donald Trump predict learned helplessness?

Current Study

Procedure

After receiving IRB approval from two prominent southern universities, researchers administered online surveys to students enrolled in various communication courses at both universities. Surveys were programmed in to Qualtrics; students received course credit for participating. All responses were anonymous and to receive credit, students had to show a printout or screenshot of the closing page of the survey to the researchers. Data were then loaded into the Statistical Package for the Social Sciences (SPSS) for analysis.

Participants

Participants ($N = 454$) were 56% female and 44% male. Seventy percent were White/Caucasian, 18% Black/African American, 3% Hispanic, 3% mixed races, 4% other races, and 2% preferred not to say. Ninety-four percent were never married and 96% were ages 18–24.

Measures

Measures of the attributes of imagined interactions were created from an abbreviated version of Madison and Porter's (2016) parasocial relationship (PSR) scales which themselves were derived from Honeycutt's (2010) imagined interaction scales. We took the top-two highest-loading items from their factor analyses to create 2-item scales measuring each of the functions of parasocial relationships. We repeated the procedure using Madison and Porter's (2015) factor analysis of functions of PSRs to produce 2-item attribute scales. Additional items were then added to the conflict, self-understanding, and catharsis scales from Honeycutt's (2010) II scales to create more robust measurements of the functions, and were contextualized to reflect imagined interaction with President Donald Trump. Each item was measured on a 5-point scale ranging from "Never" to "All the time" as possible responses. An example of an item from the frequency scale includes, "I imagine myself interacting with Donald Trump many times throughout the week" and an example from the Self-Understanding scale includes, "Imagining a conversation with Donald Trump helps me understand my feelings about him."

We assessed depression using the Zung (1965) self-report depression scale. The Zung (1965) includes a ten positively-worded items and ten negatively-worded items. Negatively-worded items were reverse coded so higher scores reflected greater depression. Items were measured on 4-point scales ranging from "a little of the time," "some of the time," "good part of the time," and "most of the time." The Zung (1965) self-report depression scale is an additive index; scores of 25–49 indicate a normal range; 50–59 indicate mildly depressed; 60–69 indicate moderately depressed; 70 and above indicate severely depressed.

The Learned Helplessness Scale (LHS) came from Quinless and McDermott-Nelson (1988) and included 19 items. Responses were measured using sliders, which assess learned helplessness from 0 to 100. Examples of items included, "I cannot find solutions to difficult problems" and "I do not try a new task if I have failed similar tasks in the past." Negatively-worded items were reverse coded so that higher scores indicated higher levels of learned helplessness. Poorly performing scale items were removed to enhance reliability.

For those of you who are statistically inclined, Table 10.1 presents the scale properties of this study. Tables 10.2 and 10.3 present regression analysis results.

Table 10.1. *Scale Properties.*

Variable	*N-Scale Items*	*N*	*M*	*SD*	*Cronbach's Alpha*
Functions					
Self-Understanding	6	445	1.67	.86	.92
Conflict Linkage	7	437	1.67	.81	.86
Catharsis	7	454	1.54	.83	.87
Attributes					
Frequency	2	454	1.39	.76	.92
Retroactivity	2	445	1.67	.91	.91
Variety	2	454	1.77	.95	.79
Valence	2	445	1.88	1.20	.94
Specificity	2	443	1.51	.83	.78
Like Trump's Policies	2	454	2.73	.62	.77
Depression	20	436	40.00	8.72	NA
Learned Helplessness	19	454	34.44	15.71	.93

Results

RQ1 asked, "Which functions and attributes of IIs with Donald Trump predict liking Trump policies?" To answer this question we ran an OLS regression to assess the impact of the predictor variables on liking Trump's policies. Conflict linkage and positive valence in IIs with Donald Trump were mild yet significant predictors of liking his policies as revealed in Table 10.2. The Beta values (B) are standardized regression coefficients that can range from −1 to 1. Values indicate the magnitude of the prediction in terms of negative or positive association.

RQ2 asked, "Which functions and attributes of IIs with Donald Trump predict depression?" To answer this question we ran an ordinary least-squares regression to assess the impact of the predictor variables on depression. As revealed in Table 10.3, retroactive IIs emerged as a significant positive predictor of depression while valence emerged as a significant negative predictor. The negative association suggests that those suffering from depression in

Table 10.2. *Regression of Functions and Attributes on Liking Trump Policies.*

Variable	B	SE(B)	β	t	Sig.(p)
Functions					
Self-Understanding	–.02	.06	–.03	–.34	.74
Conflict Linkage	.15	.06	.19	2.53	.01*
Catharsis	–.02	.07	–.03	–.30	.76
Attributes					
Frequency	–.06	.06	–.07	–.94	.35
Retroactivity	.03	.06 .05	.52	.60	
Variety	.08	.05	.12	1.52	.13
Valence	.08	.04	.15	2.14	.03*
Specificity	–.00	.07	–.00	–.03	.98

R-Square = .10; $F(8, 420) = 5.50$, $p < .01$; *$p < .05$

Table 10.3. *Regression of Functions and Attributes on Depression.*

Variable	B	SE(B)	β	t	Sig.(p)
Functions					
Self-Understanding	–.06	.05	–.12	–1.34	.18
Conflict Linkage	.05	.04	.09	1.11	.27
Catharsis	.08	.05	.13	1.49	.14
Attributes					
Frequency	.01	.04	.01	0.18	.86
Retroactivity	.11	.04	.22	2.49	.01*
Variety	–.06	.04	–.13	–1.56	.12
Valence	–.06	.03	–.18	–2.38	.02*
Specificity	–.05	.05	–.09	–0.88	.38

R-Square = .07; *$p < .05$

association with IIs with Donald Trump may be brooding over the negative things people imagine him to say.

RQ3 asked, "Which functions and attributes of IIs with Donald Trump predict learned helplessness?" To answer this question we ran an ordinary least-squares regression to assess the impact of the predictor variables on learned helplessness. Cathartic IIs emerged as the only significant predictor of learned helplessness as revealed in Table 10.4. Self-understanding, however, emerged as a marginally significant negative predictor.

Table 10.4. *Regression of Functions and Attributes on Learned Helplessness.*

Variable	B)	SE(B	β	*t*	*Sig.(p)*
Functions					
Self-Understanding	–2.73	1.61	–.15	–1.69	.09
Conflict Linkage	–.25	1.50	–.01	–.17	.87
Catharsis	5.28	1.93	.24	2.74	.01*
Attributes					
Frequency	1.47	1.58	.07	.93	.35
Retroactivity	–.07	1.54	–.00	–.04	.97
Variety	–.47	1.40	–.03	–.34	.74
Valence	–1.35	.96	–.10	–1.41	.16
Specificity	.79	1.82	.04	.44	.66

R-Square = .04; $F(8, 420) = 2.17$, $p < .05$; *$p < .05$

In summary, conflict IIs with positive valence predicted liking Trump policies. Retroactive IIs with negative valence predicted depression while catharsis IIs predicted learned helplessness. Results of this study show that people can respond to their candidate's electoral defeat in a variety of negative ways which include negative imagery. Based on these results, we offer the following suggestions for those who wish to move past the crippling feelings that come from electoral defeat.

Applications to Mental Health Status in View of Stress and Trauma

In this section we will explore the major findings of this study and apply them to improving the status of people's mental health after electoral defeat. The first finding was that positive-valenced conflict IIs predict liking Trump policies. This finding can be interpreted in a variety of different ways. First, it may be that people who like Trump's policies simply enjoy imagining conflict or may have what researchers have called "high-conflict personalities" (HCPs), which are treatable with psychotherapy. "High-conflict personalities," as Eddy (2017) argues, are fundamentally adversarial personalities" (Paragraph 1).

> They don't see their part in their own problems and instead are preoccupied with blaming others … They all have the basic HCP pattern of: 1) Targets of Blame, 2) a lot of all-or-nothing thinking, 3) unmanaged emotions and 4) extreme behaviors. In addition, they also have traits of 5 personality disorders. Some may just have traits

and others have a full disorder. This can make them very difficult, but also more predictable." (Paragraphs 1–2)

The main difference between HCPs and established personality disorders, Eddy (2017) argues, are that HCPs have targets upon which they place blame for their own problems. Such targets of blame in our current era (with their stereotypes) include Muslims (plotting terrorist attacks or promoting Sharia Law), immigrants (for "stealing" jobs), police (brutality), African Americans (unemployed drains on the welfare system), LGBTQIAs (often confused with sexual predators), and any number of convenient others. One need only tune in to American Family Radio for a list of current social targets and advocacy for the Trump administration.

Second, many people view conflict as an engine of progress (Heffernan, 2013) and even necessary for survival. It is possible that people with high conflict in their IIs are optimistic about conflict rather than seeking to avoid it, and optimism about conflict is leading to liking controversial policies. As one student pointed out, many people find themselves aghast by Trump's social etiquette, but find many of the administration's policies, such as tax code, to be practical improvements over policies from previous eras. The controversy and conflict surrounding policy change may be viewed as necessary for progress among many people.

Third, it is also possible that some people who like Trump policies are "mirroring" the thinking behind his often off-color political rhetoric. Such rhetoric may provide a sense of identity that therefore manifests itself in IIs. For such people, Trump may be acting as a role model for the success of others. These, as well as the others covered in this section were what we will call the "winners." But what of the "losers?"

The second critical finding in this study was that retroactive negative-valence IIs lead to depression. This finding implies what conventional wisdom suggests: "resentment is like taking poison and waiting for the other person to die." This particular set of II attributes regarding depression may indicate holding on to anger and resentment, turning inward, and slipping in to depression. Considering the nature of "locker room talk" and overtly racist rhetoric so commonly associated with our current president, it is likely that such rhetoric may trigger past trauma, such as sexual assaults and racial discrimination, making many of Trump's performances more personal for victims.

The third major finding in this study—catharsis IIs as predictors of learned helplessness—can be interpreted in at least two different ways. First, catharsis IIs may offer an escape alternative to actually trying to influence one's world.

People suffering from learned helplessness in light of electoral defeat may be trapped in a cycle of thinking their IIs may substitute for action or activism. In reality, catharsis IIs may be creating greater learned helplessness.

In light of these findings, we offer several solutions for coping with electoral trauma. Each of them address the different domains of existence: cognitive, affective, and behavioral. While each approach may have its individual merits, a comprehensive approach to tackling election defeat is recommended.

In the cognitive domain, we suggest practicing mindfulness and becoming aware when IIs may be turning in to something unpleasant or even pathological. Some studies (e.g., Madison, Covington, Wright, & Gaspard (2018) show that many people are increasingly turning to "hatewatching"—watching things and people they hate for entertainment. The danger of this is that we form parasocial relationships with people whom we see on television and maintain those relationships through IIs (Madison & Porter, 2015; Madison & Porter, 2016; Madison et al., 2018). Repeatedly exposing ourselves to things we detest has the potential to retrigger trauma and negative-valence retroactive IIs, leading to depression. In other words, simply avoiding the object of one's anger can help ease the trauma of electoral defeat. The alternative may lead to, as Seligman's (1968, 1972) dogs found from repeated shocks, a state of learned helplessness. As Goldberg (2017) suggests, avoiding exposure may be one of the best means of coping.

In the affective domain, we suggest talking about one's emotions with friends and family. Honeycutt and Mapp (2011) advise communicating a variety of emotions during hurricane aftermaths when tensions may be running high. Sharing one's pain with others is an age-old means of reducing it, and the same process should be helpful in times of electoral defeat and associated trauma.

Finally, in the behavioral domain, we suggest actively participating to make changes in the world that one is capable of making, such as protesting, participating in marches, or volunteering. This will look different for everyone, but the point is to stay involved in the positive things in one's life and helping share positive experiences.

Limitations and Future Research

Some of the limitations in this study included homogeneity in the sample. Participants were mostly white college students in the southern region of the U.S. Results of repeating the study may differ in "blue" states or areas associated with more "liberal" ideologies. Future research should seek greater heterogeneity in the sample to be able to better generalize to larger populations. Second, we did not control for various personality disorders and other mental illnesses that may be occurring in the sample.

Third, the data are cross-sectional and correlational. While researchers can certainly gain important insights from cross-sectional data, repeated and longitudinal study may yield more accurate results and account for the changing dynamics of human imagination over time. Future research should explore II functions and attributes over time, particularly in response to media-rich environments. The richness of the current media environment, as various people have argued, may be problematic in itself, and among humans may even produce effects similar to those in the electrocution cages used by Seligman et al., (1968).

As Goldberg (2017) recommends, people who have strong emotional responses to figures they see on television should avoid immersing themselves, which may pull more triggers and perpetuate misery. Media researchers should continue this line of work to sift out the effects that repeated exposure to undesirable content may have on human imagination and happiness. "Unplugging" from mobile and other screen devices may be the best defense against learned helplessness, particularly if the user has experienced extreme trauma.

Summary

This study identified the uncomfortable state of living in an unprecedented electoral world and a connection to imagined interactions. We found that an appreciation for conflict IIs and/or having a high-conflict personality predicted liking Trump's policies among the election's "winners." Among the losers, however, negative retroactive IIs—ruminating on electoral loss to a controversial reality star predicted depression. Moreover, we suggest that catharsis II's while possibly improving a person's outlook, may also promote deeper levels of learned helplessness. Solutions to depression induced by these types of IIs among the "losers" may be alleviated through mindfulness and recognizing when our imaginations are turning against us or going out of control, communicating our emotions with friends and family, and actively participating in society through political activism or other means.

Discussion Questions

1. *How might hatewatching, also known as "ironic consumption," and emergent parasocial relationships—the one-sided relationships we form with people whom we see in the media—serve to reduce the trauma associated with electoral defeat?*
2. *What functions did your own imagined interactions related to the 2016 presidential election serve in your life?*
3. *How can you implement imagined interactions for a client experiencing election-related stress, depression, and/or learned helplessness.*

References

American Psychological Association (2016). *Stress in America: U.S. presidential election 2016.* Retrieved from http://www.apa.org/news/press/releases/stress/2016/ presidentialelection.pdf

American Psychological Association (2017). *Stress in America: The state of our nation.* Retrieved from http://www.apa.org/news/press/releases/stress/2017/state-nation.pdf

American Psychiatric Association (2017). *What is depression?* Retrieved from https://www.psychiatry.org/patients-families/depression/what-is-depression

Clark, D. A., & Beck, A. T. (1999). Depression symptoms and disorders: Diagnostic and conceptual considerations. In D. A. Clark, D. A., A. T. Beck, & B. A. Alford (Eds.), *Scientific foundations of cognitive theory and therapy of depression* (pp. 1–21). New York, NY: John Wiley & Sons.

Eddy, B. (2017). Five types of high-conflict personalities: And their targets of blame, and sometimes violence. [Blog post] Retrieved 15-May, 2018 from https://www.psychologytoday.com/us/blog/5-types-people-who-can-ruin-your-life/201711/five-types-high-conflict-personalities

Goldberg, C. (2017). Psychologist: No, it's not post-election stress 'disorder.' *WBUR.* Retrieved from http://www.wbur.org/commonhealth/2017/03/10/psychologist-not-post-election-stress-disorder

Heffernan, M. (2013). Dare to disagree. *TED Radio Hour.* Retrieved 5-May, 2018 from https://www.npr.org/2013/08/23/174037793/is-conflict-good-for-progress

Honeycutt, J. M. (2010). *Imagine that: Studies in imagined interactions.* Cresskill, NJ: Hampton Press.

Honeycutt, J. M., & Mapp, C. M. (2011). Families overcoming trauma and emotional aftermath from hurricanes using effective communication. In L. M. Webb, & F. C. Dickson (Eds.), *Communication for Families in Crisis: Theories, Research, Strategies (pps. 361–379).* New York, NY: Peter Lang.

Madison, T. P., Covington, E. N., Wright, K., & Gaspard, T. (2018, August). *"They're turning the frogs gay!" Credibility and attributes of parasocial relationships with Alex Jones.* Paper presented at 2018 Association for Education in Journalism and Mass Communication (AEJMC) annual conference. Washington, D. C.

Madison, T. P., & Porter, L. (2015). The people we meet: Discriminating functions of parasocial interaction. *Imagination, Cognition, and Personality*, 35, 47–71. doi: 10.1177/0276236615574490

Madison, T. P., & Porter, L. (2016). Cognitive and imagery attributes of parasocial relationships. *Imagination, Cognition, and Personality*, 35(4), 359–379. doi: 10.1177/0276236615599340

Nuvvula, S. (2016). Learned helplessness. *Contemporary clinical dentistry*, 7(4), 426–427. doi: 10.4103/0976-237X.194124

Psychology Today (n.d.). *Stress*. Retrieved from https://www.psychologytoday.com/us/basics/stress

Quinless, F. W., & McDermott-Nelson, M. A. (1988). Development of a learned helplessness scale. *Nursing Research*, 37, 11–15.

Seligman, M. E. (1968). Chronic fear produced by unpredictable electric shock. *Journal of Comparative and Physiological Psychology*, 66(2), 402–411. doi: 10.1037/h0026355

Seligman, M. E. (1972). Learned helplessness. *Annual Review of Medicine*, 23, 407–412. doi: https://doi.org/10.1146/annurev.me.23.020172.002203

Seligman, M. E., Maier, S. F., & Geer, J. H. (1968). Alleviation of learned helplessness in the dog. *Journal of Abnormal Psychology*, 73(3), 256–262. doi: 10.1037/h0025831

Sweeton, J. (2016). Post-election stress disorder in women. *Psychology Today*. Retrieved from https://www.psychologytoday.com/us/blog/workings-well-being/201611/post-electionstress-disorder-in-women

Teodorescu, K., & Erev, I. (2014). Learned helplessness and learned prevalence: Exploring the causal relations among perceived controllability, reward prevalence, and exploration. *Psychological science*, 25, 1861–1869.

Zung, W. W. (1965). A self-rating depression scale. *Archives of General Psychiatry*, 12, 63–70.

· 11 ·

EPILOGUE

Tips on Using IIs to Deal with Trauma

James M. Honeycutt

The vast array of findings reported in the chapters in this book indicate that IIs are a type of self-therapy that can be used to deal with stress and trauma in a variety of circumstances. People have not systematically investigated how we can invigorate ourselves or depress ourselves through inner talk. Resiliency can be enhanced through using combination of II features. Elsewhere, I have noted that when one uses IIs, one experiences anxiety relief (Honeycutt, Vickery, & Hatcher, 2015). Both catharsis and rehearsal allow individuals to think through possible outcomes of interactions before the actual encounter. In catharsis, thinking through outcomes allows for the release of emotions and anxiety; for rehearsal, thinking through the outcomes prepares individuals with a script for how to engage in the interaction. Following is a review of practical advice for using IIs to cope with trauma and stress.

Benefits of Proactive IIs

Proactive imagined interactions help individuals rehearse strategies, reduce primary tension (which occurs before or at the beginning of interactions), and gain others' viewpoints. It is associated with empathy. Rehearsal increase successes and reduce embarrassment. Before asking someone out, we usually rehearse what to say, and what to say if they say no. Relatedly the chapters throughout this book provide recommendations for trauma in various areas that were reviewed (e.g., conflict and abuse, loss, and policy concerns). For example, people who disagree on climate change policy can use IIs to vent their frustrations when the policies that are instituted result in anger. Following is a list that combines the areas into an overall archetype for using IIs to deal with trauma.

Practicing with IIs boosts confidence even when actual encounters differ from practiced ones (Honeycutt, 2000). This occurs through the reduction of EVALUATION APPREHENSION (the fear of being judged negatively). A student, who practiced informing her father about moving off-campus, wrote "I thought that all of that 'practicing' was just a waste of time, since I did not use what I had practiced, but I think I was a little more confident about the discussion since I had gone over in my head the points of view that I wanted to get across."

Tips for Proactive IIs

Relax before anticipated encounters. Specifically imagine the encounter's scene and what you and the others say. Imagine the encounter from start to finish. And, when possible, consider going beyond IIs to role-playing rehearsals.

Benefits of Retroactive IIs

Retroactive imagined interactions help individuals understand what took place, review strategies, and reduce secondary tension (occurring as a result of the interaction). For example, Chris over their speech's unexpectedly warm reception and realizes classmates judged the speech on behavior, not subjective angst. As Chris replays what she said, and how she said it, she decides to approach her next assignment pretty much the same way, except for adding a final summary to help clarify her main idea. But even when Chris, speech bombs, replaying it several times helps. It releases her pent-up feelings and emotions—called CATHARSIS, reducing the events' negative impact, and lessening subsequent speaking traumas. Behaviorists use a similar approach called IMPLOSION THERAPY. Patients are directed to imagine their phobias as graphically and specifically as possible. They usually find repeated exposure collapses negative effects.

Tips for Retroactive IIs

Return to the situation. Mentally recreate the encounter's context. In fact, you might develop the habit of jotting down refresher notes after the event takes place. Try to identify what you did well. Identify key factors in the interaction. Think of alternative actions you could have taken to improve consequences. Finally, role-play the encounter from the other's point of view to work on empathy.

Because IIs are a type of mental imagery, they can be used as a type of meditation. Recall, that they represent mindful volitional cognition. Even though, you can think positively or negatively, thinking positively may be easier said than done. Human survival and mental health require a balance between optimism and pessimism. Excessive optimism can result in dangerously risky behaviors while undue pessimism makes life miserable (Hecht, 2013). In order to overcome negative IIs, a few tips are offered.

What Should You Avoid When Practicing IIs?

There are three major things to avoid when practicing IIs: catastrophizing, keeping conflict alive, and egocentrism.

Catastrophizing

After a traumatic event, it is human nature to have panic attacks, inability to focus, and feel depressed. After tragedies, stressful episodes; the fundamental asking of the why this happened to me often provides the answers to the fundamental questions of who, what, where, when and how. Collectively, these basic questions are referred to as the "five W's and H" are used to inquire about crises (see https://en.wikipedia.org/wiki/Five_Ws).

When negative mood happens, old habits of negative thinking often start up again, negative thinking gets into the same rut, and a full-blown episode of depression may be the result. Catastrophizing occurs when what is imagined is quite negatively discrepant from what is likely to, or actually did, occur. For example, you might feel guilt or shame in requesting assistance from family members after the loss of a job in order to make ends meet. You could imagine them saying, "No, you should live on a limited budget," and steps out. But, in real life, they simply hands over the money. Catastrophizing often results from poor self-concept or overgeneralizing. That is, "No one likes me" and

"Stanford hasn't accepted me; no school will accept me." Such catastrophic expectations/assessments ultimately become SELF-FULFILLING PROPHECIES when real life interactions are avoided. That is, these beliefs cause you to behave in a manner that causes them to become true.

Keeping Conflict Alive

Recall that the conflict-linkage functions helps us deal with arguments and grievances. We revisit old conflicts and may plot or justify revenge. For example, the chapter on hurricane evacuations (Chapter 8) was about how people risk to hurricane notices. If you have been repeated denied FEMA relief after a hurricane has destroyed your house, you may continually imagine the denials. "The FEMA agent is unreasonable and not sympathetic. Government bureaucracy is a sham. May they reap, what they sow." Such thinking tends to extend and rekindle conflicts. Look for alternatives instead. Think compromise and tension reduction (catharsis function). Try to terminate the conflictual IIs and bury the hurt. When a door is closed, a new one may open.

Egocentrism

This occurs when we give ourselves a much more central role in imagined interactions than what is likely to, or actually did, occur. That is, we tend to overestimate our control over events (the ILLUSION OF CONTROL BIAS), our contributions to jointly produced products (the SELF-CENTERE BIAS), and our credit for success (the SELF-SERVING BIAS). For example, it is rare, and almost unnatural, to imagine ourselves listening to others' long monologues or lectures. We tend to "see" ourselves talking, while our partner listens. Yet, in reality conversations are more evenly divided. Concentrating too much about what we want to say in IIs leaves us unprepared when partners say more than anticipated and lacking responses to probes, praise, questions, or compliments. Only by recognizing our egocentric tendencies, and deliberately concentrating on others their words and points of view—can we develop conversational sensitivity and active listening.

In concluding, IIs can be used as a type of self-therapy in dealing with trauma and stress. Social networking is helpful through social media. People can be trained how to use them for therapeutic benefits. Ultimately, if a person can afford it with the rising cost of healthcare, a combination of IIs, cognitive behavioral therapy, and psychotropic medicines are more productive than sole use of one component. This is particularly relevant during the 21st century because individuals create their own realities due to social media technology, internet prevalence, and the ability to be exposed to thousands of information sites at the touch of a finger.

Discussion Questions

1. *Have you discussed any stress on Facebook compared to other sources (e.g., family, offline friends, practitioners)? Which medium did you find most or least helpful?*
2. *When was the last time that you catastrophized about an event? Did it actually, help you to overcome the situation?*
3. *Do you know some people who catastrophize as a personality type, to the extent that when bad things happen, they are pessimistic and imagine bad outcomes? Discuss who these people are and if they can be encouraged not to catastrophize.*

References

Hecht, D. (2013). The neural basis of optimism and pessimism. *Experimental Neurobiology, 22*(3), 173–199. http://doi.org/10.5607/en.2013.22.3.173

Honeycutt, J. M. (2000). It's the thought that counts. In C. G. Waugh (Ed.), *Let's talk: A cognitive-skills approach to interpersonal communication* (pp. 18–20). Newark, DE: Kendall-Hunt.

Honeycutt, J. M., Vickery, A. J., & Hatcher, L. C. (2015). The daily use of
imagined interaction features. *Communication Monographs*, 82(2), 201–223. doi: 10.1080/03637751.2014.953965

CONTRIBUTOR BIOGRAPHIES

James M. Honeycutt is a Distinguished Professor Emeritus at Louisiana State University. He received his Ph.D. from the University of Illinois. He has authored and edited over ten books and 135 publications. He is senior managing co-editor of the journal *Imagination, Cognition, and Personality*. His research included cardiovascular indicators of relational conflict and dealing with trauma in terms of imagined interaction. His hobbies include Golden Doodles, statistical modeling, reading, and mixing music. Address all correspondence to James Honeycutt at sphone@lsu.edu.

Ryan D. Rasner (MA, University of Wyoming) is a doctoral candidate at LSU. His research focuses on observational modeling of relationships, relationship development, evolutionary communication, cognition, and physiology. Hobbies include hiking, swimming, dogs, and music. Address correspondence to rrasne1@lsu.edu.

Jonathon K. Frost is a doctoral candidate at Louisiana State University. His research focuses on social cognition and misunderstanding, with a growing emphasis on mental health stigma and its antecedents and ramifications. His hobbies include dogs and video games, and he is a proud member of the Baton Rouge APA pool/billiards league. Address correspondence to jfrost7@lsu.edu.

Jake Harwood is a Professor of Communication. He received his Ph.D. in Communication from the University of California at Santa Barbara. His research focuses on intergroup communication with a particular focus on age groups, and on the role of music in intergroup relations. He is the author of "Communication and Music in Social Interaction" (Cognella, 2018) as well as "Understanding Communication and Aging" (2nd Edition, Cognella, 2018). He has published over 100 articles and book chapters. He teaches courses in research methods/statistics, intergroup communication, communication and music, and intergenerational communication. His graduate research team works on projects related to interpersonal and mediated intergroup contact, and the role of music in interpersonal and intergroup relations. One of his hobbies is music. Address correspondence to jharwood@email.arizona.edu.

Pavica Sheldon is an associate professor and chair in the Department of Communication Arts at University of Alabama in Huntsville. She holds a B.A. in Journalism from the University of Zagreb, an M.M.C., and a Ph.D. in Communication Studies from Louisiana State University. She is an author of two books and 40 peer-reviewed articles on the uses and effects of social media. Her hobbies include cooking, exercising, and photography. Address correspondence to ps0027@uah.edu.

Andrea J. Vickery is visiting faculty in the Department of Rhetoric and Communication Studies at the University of Richmond. She teaches courses on interpersonal communication and quantitative research methods and conducts research on mental imagery, supportive communication, listening, and personal relationships. Her Ph.D. and MA are in Communication Studies from Louisiana State University and she holds a BS from Chapman University. Her hobbies including spending time with her family (pets included), and running local trail and road races from 5Ks to half-marathons in the Richmond area. Address correspondence to avickery@richmond.edu.

Michael F. Rold received his Ph.D. in communication studies from Louisiana State University in 2014. He is a Lecturer in the Department of Communication at Texas A&M University where he currently teaches courses in media theory and media campaigns. In his spare time he enjoys running, playing racquetball, strumming his guitar, and entering weekly trivia competitions with his colleagues. Address correspondence to mrold1@tamu.edu.

Kayla J. Hastrup received her Master's degree from Virginia Tech. She is currently a Ph.D. Candidate at Louisiana State University. Research interest areas include rhetorical theory and criticism, mass communication, media studies, and public opinion. Aside from her academic interests, Kayla enjoys listening to podcasts and audiobooks, swimming, assembling jigsaw puzzles, and watching TV. Address correspondence to khastr1@lsu.edu.

Stephanie Houston Grey received her Ph.D. from Indiana University. Her work focuses on the rhetoric of science and technology, environmental rhetoric and the discursive and communicative dimensions of food politics. She is researching the various dimensions of a proposal to conduct hydraulic fracturing drilling operations in Chaco Canyon, New Mexico, a UNESCO World Heritage Site. Hobbies include traveling and enjoying the North shore of New Orleans. Address correspondence to houston@lsu.edu.

Michael Navarro received his MA from Louisiana State University and is a doctoral candidate. His research interests are in risk communication and human intransigence in the face of warnings. His hobbies are rooting for the Texas Rangers baseball club from his hometown of Dallas and online gaming where he does consulting. Address correspondence to mnava12@lsu.edu.

Laura B. Carper received her Master's degree in Organizational Communication from Southeastern Louisiana University. She is currently working on her PhD at Louisiana State University. Research interests include stigma, social ties, and overall health with participants of WIC and SNAP, as well as how risk messages are conveyed to the public. Hobbies include playing with her kids, watching her many fandoms (mainly Star Trek), playing Nintendo, and baking. Address correspondence to lcarpe6@lsu.edu.

T. Phillip Madison lives with his wife and children in Lafayette, Louisiana. He received his PhD from Louisiana State University. He is currently at the University of Louisiana at Lafayette. He has taught undergraduate courses in Social Media, Social Media Strategies and Tactics, Strategic Media, Principles of Public Relations, and Adobe CS5. He has taught graduate courses in PR Publics, PR Campaigns, Research Methods, and Data Analysis, while his general research interest is in media effects, focusing on parasocial relationships. His hobbies are fishing. Address correspondence to tpm6613@louisiana.edu.

Emily N. Covington is pursuing a Master's of Science in Communication at the University of Louisiana at Lafayette. Her research interests include political discussion, hate-watching, and social movements. In her spare time, she enjoys running, cooking, and being tolerated by her two cats, Piper and Oscar. Address correspondence to emilyncovington@gmail.com.

Philip J. Auter is the Hubert Bourgeois Endowed Professor in Communication at the University of Louisiana at Lafayette. He received his PhD from the University of Kentucky. His research interests are in digital and social media including intercultural communication. Address correspondence to auter@louisiana.edu.

SUBJECT INDEX

A

B

C

D

E

F

G

H

I

J

L

M

N

P

R

S

T

V

AUTHOR INDEX

A

B

C

H

I

J

K

L

M

N

O

P

Q

R

S

T

V

W

Y

Z

Health Communication

Gary L. Kreps, Series Editor

This series examines the powerful influences of human and mediated communication in delivering care and promoting health.

Books analyze the ways that strategic communication humanizes and increases access to quality care as well as examining the use of communication to encourage proactive health promotion. The books describe strategies for addressing major health issues, such as reducing health disparities, minimizing health risks, responding to health crises, encouraging early detection and care, facilitating informed health decisionmaking, promoting coordination within and across health teams, overcoming health literacy challenges, designing responsive health information technologies, and delivering sensitive end-of-life care.

All books in the series are grounded in broad evidence-based scholarship and are vivid, compelling, and accessible to broad audiences of scholars, students, professionals, and laypersons.

For additional information about this series or for the submission of manuscripts, please contact:

Gary L. Kreps
University Distinguished Professor and Chair, Department of Communication
Director, Center for Health and Risk Communication
George Mason University Science & Technology 2, Suite 230, MS 3D6
Fairfax, VA 22030-4444
gkreps@gmu.edu

To order other books in this series, please contact our Customer Service Department:

(800) 770-LANG (within the U.S.)
(212) 647-7706 (outside the U.S.)
(212) 647-7707 FAX

Or browse online by series:
www.peterlang.com

www.ingramcontent.com/pod-product-compliance
Ingram Content Group UK Ltd.
Pitfield, Milton Keynes, MK11 3LW, UK
UKHW021838100926
8556IPUK00004B/419

9 781433 153631